PAGEANT IN THE
WILDERNESS

Pageant in the Wilderness

The Story of the Escalante Expedition
to the Interior Basin,
1776

Vélez de Escalante, Silvestre

Including the Diary and Itinerary of
Father Escalante Translated
and Annotated

F
786
V513

↑ 818488

BY
HERBERT E. BOLTON

LIBRARY OF
LAMAR STATE COLLEGE OF TECHNOLOGY

Utah State Historical Society
Salt Lake City, Utah
1950

Also published as *Utah Historical Quarterly*, Vol. XVIII

COPYRIGHT 1951
UTAH STATE HISTORICAL SOCIETY

PREFACE

THIS DYNAMIC STORY of Father Escalante's trek into the Great Basin, by Dr. Herbert E. Bolton, represents the results of a long lifetime of interest, writing, and exploration in Spanish activities in the great Southwest. For the Utah State Historical Society it also represents the hope and interest of many years. More than a decade ago this Society ventured to bring to print its first articles dealing with the explorations of the initial white travelers in the Intermountain Basin. A couple of years later it undertook to publish the results of the researches of the late Herbert S. Auerbach, who had spent considerable time and effort in translating and annotating the journal of Father Escalante, as well as collecting and interpreting several of the contemporary maps of the Escalante expedition. A testament to the excellence of the Auerbach volume and to the importance of the first white explorations in the region, this book quickly went out of print. Faced with continued requests for the Escalante story, the Board of Control of this Society, under the leadership of its president, Joel E. Ricks, arranged to publish the adventures of Father Escalante as translated and interpreted by the eminent historian of the West, Professor Bolton. Despite Bolton's own statement that "there never was and never will be a definite monograph," this Society feels that the present study very nearly approaches the ideal and final word.

The author has not only translated the Escalante journal with great care and insight, he has carefully identified the campsites in terms of modern geography. As if this were noe enough, he has written an historical introduction which not only places the Escalante expedition in its proper historical setting, but depicts this trek as a great adventure, which in truth it was.

Dr. Bolton is directly responsible for the inclusion of the two maps which accompany this volume. The Miera map reproduced from a colored copy made from Miera's original was discovered by the author and is here reproduced for the first time. The Trails map which delineates the route in terms of modern place names and geography was drafted by Dr. Bolton himself. The intimate knowledge of the entire region repre-

Preface

sented in the map results from carefully retracing the trail in person.

In addition to the acknowledgments mentioned elsewhere by the author, the Society feels greatly indebted to a whole host of individuals who have contributed much to any excellence which this book may possess. Many individuals freely allowed use of illustrative material. Mr. Keith Eddington for his oil painting reproduced as the frontispiece especially should be named.

It is hoped that this volume will be received by both scholar and casual reader, the former for the excellent translation of the Escalante journal, and the latter for the simple yet dramatic delineation of the great trek, which we can follow step by step in the historical introduction.

Arlington R. Mortensen

FOREWORD

IN THE PREPARATION of Escalante's narrative for publication I have included a short background sketch to give the *Diary* its setting in time and place, and to clarify matters which, though obvious to Escalante's contemporary audience, may be less apparent to present-day readers whose historical and ideological orientation are different from that of the bold eighteenth century explorer who wrote the superb account of his "Splendid Wayfaring." I have retraced the entire route followed by Escalante and his companions, much of it several times, recorded the major human incidents of the long trek, and told of the Indians they encountered. Since a considerable part of the area traversed had been the home of prehistoric peoples, I have included a nontechnical indication of some of the antiquities along the way.

I owe a large debt of gratitude to the officers of the Utah State Historical Society for their generous cooperation, and to my many good companions on the Escalante trail, of whom I would here include a list if I could make it complete. These companions not only gave me important aid in my research, but they helped to make an unforgettable and deeply cherished episode in my life. To Dr. George P. Hammond, Professor of History, and Director of the Bancroft Library, I am indebted for many courtesies and helpful service. For most valuable assistance in the preparation of the book I wish to express my deepest gratitude to Miss Virginia E. Thickens and Miss Margaret Mollins.

HERBERT E. BOLTON

Berkeley, 1951.

CONTENTS

PREFACE ix
FOREWORD xi
HISTORICAL INTRODUCTION
    I. A Road to California 1
    II. The Adventure Begins 9
    III. To the Colorado Border 16
    IV. Down San Juan River and Past Mesa Verde.. 23
    V. River of Sorrows 29
    VI. Across Tabehuache Sierra and Down Uncompahgre River 34
    VII. Silvestre Becomes Guide 41
    VIII. Up the Mountains to the Sabuaganas 44
    IX. Domínguez Talks at San Antonio 46
    X. Northwest to Green River 51
    XI. Westward to Utah Lake 59
    XII. Paradise Valley 70
    XIII. Forward to Monterey 74
    XIV. The Bearded Utes 77
    XV. A Guide Deserts 81
    XVI. Backtrack Toward Santa Fé 86
    XVII. To the Virgin River 90
    XVIII. Along the Base of Hurricane Cliff 98
    XIX. The Crossing of the Fathers 110
    XX. To the Hopis and Santa Fé 120
    XXI. The Sequel 126
    Miera's Map 128
    Astronomical Observations 129
DIARY AND ITINERARY 133
MIERA'S REPORT 243
BIBLIOGRAPHY 253
INDEX 259

ILLUSTRATIONS

Father Escalante Discovers Utah Valley xv
Escalante's Crossing of the Green River 57
The Valley of Paradise 71
A Bearded Indian 79
Yuta Indian Girls 79
Scene in Southwestern Utah 95
The Crossing of the Fathers 119
Father Escalante Stayed Here 123
Split Mountain and the Green River 169
Mt. Timpanogos 179
Pahvant Butte 191
Monument Valley 229

MAPS

Miera's Bearded Indian Map .... Back Pocket
The Trail of Escalante .... Back Pocket

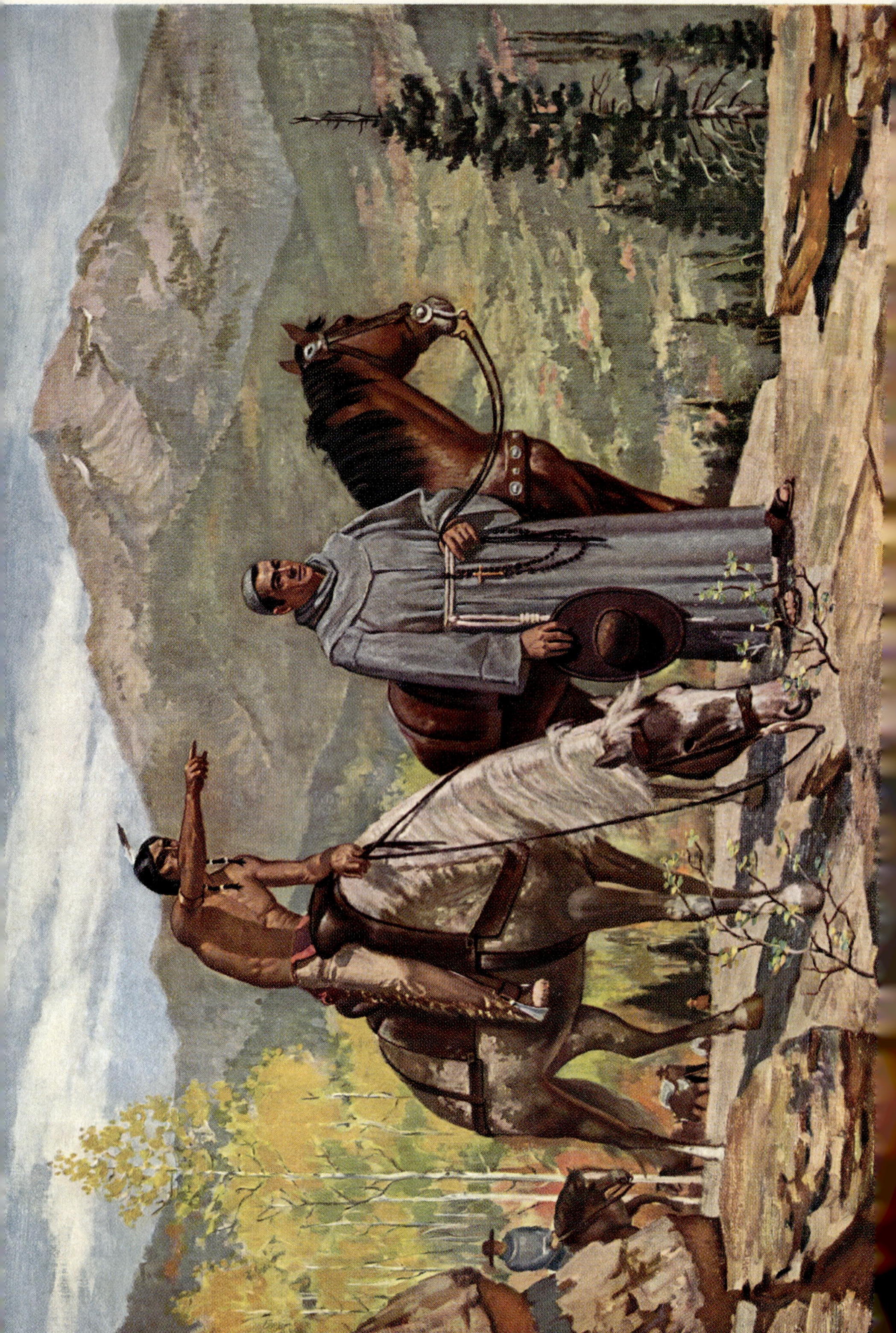

FATHER ESCALANTE DISCOVERS UTAH VALLEY
—From an oil painting by Keith Eddington

"We ... climbed a small hill, and beheld the lake and the wide valley of Nuestra Señora de la Merced de los Timpanogotzis. ..."
—From Father Escalante's diary, September 23, 1776

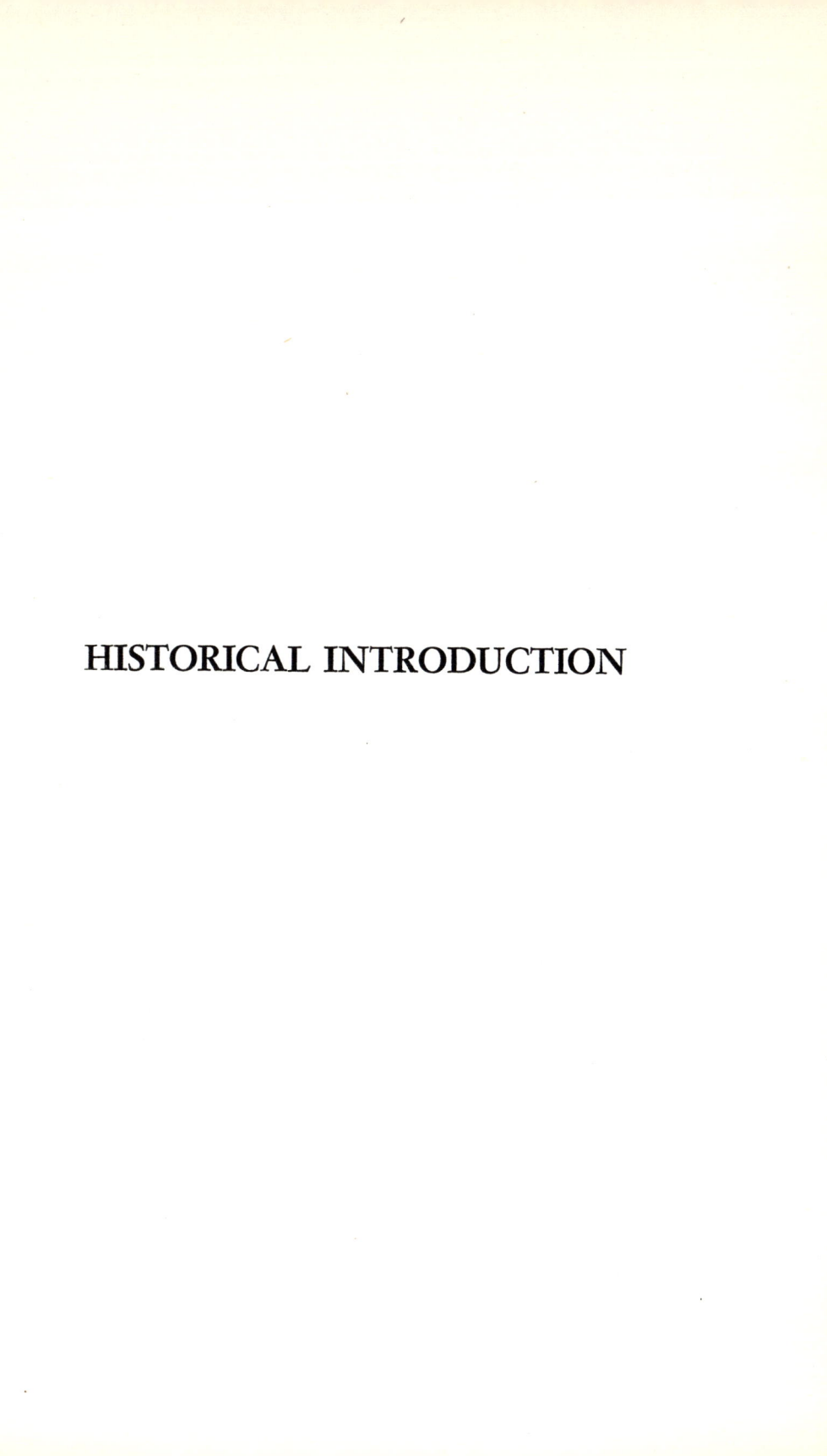

HISTORICAL INTRODUCTION

Pageant in the Wilderness

I

A ROAD TO CALIFORNIA

HISTORICAL EPISODES, like rivers, represent the coming together of numerous small streams of influence from different directions. This was true of the famous Escalante Expedition from Santa Fé to the Utah Basin in 1776, year of the Declaration of Independence by thirteen of England's thirty colonies in America. It was a spectacular chapter in the history of the Far West and in the opening of the Continent to European civilization. Unlike many chapters in the early history of North America, the episode lacked entirely the noise and carnage of battle.

The Spanish province of New Mexico, founded by Oñate in 1598 with a colony from Old Mexico, was established in the midst of sedentary natives who lived in compact and stable towns or pueblos, to use the Spanish term, hence their designation as Pueblo Indians. When California was founded more than a century and a half later, officials in Mexico City and colonists on the frontier recognized the desirability of opening communication between Spain's old province in the heart of the Continent and the new one on the Pacific Coast. The men who made the most heroic effort toward putting this idea into effect were two Franciscans, Fray Silvestre Vélez de Escalante, missionary at Zuñi in New Mexico, and Fray Francisco Garcés, who at the time was serving as a link between Sonora and California, with his base of operations at San Xavier del Bac, in the region that is now Arizona. We call the former of these two men Escalante, but by his contemporaries he was known as Vélez. Two others, Fray Francisco Atanasio Domínguez and Captain Miera y Pacheco, played important parts in carrying the project through.

Our story starts in New Mexico, land of the Pueblo Indians and of the Spanish pioneers of the Southwest. Early in 1775 the governor of that province, writing from his capital at Santa Fé, asked Father Escalante for a report regarding communication between New Mexico and Sonora, a road from New Mexico to Monterey, capital of recently founded California, and the subjugation of the Moquinos, or Hopis, who, having long been hostile to Spanish authority and to Christian missionaries, were an obstacle to the desired communication between Santa Fé and the Pacific Coast. To obtain data for the report, Escalante with a small party made a horseback journey from Zuñi to Hopi Land, and wrote a diary that is full of information regarding the trail and affairs at the now famous Hopi Mesas, or plateaus, in Arizona. Later in the same year,[1] Escalante wrote to New Mexico's Governor Mendinueta that the purpose of his trek to Hopi Land had been to inquire about a route to Monterey by way of "the great river of the Cosninas, which I judge to be the Colorado." The Cosninas were the Indians now better known as the Havasupais who, like the Hopis, still live just where they did then, quite in contrast with many North American tribes who have had neighbors of European stock.

Escalante reached the Mesa of Gualpi on June 25, and two days later, having climbed the long steep trail up the rugged cliff, he entered the pueblo of Oraibe, whose people were sullen. He tried to tell them about the Christian Faith, but they refused to listen. Then, turning to the main object of his jaunt, he asked about the road to the Cosninas. It happened that some men of that tribe had recently been at Oraibe and had just returned to their own country in the west. In fact, one young Cosnina was still at Gualpi, and with him Escalante had an historic chat.

The friar lighted a *cigarro*, he and the Cosnina alternately puffed on it as long as it lasted, "and then they smoked another." Meanwhile the Indian told Escalante about his homeland in the west, made him a map of the trail from Oraibe to the Cosnina settlement in Havasupai Canyon, showing the turns, the days' journeys, watering places, villages, the size of the country, the course of the Colorado River, and neighboring tribes. All this he mapped with charcoal on an equestrian breastplate, belonging

---

[1] October 28, 1775.

apparently to one of the soldiers in the friar's escort. Escalante wrote to the governor at Santa Fé, "I do not reproduce the map here, because after I have seen all those places I hope to make one myself." The conference ended, the Cosnina said, "Padre, now my heart is at peace." With the information acquired, Escalante rode back to Zuñi and thence to Santa Fé to confer with the governor. He little dreamed what an Homeric adventure was in store for him as a sequel to that friendly smoke with the young Cosnina Indian from the Colorado River.

While Escalante was endeavoring to win favor with Hopis and Havasupais, Father Garcés, a far western Daniel Boone in Franciscan garb, and a contemporary of the famous Kentuckian, with high adventure was exploring a route from California that met Escalante's rugged trail in Hopi Land. Having ascended the Colorado River from Yuma to the Mojave Indians, who lived and still live a short distance north of the sharp pointed Needles, with one horse and Mojave guides he swung west and south and again west to recently founded San Gabriel, went thence over the mountains to San Joaquin Valley by a trail parallel to but generally east of the modern Ridge Route, and back to the Mojaves via Tehachapi Pass, of which he was the discoverer. From boyhood experience with Spanish mustangs used by the Winnebago Indians of Wisconsin, I have imagined that Garcés' horse was buckskin colored, with a dark stripe along his backbone. While in the vicinity of later founded Fresno in the San Joaquin Valley, Garcés saw what he thought was a pass through the eastern sierras, and it intrigued him. Might not that gap offer a route from California to New Mexico, or *vice versa*? This visit to San Joaquin Valley and back was a jaunt of several hundred miles over unexplored country before he got started on another chapter in his "Splendid Wayfaring," to borrow a pertinent phrase from eloquent Neihardt.

From Colorado River Garcés now set forth east and north with his faithful horse and one Mojave guide to open a route to the Hopis and Santa Fé, and incidentally to see what he could see, which with him as with Boone was always a major urge. He and Escalante were working on opposite ends of the same problem. Adventure rode with restless Garcés. Like many another Franciscan all the world over, he manifested his zeal for saving souls both by physical endurance and by religious ministrations.

He served God by the sweat of his brow as well as by pious vigils and long sermons, and this human approach was an important factor in his notable success. Many ingredients enter into the end product which we call salvation.

On June 5, 1776, a year big with destiny on both Atlantic and Pacific shores, Garcés crossed the mighty Colorado River at a place just north of the sharp pointed Needles, bound for the Havasupais, who lived along his route to Hopi Land, where he would meet Escalante's trail. Traveling northeastward, he crossed Sierra del Sacramento, now called Black Range, and descended into the valley beyond. From here northward for a long distance he was on or close to the route of the Santa Fé Railway, built in another century by another people. Two days later, near the site of present-day Kingman, Arizona, Garcés visited the Hualapai Indians, who still live in the same vicinity. He spoke to them about God "of whom they already had some knowledge." He was encouraged here also by evidence of trade with the Spaniards of New Mexico, for it seemed to promise him an open road to his objective. The Hualapais wore Hopi shirts and Castilian belts, and had awls and other Spanish tools obtained in Pueblo Land, showing communication between the two regions hundreds of miles apart. Going forward, Garcés ascended Hualapai Valley, passed the sites of Hackberry and Truxton Wash in Arizona, and on June 11 arrived at the place now called Peach Springs, where the Santa Fé Railway turns sharply east, leaving Garcés' trail, which continued north.

Traveling now through junipers and pines, the friar in his flowing skirts and wide-brimmed sombrero reached Aubrey Cliffs, and passed a well or pond covered with roses,[1] where they still bloom in season. The site is easily identified today. He then swung northeastward over rough terrain and entered Havasupai Canyon, into which with fearless heart he descended by a fearsome trail, and visited the friendly Indians then and still living there. Three-quarters of a century later Lieutenant Whipple, an American officer with a detachment of Federal soldiers, reached the head of the same canyon at the same site, attempted to descend by the same trail, but gave up the task as too difficult for Yankee soldiers, though not for a lone Franciscan friar. Long afterward I made

---
[1] Poza de las Rosas.

the same descent on horseback with two genial young officials of the Santa Fé Railway, and we all nursed sore muscles for many days afterward.

Climbing out of the Hualapai abyss by an equally rugged trail up the eastern wall to "Hilltop," as the Indians now call it, Garcés rode east, then north one day to Quetzal Point, looked east into the awesome gorge of Grand Canyon, and spent another day traveling southward retracing the side trip. Coues, who edited Garcés' diary, assumed that on these two days Garcés was traveling east, instead of north and south, with the result that for the rest of the eastward march he put the friar two days' travel ahead of his actual position.

Garcés again turned east, crossed Little Colorado River, and on July 2 reached the famous pueblo of Oraibe, where he was given a cold reception by the sullen natives, not even being permitted to enter a house to sleep. Next day near midnight he wrote a letter and sent it by a bribed young Hopi to the minister of Zuñi, who was no other than Escalante, proposing an attempt to open communication with California. The original letter, written on a small piece of paper, is now in the archives of Mexico City. It is of interest to remember that midnight of July 3 at Oraibe was early morning of July 4 in Philadelphia, the day when the Liberty Bell was rung. Garcés perhaps knew that Escalante was planning just what he himself was recommending—a road from New Mexico to California. It is clear from other correspondence that one project in the minds of both Escalante and Garcés was the founding of Spanish settlements at Yuma and along the Gila River as a means of keeping open communication between Sonora and New Mexico. Garcés now retraced his lonely way to Yuma, after a pioneer jaunt equal in distance and difficulty to any made by his famous contemporary and brother in spirit, Daniel Boone. Before he got back to his post, a rumor that he had been killed or was lost spread far and wide.

When our story opens, Fray Francisco Atanasio Domínguez was a recent comer to New Mexico, having been made superior of the Franciscan missions there. Escalante had arrived in the province earlier and was now stationed at Zuñi. Both were members of the missionary province of the Santo Evangelio, or Holy Gospel, of Mexico. Domínguez was a native of that country, which he affectionately called "the delightful cradle of my childhood." Escalante's birthplace and his early life are unknown to us, we are sorry to say, for the records are not yet available. Both of these men deserve and some day, perhaps, will be given full-length biographies, for, contemporaries of Junípero Serra, they were great Western pioneers.

Early in 1775 Domínguez had been sent by his superiors in Mexico to inspect the Franciscan Custodia or subprovince of New Mexico, give a detailed report of the missions there, and correct any abuses he might encounter. This does not imply that affairs there were under suspicion, and his inspection may have been just a routine matter. An important enterprise, however, was in the air. Domínguez was instructed also to discover a route between the old province of New Mexico and recently founded California. In the same connection, he was charged to learn whether Garcés in the course of his lone horseback ride from California to Oraibe had made contact with Father Escalante of Zuñi, as we have seen that he had by his letter of July 3, 1776. It is possible that by way of Yuma, before starting on his long ride, Garcés had received instructions similar to those which Domínguez bore for Escalante.

On his way from Mexico to Santa Fé, Domínguez arrived at El Paso in September, 1775, and before the end of March he set forth on his official visitation. In June he summoned Escalante from Zuñi to Santa Fé, to plan an expedition to explore a route from New Mexico to Monterey in California. How that order was carried out is the story told in this book.

Through his own experience and that of Garcés, Escalante had found the road west to California blocked by Hopi resistance and by hostile Apaches along Gila River, so he took a more roundabout trail, which made him one of the great adventurers of his day, comparable to the more publicized David Livingstone in Africa several decades later. For a number of years before our story opens, New Mexico traders had made expeditions north into the area that is now Colorado, exchanging with the Indians Spanish goods for peltry, as so well has been told by Joseph J. Hill in published articles. One such expedition was made in 1765 by Juan María de Rivera under orders from Tomás Vélez Cachupín, then governor of New Mexico. Rivera's report of the trek has not been discovered, but its contents are known through references made to it by later travelers over the same trail. In this way we are able to follow the general course of Rivera's route from Santa Fé northward to San Juan River and across the northern spur of La Plata Mountains, in present-day Colorado, which already had been prospected and given their present name because of finding in them silver ore, *plata* being the Spanish word for silver. Continuing northwest, down Dolores River, Rivera then swung eastward across Uncompahgre Plateau and River and down the latter to the Gunnison. Here, after sending two of his men beyond that stream in search of Yuta Indians with whom to trade, Rivera began his return to Santa Fé, presumably retracing his outward trail. He made an historic journey and one that had an epic sequel.

In the next decade other traders from New Mexico, with or without government permission, made expeditions over the same route, deepened the trail, and brought back to Santa Fé new stories of adventure and of profit or loss as the case might be. For example, Pedro Mora, Gregorio Sandoval, and Andrés Muñiz, in 1775 went northwest then northeast as far as Gunnison River, "where at the mouth of the Uncompahgre they examined the young cottonwood on which Rivera had carved a cross, together with the initials of his own name and the year in which he was there." This was an unmistakable trail mark. All the Spaniards here named had been with Rivera on his trading jaunt ten years earlier.

That there had been still other expeditions to the far north in the decade after 1765 is plain. We are told, for example, that Spaniards from New Mexico frequently traded with these distant tribes in violation of orders issued by the governors, and that they made a practice of going to the Yutas and remaining with them "two, three, and four months at a time" for the purpose of gathering peltry, and to see what they could see.

Thus by 1776, the region east of Colorado River and as far north as the Gunnison appears to have become fairly well known to Spanish traders of New Mexico. Hill writes: "This is clear from the fact that most of the more important physical features of the country were referred to in the diary of Escalante by names that are still on the map, and in a way that would lead one to think . . . those names were more or less in common use at that time. It was also definitely stated by Nicolás de la Fora, who accompanied the Marqués de Rubi on his tour of inspection of the northern

Spanish provinces in 1766-67, that the country to the north along the Cordillera de las Grullas,"[1] as the Rocky Mountains then were called, "was at that time known to the Spaniards for a hundred leagues above New Mexico."

---

[1] The Cranes.

II

THE ADVENTURE BEGINS

Finding a direct route to California blocked by Hopi and Apache resistance, Domínguez and Escalante turned to this traders' and trappers' trail, hoping to reach their goal by a northern approach, and in the summer of 1776 the historic trek was launched. It was a bold enterprise. The aim of the expedition was twofold. The primary interest of the Spanish government was the opening of communication between old Santa Fé and California. Escalante had dreams of Indian missions between Pueblo Land and the Pacific Coast, where Serra and Palóu had just begun their celebrated work, and where Anza with heroic endeavor was founding San Francisco. The Ute Indians had shown intelligence and a friendly spirit. Another tribe Escalante had in mind were the gentle folk of deep Havasupai Canyon, recently visited by Father Garcés. Moreover, the whereabouts of Garcés was not known in New Mexico, and it was feared that in his lone excursions he had met some disaster. And it is clear that Escalante had a goodly measure of wanderlust and was, in fact, a typical missionary adventurer of his day, comparable to Kino of an earlier generation.

On June 7 Domínguez and Escalante decided to make the expedition from Santa Fé to Monterey, and to look for men suitable for the undertaking. They reported their plan to Governor Otermin, who not only approved it "but also opened his heart and his hands," promising to furnish supplies and everything else needed for the adventure. Men had already been selected for the expedition and the 4th of July, 1776, was set for the day of departure. But there were delays. On June 20 the presidial soldiers were sent on a campaign against hostile Comanches, accompanied by Escalante as chaplain. The campaign lasted eight days, the men returning fatigued and some of them wounded. Three days after his return to Santa Fé from the campaign Escalante went to Taos on urgent business, while Domínguez was attending to other affairs at Isleta. From there Domínguez made a hurried visit to Taos, where Escalante had fallen ill with a pain in his side, "which was so severe that he was in great distress." When

Domínguez arrived at Taos, Escalante was out of danger but not strong enough to travel so Domínguez ordered him to rest there another week. Meanwhile the Garcés affair at Oraibe and an inquiry at Zuñi had occurred. In the light of that episode Domínguez, Escalante, and Governor Mendinueta still thought the expedition to Monterey would be useful, and went ahead with their plans. Domínguez wrote: "For even though we may not achieve our purpose, which is to explore a road from this kingdom to Monterey, much advance will be made by the knowledge we can acquire of the lands through which we shall travel, and it will be very useful in subsequent attempts. Moreover, we plan to return through Cosnina, to confirm that nation in its good intention to be christianized, and to separate it entirely (if God so favors us) from the Moquinos, who are so opposed to the conversion of themselves and of others. At the end of the last copy is the plan of the journey and the list of persons who are to accompany us and to whom we are giving mounts, which, together with the mules that carry our supply of provisions that I have obtained through my solicitude. All the rest I shall lay before Your Reverence upon our return.

"Now I merely inform you that today, Monday the 29th of July, we shall set out from this villa of Santa Fé on our journey. We are happy and full of hope, trusting only in your fervent prayers, and that as our father you will have our brothers in that very holy province bear us in mind in their offerings and prayers. In ours we shall not forget them nor Your Reverence, for whom we ask of God our Lord the greatest understanding and success, so that as hitherto you have been like Elijah, we your followers may be Elishas, clothed in the spirit of Your Reverence, our Father Elijah, and that he may preserve to us your important life many more years."

In the historic band who now set forth from Santa Fé on this epic jaunt there were ten persons. Official head of the expedition was Father Francisco Atanasio Domínguez, Superior of the New Mexico Franciscans and commissary visitor or inspector for the Province of the Holy Evangel,[1] whose headquarters were in Mexico. Father Domínguez, aided by Governor Fermín de Mendinueta, provided mounts and pack animals for the long hard

---

[1] Santo Evangelio.

trek in prospect. On the way Escalante wrote the superb diary that gave the expedition its place in history, and for that reason he became better known to fame than Domínguez, his superior, as so often happens, for good paper and ink outlast the human body, or the memory of human exploits, otherwise we should know comparatively little about our early history. In the intrepid company was veteran Don Bernardo Miera y Pacheco, engineer, retired captain, and citizen of Santa Fé. He was custodian of the astrolabe that was carried, and with it he made astronomical observations on the way. He also drew an illuminating map, and wrote an important account of the area traversed in the expedition, especially of the Utah region, thus greatly supplementing Escalante's diary.

Besides these three notables in the expedition, there were Don Pedro Cisneros, alcalde mayor of the Pueblo of Zuñi; Don Joaquín Laín, also a citizen of Zuñi; Lorenzo Olivares of El Paso; the brothers Lucrecio and Andrés Muñiz, Juan de Aguilar, and Simón Lucero, who bore no official titles and whose residences are not given in the narrative. Some of these men were chosen because as traders and trappers they had been over part of the trail to the far north. All of them, we may be sure, were comparatively young, for the march ahead of them was long and difficult, and this was not an old man's job. Andrés Muñiz, who the previous year had been north as far as Gunnison River and knew the Yuta language, went as interpreter. He proved to be highly important on the expedition, for most of the way through the regions that are now the states of Colorado and Utah, till after the explorers crossed the Colorado River on the homeward trek, all the Indians spoke dialects of the Yuta tongue.

Because of the conspicuous but less publicized role he played in the expedition, and of the intelligent map and report he made of what he saw on the long journey, Miera y Pacheco deserves special notice here. Don Bernardo was already a veteran of more than thirty active years on the New Mexico frontier, long antedating both Domínguez and Escalante. Born in the mountains of Burgos in Old Spain, he came from a prominent family of warriors. His grandfather, Don Antonio Pacheco, governor of Navarre and colonel of a regiment of infantry in Lombardy, was killed in a siege of Mantua. His father, Don Luís de Miera, raised a company of cavalry at his own expense in the service of King Philip V, in one of his numerous and sometimes bloody wars. The grandson, Don Bernardo, arrived in America in 1743 and became a soldier at El Paso, whence he took part in four campaigns against Apaches, Sumas and their allies who infested that border. So we conclude that in 1766 he must have been what we would call middle-aged, perhaps in his forties. In a war against the Gila Apaches, as engineer and captain of militia, he had made a map of the region covered in the campaign. Two years afterward he went east from El Paso with Captain Rubén de Solís to map the banks of the Río Grande and Conchos rivers. For this work he was allowed a salary of eight pesos a day, but he declined to accept it, preferring to serve the King of Spain without remuneration, so we infer that he was relatively well-to-do.

Later, accompanied by his family, Don Bernardo went in 1754 with Governor Marín del Valle to Santa Fé, where he served as alcalde and as captain of the frontiers of Galisteo and Pecos along the old Coronado trail, opened more than two centuries before our present story begins. In this capacity he made campaigns against the Comanches of the eastern border of New Mexico and mapped the regions covered in his forays. Still later he went to Moqui, apparently with Escalante, to talk with some Tanos Indians who said they wished to become Christians. As a result of this visit he drew a map of Hopi Land and recorded a conversation with some Cosninas who had come there to trade.

Don Bernardo drew a map of the northern provinces of Mexico, which he sent to the king by Bishop Tamarón after that prelate's visit to New Mexico in 1760. The king in turn sent the map to Nicolás de la Fora, captain of engineers, who came to the Spanish frontier of North America with the Marqués de Rubí on his famous expedition of 1766. Miera says he also made a map of the Navajo country. Did he mean the one he drew in the course of the Escalante expedition, or was it an earlier one that has not come to light? For four years energetic Miera was alcalde and captain of militia in New Mexico under the administration of Tomás Vélez Cachupín, who was governor of New Mexico between 1762 and 1767.

Finally, "led by the love and desire of placing himself at the service of the King and of extending the Faith," and equipped with a compass to determine directions and an astrolabe for taking latitudes, in 1776 Captain Miera joined Domínguez and Escalante as astronomer and cartographer on their historic expedition bound for California, and in it he played a conspicuous part. Several times he went ahead of the friars in difficult areas, selected routes and campsites, and sounded out the temper of the Indians. Once at least he got lost, to the dismay or perhaps the amusement of his companions. On the way he observed latitudes at numerous places, apparently the first time this was done in all the vast area traversed by the wayfarers in the areas that are now Colorado and Utah. These observations are shown in a table on page 129. He also made an ingenious and illuminating map of the regions explored on the way, and wrote a report which, alongside of Escalante's diary, is one of the precious treasures of far western American history for that historic year of 1776. As a result of his long service and of his many reports and maps, the archives of Mexico and Spain are replete with the writings and cartography of Miera y Pacheco, which would furnish data for a well documented and significant biography of Don Bernardo. We shall hear more about him as our story unfolds.

The adventurers now bound for California were equipped with saddle horses for the men, and with pack animals to carry baggage and provisions, which must have been considerable in view of the long jaunt in prospect. How many mules and horses the wayfarers had is not stated, but there must have been numerous extra mounts. One of them especially showed astonishing hardihood, as our story will relate. To supplement the food transported on mule-back and to provide fresh meat on the way, a herd of cattle was driven along, and they caused some of the diversions as well as the tribulations of the long trek, for on occasion cattle can be ornery beasts. In fact, we conjecture that the herdsmen, when out of hearing, on more than one occasion used language that would not have been considered fit for the ears of Fathers Domínguez and Escalante, who themselves were no tenderfeet.

There is little mention of killing wild game for food on the way, but perhaps this was regarded as a matter of course and not worth writing about. Before the expedition ended, the supply of cattle and other provisions was exhausted and the wayfarers lived off the country the hard way. In this state of affairs, on one occasion even a porcupine they captured was considered a welcome even though a prickly morsel. Nothing is said of weapons, for this was a peaceful errand, but it is inconceivable that the travelers should have embarked on such an adventure wholly unprepared for emergencies, especially since there was a professional soldier in the party, and since some of the natives on the route were known to be hostile to Europeans. And even pious friars, while they trusted in God, could not wholly neglect to keep their powder dry.

Although we find no specific statement on this point, we infer that Escalante's plan was to follow the trappers' trail northwest past Mesa Verde, descend Dolores River some distance, turn west to Green River and the Colorado, thence to Monterey, if they were lucky enough to hit it, through the pass in the High Sierra which Garcés thought he saw when he was in the San Joaquin Valley. Perhaps, on the other hand, Escalante's ideas on this last point were not so definite as this conjecture of mine.

For its patron saints the expedition chose the Virgin Mary, Our Lady of the Immaculate Conception, and her spouse the Patriarch Joseph. The start was made on July 29 from Santa Fé, then a city more than a century and a half old and therefore now in 1951 nearly twice the age of San Francisco. Mounts were fresh, and riders exuberant with the prospect of adventure and a look at the Pacific Ocean from the California shore. Before the departure there was a Solemn Mass. We would like to think that when the procession was about to set forth from the historic old Plaza, which is still in use today, there was a ringing of church bells, an assemblage of citizens, a loud chorus of adieus, many embraces and "God bless you's," and a shedding of tears by relatives, friends, and sweethearts. But no mention of any such demonstration was made in the diary, a fact that may be due to self restraint on the part of Father Escalante, the diarist. The drove of cattle designed to serve as food for the explorers presumably had been sent a few hours or a day ahead to be overtaken on the way.

In the English colonies on the Atlantic seaboard it was sometimes the custom to "procession"—that is, for the citizens in a body to retrace the boundaries between colonies, as is told in classic form by Byrd of Westover, ancestor of our Admiral Byrd, in his famous book called *The Dividing Line*. With Escalante's great diary in hand, this could be done today for longer or shorter stretches by present-day residents on the Escalante route, thus reliving the spectacular episode of 1776 and keeping its memory fresh.

III

TO THE COLORADO BORDER

Having finished their adieus, Escalante, Domínguez, Captain Miera, and their companions climbed the juniper-covered ridge north of Santa Fé, looked up at snow-covered Sangre de Cristo Mountains on their right, and at Valle Grande Range across the river on their left, passed the Indian pueblos of Tesuque, Nambé, Pojoaque, and San Ildefonso, and after a march of nine leagues, or some twenty-three miles north-northwest, crossed the Río Grande and spent the night at the pueblo and mission of Santa Clara. This was historic ground, as Hammond and Rey[1] so well have told us. A short distance north of here, on the east bank of the river, was the cradle of Spanish New Mexico, at the site of old San Juan de los Caballeros, where Juan de Oñate, in 1598, established his capital nine years before Jamestown was begun, some twelve years before the capital of New Mexico was moved to Santa Fé, and a whole century and three-quarters before the Escalante expedition or the founding of San Francisco. So our story falls just half-way between the arrival of Oñate and the year 1951.

Next day[2] the wayfarers left Santa Clara, continued northwest, passed the sites of present-day Española, Chamita, and Hernández, and marched up the valley of Chama River by a trail which, before the day of modern highways, was rough, tortuous, brush-covered, and punctuated by numerous steep pitches that slowed the pace of the wild and as yet not trail-wise stock. On the right still loomed snow-covered Sangre de Cristo Mountains, and on the left ran broken Valle Grande Range, some of its peaks rising above ten thousand feet. Having continued north-northwest up Chama River and traveled nine leagues that day, they reached the mission of Santa Rosa de Abiquiú, the last Spanish settlement seen by the wayfarers until they returned to civilization five months later, after a jaunt of nearly two thousand miles. Here the travelers halted one day and two nights "because of certain circumstances"

---
[1]George P. Hammond and Agapito Rey, *Narratives of the Coronado Expedition, 1540-1542* (Albuquerque, 1940).
[2]July 30.

not explained. Meanwhile a Solemn Mass was said in the little old church, imploring for the journey ahead the aid of the celestial patrons of the expedition.

Abiquiú was a famous outpost standing on the left bank of Chama River, beneath jagged red and gray cliffs that towered above the town which then was the last Spanish settlement toward the northwest. That border having long been infested by Comanches and Apaches, a colony of non-Christian Indians called *genízaros* or janissaries, a term brought from the Near East, had been established at the site to protect the frontier. In 1763 a *causa célebre* arose at the mission when an Indian called Juachinillo, or little Joaquín, was accused of witchcraft, by means of which he was said to have upset the fastidious stomach of Fray Juan Joseph de Toledo, the missionary then in charge. The records of the trial held before Carlos Fernández, alcalde mayor of La Cañada, filled more than a hundred manuscript pages.

The region from Abiquiú to the present border of the State of Colorado was one that had long been fought over by Spaniards against Apaches and Comanches, and in 1776 it apparently was not permanently occupied by any sedentary Indians, but instead was *tierra de guerra*—a land of war. So Miera the soldier was on the *qui vive*. In fact, the year after Escalante passed through the area, Juan Bautista de Anza, after leading his famous colony to San Francisco, became governor of New Mexico and made a campaign against the Indians of this very region through which Escalante was now passing. Anza's governorship in New Mexico is another illustration of the intertwining of the history of California and New Mexico in this early period.

By now the cattle, horses, and men were becoming trail-wise, the cattle sometimes in excessive measure. Leaving Santa Rosa de Abiquiú after Mass,[1] the wayfarers traveled west nearly two leagues along the bed of Chama River, then swung northward to avoid its rough canyon and the rugged Mesa de los Viejos[2] farther up its course. Continuing in that direction three and one-half leagues, over a road made difficult by stony mesas, the travelers took siesta on the north side of the valley of La Piedra Alumbre[3]

---
[1] On August 1.
[2] Plateau of the Ancients.
[3] Alum Rock.

near Arroyo Seco. Then, after going a short distance farther north, they swung northeast through a wooded canyon and camped on the bank of Arroyo Seco, having traveled seven leagues for the day, their fatigue having been relieved by a welcome shower which Escalante gratefully mentioned. Camp was pitched at the edge of the mesa or plateau closing Abiquiú Valley on the north. These details of the route described by Escalante illustrate the care he took in making the record. He was a good topographer and a superb diarist. Presumably Miera, the experienced engineer, helped with the report of topography, distances, and directions. No Indians were seen after the first day out from Abiquiú until August 23, when they met a lone Yuta Tabehuache from the far northeast. This fact may dispel any notion that everywhere in primitive America the woods were full of Indians.

August 2 had its diversions and its irritating incidents. Four leagues northeast up the canyon the wayfarers entered a dense grove of small oaks in which four ornery critters hid, and where the trail was temporarily lost. These are not Escalante's exact words, but they seem to express his feelings. Then followed, in pleasant contrast, a plain decorated by "purple and white flowers resembling carnations, groves of limes, choke-cherries, and manzanita berries, some white and some black." Clearly, Escalante was color conscious, had a romantic as well as a zealous soul, and this laudatory paragraph in his diary is highly prized by present-day residents in the vicinity through which he was passing, and where he is now a legendary hero.

Having found the hiding cattle, the travelers went forward, passed the site of Canjilón, and took siesta at Río Cebolla, where they found plentiful water in pools. Now swinging northwest three leagues over good terrain, they camped on the Río de las Nutrias, "where beavers lived," as Escalante tells us. The stream still bears the name, reminiscent of the clever animals which now are not so numerous in the area as they were in 1776, when Escalante passed that way. To creatures of the forest, man is a scourge.

August 3 brought new adventures that relieved the saddle galls, the blistered feet, and the homesickness of the wayfarers. Swinging northwestward they passed Tierra Amarilla, then a patch of red earth in the road but now a lively town, forded the

Chama River, perhaps at La Puente[1] below the site of Park View, and took siesta on its western bank.

Here a new diversion broke the monotony of travel, but by one of the participants it was not greatly enjoyed. Everybody likes a joke on the other fellow. Near the river they encountered large sinkholes, hidden by small stones on the surface, as if by nature's prankish design. In one of these treacherous pools the horse of Cisneros was completely submerged and Don Juan got a good soaking, while his companions doubtless laughed, at the same time that they generously helped him out. Escalante here notes, "the meadow of the river is about a league long from north to south, and is of good land for crops, with opportunities for irrigation. It produces much flax, and good and abundant pasturage. And there are also the other advantages necessary for the founding and maintenance of a settlement." The nearby town of Park View is the verification of this optimistic prediction.

After siesta the travelers went forward, climbed the western bank of the river and entered a small valley then called Santo Domingo in honor of the saint whose day they were celebrating by their patriotic trek. Not far away three mesas covered with pine curved around from north to south "to form a semi-circle reaching the river." These mesas which they aptly called "The Trinity," are plainly seen north of El Vado and west of Park View. The guides told the travelers that beyond the mesas there were two small lakes. They were apparently the ones now called Burford Lake west of El Vado, and Boulder Lake a few miles farther north. What the Indians called them is not recorded.

Escalante was now in the area today included in the Jicarilla Indian Reservation, whose people were so-named by the Spaniards because they made *xicarillas,* or little baskets. Here today a traveler may see a contented Indian woman sunning herself outside of a comfortable log house and reading a Sears-Roebuck catalog, which in popularity in the area is a keen competitor of the Bible and the movie. At the reservation headquarters a traveler now hears hearty stories about the pioneer days and tenderfoot visitors. Some of the tales are diverting but not all are intended for publication. The plodding wayfarers continued northwest through the valley and entered a small grove of pines. Here a loaded mule

---

[1] The bridge.

strayed away and did not appear until sunset, and because of the delay the wayfarers camped unhappily on rough ground at La Santísima Trinidad.

Next day[1] the travelers rode through a pine forest between two semi-circular mesas, separated at the north by a narrow gap, and passed Laguna de Olivares, whose water, though unpleasant to the taste, was fit to drink. Why the name of Olivares was thus put on the map is not explained in the diary, but there was doubtless some human incident involving Olivares and out of which Escalante cheated us. The lake was a small one, about a quarter of a league long and two hundred yards wide. It is now called Horse Lake. Going forward by a circuitous route but generally northwest, the travelers passed near the sites of Monero and Lumberton, along the route of the Denver and Rio Grande Railroad. At Lumberton they turned west and camped in Cañon del Engaño,[2] as they ruefully called it, near the site of Dulce.

Only a painstaking diary such as that of Escalante would enable us to identify this winding trek a century and three-quarters after the event. Arroyo del Belduque,[3] mentioned in the diary, is a small stream just south of the state line, the ancient origin of whose name is uncertain but intriguing, for it doubtless embalms some diverting episode. Piedra Parada,[4] which is also mentioned, is a conspicuous obelisk just north of the Colorado boundary. Both places were landmarks long before 1776, and so well known that Escalante did not feel called upon to explain their names. Dr. Alfred Thomas, in his excellent book called *Forgotten Frontiers,* has set forth interesting data regarding the early history of this very region.

The last day[5] on the soil of present-day New Mexico, which is much smaller now than in 1776, was a hard one for the wayfarers. Leaving the Canyon of Deceit and traveling half a league, they arrived at Río de Navajó, which, says Escalante, "rises in the Sierra de la Grulla and flows southwest to this place." The Sierra de la Grulla is one of the great ranges of the Rocky Mountains. From the place where they reached the Río de Navajó the

---

[1] August 4.
[2] Deceitful Canyon.
[3] Hunting Knife Creek.
[4] Standing Rock.
[5] August 5.

travelers continued westward. The day's march was over difficult terrain, "in canyons, over hills, and through very difficult forests." Here the guides lost their bearings, "and seemed to have forgotten the slight knowledge they had appeared to possess," thus putting a hard strain on Escalante's temper. They then swung northwest, traveled three leagues without a trail, crossed the Colorado line that was drawn long afterward, reached the San Juan River, forded it, and camped on or close to the site of the present town of Carracas, named much later, perhaps by or for some native of the capital of Venezuela, in South America. American place names are as conglomerate as the peoples who have occupied our country.

The campsite was poetically called Nuestra Señora de las Nieves,[1] in allusion to the snow-capped Rockies to the northeast. And what a panorama the travelers beheld as they raised their eyes! In the Continental Divide to the northeast, from which the Navajó, San Juan, Blanco, Conejos and other streams descend, there is a galaxy of snow-covered peaks over ten thousand feet high, forming one of the most scenic areas of the Rocky Mountains: Banded Peak, 12,760 feet; Nigger Mountain, 11,195 feet; Conejos Peak, 13,180 feet; Red Mountain, 12,006 feet; Cornwall Mountain, 12,291 feet; Silver Mountain, 12,450 feet; Summit Peak, 13,272 feet; and others nearly as lofty. If we have omitted somebody's favorite we apologize.

In order to make an astronomical observation, the first recorded by Escalante after leaving Santa Fé, and probably the first ever undertaken in all that vast region north of New Mexico, the travelers halted here until the afternoon of August 6, a welcome rest for men, cattle, and horses. Escalante wrote in his faithful diary, "the observation was made by the meridian of the sun, and we found the campsite to be in 37° 51' North Latitude"—an estimate more than half a degree too high, which was not bad considering all the circumstances. Miera made the observation, but Escalante's record of the event is an inclusive "we," indicating perhaps that he and Domínguez took a hand in the operation.

While camp was at Las Nieves, Escalante went upstream in the afternoon to examine the site where the Navajó and San Juan rivers join, "and found it was three leagues as the crow flies due

---

[1] Our Lady of the Snows.

east of Las Nieves, and that on the banks of both rivers, right at the junction, there were good advantages for a fair-sized settlement." Escalante adds, "The San Juan River carries more water than the Navajó, and they say that farther north," in the vicinity of Pagosa Springs, "it has fine . . . meadows because it runs through a more open country. Now joined, the two streams form a river as large as the Río del Norte in the month of July. This stream is called the Río Grande de Navajó because it separates the province of this name from the Yuta nation," who lived farther north in the vast region that are now the states of Colorado and Utah. He adds, "Downstream from the meadow of Nuestra Señora de las Nieves," that is, at Carracas and farther west, "there is good land with facilities for irrigation and everything else necessary for three or four settlements, even though they might be large ones." With an eye for natural beauty as well as for practical assets, he commented, "On either bank of the river there are dense and shady groves of white cottonwood, dwarf oak, choke-cherry, manzanita, lime and garambullo. There is also some sarsaparilla, and a tree that looked to us like the walnut."

IV

DOWN SAN JUAN RIVER AND PAST MESA VERDE

From the New Mexico border to northern Colorado Escalante and his companions saw no Indians, but they traversed a region rich in antiquities—the vestiges of an early population. The distinguished scientist Frank H. H. Roberts, tells us that down to the end of Pueblo III period, the San Juan area, for its archaeological remains was one of the most important in all the Southwest. "It seems to have been the center from which many of the characteristic features of the sedentary cultures were diffused, and for a long time was a leader in their development. The three great centers of Pueblo culture were Mesa Verde in southwestern Colorado, the Chaco Canyon in northwestern New Mexico, and the Kayentá district of northwestern Arizona. Besides these three major nuclei there were a number of minor districts of more or less importance. Most of the smaller areas were peripheral to and developed under the influence of the main centers." Moreover, the San Juan area had close historical ties with the Pueblo folk of New Mexico, amongst whom Escalante, Domínguez and Miera had all been working.

In the afternoon[1] the explorers left Las Nieves and traveled west down San Juan River. But Don Bernardo, not as hardy as the friars, had been having stomach trouble which doubled him up with grueling cramps, and he now became worse, so, after marching two and one-half leagues they camped on the bank of the river to permit him to recuperate. Next morning[2] Miera felt better, and the wayfarers continued west a league or more along the bank of the stream and on the slopes of the adjacent mesas, climbed a difficult hill, swung northwest, and having traveled one more league, arrived at Río de la Piedra Parada,[3] still so-called, near its junction with Río Navajó. The crossing of the stream was close to the site of the present-day town of Arboles. Here they noted a large meadow which they named San Antonio, of

---
[1] On August 6.
[2] On August 7.
[3] River of the Standing Rock.

which Escalante wrote: "It has very good land for crops, with opportunities for a settlement—firewood, stone, timber and pasturage, all close at hand." For this record Escalante's name is known to every schoolboy at Arboles, but he made no mention of the marvelous ruins which archaeologist Roberts and his associates have unearthed in recent years.[1] Of these archaeological treasures which Escalante passed by at close range and unconscious of their existence here at Piedras River, Roberts writes: "A number of the sites contain ruins of stone dwellings. Chimney Rock Mesa and lower spurs jutting out from it are literally covered with the remains of stone buildings. There is a large pueblo belonging to the third period (of Pueblo culture). On the lower level of this same formation there are 110 mounds marking the location of former unit-type or one-clan villages. . . . An even later period is represented by some of the ruins. Pottery fragments are of characteristic form found on the Pajarito Plateau in New Mexico. Two sites, one on the mesa top just above the town of Arboles, and the other on the west side of the Piedras River six miles upstream, show that they were occupied at some time during and subsequent to the Pueblo Revolt with its attendant reconquest, 1680-1700," that is to say, less than a century before Escalante and his party descended San Juan River that August day in 1776. Roberts con-

[1] Roberts, the distinguished archaeologist, writes: "The Piedra District, including the upper reaches of the San Juan River, as far as Pagosa Springs, Colorado," south of which the Escalante party had just passed, "is the most outlying of the two minor centers. It was practically unknown archaeologically prior to the summer of 1921, when a joint investigation of the ruins was begun by the State Historical Society of Colorado and the University of Denver." He says that most of the sites contain not only remains of Pueblo I and Pueblo II periods—categories well known to archaeologists—but vestiges of an even later period are found. The culture center of the district lies in and around Chimney Rock Mesa. Some of the sites show that they were occupied during or after the famous Pueblo Revolt. He adds that in Governador, Burns, and Francis canyons thirty miles south of Arboles, there are many ruins which date from the same period, and that perhaps the Piedras sites represent a northward extension of that group. "There seems to be little doubt that the latter were Jémez people"—perhaps those who were defeated by Captain Miguel de Lara in the battle of June 29, 1696, and fled to the Navajo country. In other words these ruins just recently discovered, record a chapter in the history of New Mexico. Roberts specifically dates as of "1690" two or more sites on Piedra River north of the town of Arboles. He adds, "From the junction of the Piedras and San Juan Rivers, just below the town of Arboles, there is an almost unbroken line of former house sites and ruins extending northward on both sides of the river for a distance of over fifteen miles." Frank H. H. Roberts, *Early Pueblo Ruins in the Piedra District, Southwestern Colorado.* Bureau of American Ethnology, Bulletin 96, dealing with the archaeology of the area near the place where Escalante camped on August 5, 1776.

cludes that many of the ruins in the vicinity represent settlements of runaway people from New Mexico in the upheaval caused by the Pueblo Revolt, an episode to which Hackett in his classic monograph devoted his superb scholarship.[1]

At the site of Arboles Escalante left San Juan River, on whose banks and tributaries for a long distance downstream there are many other remains of an ancient civilization. With no mention of ruins at Piedras River, for apparently he neither saw nor heard of any, Escalante on the same day[2] crossed the stream, traveled west-northwest more than two leagues, passed the sites of the present-day towns of Allison and Tiffany, and reached Río de los Pinos, so-called because of the pines growing on its banks. At the place where Escalante crossed this stream there were large meadows with abundant pasturage of grama grass, extensive lands for raising crops by irrigation, and everything that might be desired for a good settlement. The ford was apparently about halfway between the present-day towns of Ignacio and La Boca. They camped in a meadow naming it La Vega de San Cayetano.

Leaving camp on August 8, the travelers continued west-northwest, still close to the line of the Denver and Rio Grande Railroad, went four leagues, passing south of the sites of Ignacio and Oxford, and arrived at flower-strewn Río Florido, a stream smaller than Río de los Pinos, they said. At the place where they crossed it Escalante mentioned "a large meadow of good land for crops and facilities for irrigation." Continuing west two leagues and then west-northwest more than two leagues, they descended a stony slope, crossed Río de las Ánimas,[3] and camped for the night on its bank some four miles south of the site of the city of Durango, and near the southern end of Moving Mountain, which in recent years has been slowly traveling downstream, and making itself an object of lively concern to citizens and of interest to geologists. Farther down the Ánimas River, which is a tributary of the San Juan, there are many famous ruins of ancient settlements, notably at Aztec and Farmington, and at numerous places farther west, where archaeologists have uncovered extensive ruins and reconstructed a fascinating story of antiquity.

---
[1]Charles W. Hackett, *Revolt of the Pueblo Indians of New Mexico and Otermin's Attempted Reconquest, 1680-1682* (Albuquerque: University of New Mexico Press, 1942).
[2]August 7.
[3]River of the Souls in Purgatory.

Miera mentioned these in his report and on his map when he recommended that a Spanish presidio and settlement should be found "at the junction of the River of Nabajóo[1] with that of Las Ánimas along the beautiful and extensive meadows which its margins provide for raising crops, together with the convenience of the timber, firewood, and pastures which they offer." He adds, "There still remain in those meadows, vestiges of irrigation ditches, ruins of many large and ancient settlements of Indians, and furnaces where apparently they smelted metals." One need not be much excited over "firsts" in history, but might not this be the first written mention of antiquities in that great archaeological treasure house along San Juan River? Escalante's predecessors, the trappers, and traders, may have seen or heard of them, but has any earlier mention of them been recorded?

On August 9 the wayfarers set forth west, threaded the beautiful valley now called Ridge's Basin, swung west-northwest through a leafy forest, and camped for the night on Río de San Joaquín[2] near the site of Hesperus. The main highway now runs close to Escalante's trail for this day's march. The mountains round about were then and still are called Sierra de la Plata because in them silver had been reported, and the present-day town of La Plata is a short distance north of Escalante's trail. To verify these stories of silver deposits Governor Vélez Cachupín[3] had sent men from Santa Fé. They obtained some ore, "but it was not learned with certainty what metal it was." Tired horses and cattle and a heavy rain caused Escalante and his party to remain here at Río de San Joaquín for the night.

Next morning[4] Father Domínguez awoke with what perhaps would now be called neuralgia in his face and head, and he was more fit to rest than to ride a horse, but bad weather and the dampness of the place forced the travelers to move on, so they continued north, northwest, and north. Another heavy rain fell, Domínguez became worse, and the roads impassable. So, having advanced north and west four and one-half leagues for the day, they camped on the south fork of Mancos River near the site of

---

[1] Now called the San Juan River.
[2] Río de La Plata.
[3] Tomás Vélez Cachupín was governor of New Mexico from 1762 to 1767. He was succeeded by Pedro Fermín de Mendinueta, 1767 to 1778, including the period of the Escalante expedition.
[4] August 10.

the present town of Mancos, calling the stream San Lázaro. The name Mancos suggests that at some time previously Indians or skeletons with hands cut off had been seen or heard of in the vicinity, but this may be a bad guess.

At Río de San Lázaro Escalante was only a few miles from fabulous Mesa Verde, where some of the most remarkable antiquities of all North America are found. We now know that for more than a thousand years an agricultural people had lived on Mesa Verde and in the adjacent regions, and from the ruins still found in the area archaeologists have written one of the most remarkable chapters in the story of prehistoric America. But of this treasure house of archaeology Escalante made no mention. If the guides knew about the ruins, superstition and fear perhaps sealed their tongues.

On August 11, because Father Domínguez still had a fever, the travelers remained in camp at San Lázaro, unable either to go forward or to inspect "the veins of metallic rocks that were in the nearby sierra," of which they had been told by a companion who had seen them on another expedition. Which member of the party this was is not stated.

Next day,[1] Father Domínguez was better, "and in order to change terrain and climate rather than to make progress," they left Río de San Lázaro, continued northwest a league, swung west-northwest five leagues, and west two and one-half leagues, then a quarter of a league north, crossed Dolores River and camped near the site of the present town of Dolores. This was one of the longest distances covered in a day. Did it represent the eagerness of the guides to leave the vicinity of ghostly Mesa Verde which lay a short distance south of this day's line of march? With all its wonders, Mesa Verde is mighty spooky.

Next day[2] the wayfarers remained in camp, "partly in order that Father Domínguez might improve in health and partly to observe the latitude of this site and meadow of Río de los Dolores." The observation was made—the second on the trip—and Miera found they were in 38° 13½′ north latitude, which was more than two-thirds of a degree too high, owing to their primitive apparatus. Here Escalante noted "everything necessary for the establishment and maintenance of a good settlement in the way of

---
[1] August 12.
[2] August 13.

irrigable lands, pastures, timber and firewood." This place was notable for another thing. Escalante wrote in his diary for the same day that "on an elevation on the south bank of the river in ancient times there was a small settlement of the same form as those of the Indians of New Mexico, as is shown by the ruins which we purposely examined." It is significant that he did not suggest any relation between this small ruin and the great ones on nearby Mesa Verde, of which apparently he had not heard.

Of this antiquity on the left or western bank of Dolores River, Walter Fewkes, the noted archaeologist wrote: "The name Escalante Ruin, given to the first ruin recorded by a white man in Colorado is on the top of a low hill to the right of the Monticello Road, just beyond where it diverges from the road to Cortez. The outline of the pile of stones suggests a D-shaped or semi-circular house, with a central depression surrounded by rooms separated by radiating partitions. The wall on the south or east sides was probably straight, rendering the form not greatly unlike other ruins on hilltops in the neighborhood of Dolores."[1] The relic is still to be seen beside the highway. Who first gave Dolores River its name we do not know, but there is no doubt as to its appropriateness. Apparently it was so-called by the New Mexico traders who had preceded Escalante, and who fully recognized the fitness of the designation.

---

[1] J. Walter Fewkes, *Prehistoric Villages, Castles, and Towers of Southwestern Colorado* (Washington, 1919).

V

RIVER OF SORROWS

On a modern map the Dolores River looks innocent, and easy to follow. But before the day of cleared farms and surfaced highways the banks of the stream were grown with dense thickets of brush through which even cattle, especially the Spanish long horns, found difficult going. Moreover, for long distances the Dolores runs through narrow gorges between high and unscalable cliffs. It is these features that make the Dolores River a matter of affection and pride to the people who live upon its banks, but from some of the canyons, unless a traveler is equipped with the outfit of a Swiss mountaineer, the only way to get out is to go forward or turn back. Several times the Escalante party found themselves in just this predicament.

Next morning,[1] Father Domínguez was feeling better, and the caravan set forth downstream. Starting on the right bank of Dolores River, they traveled north, crossed the stream near the site of McPhee, went northwest by west five leagues through dense chamise thickets, entered a deep and rough canyon, followed it two leagues, crossed the Dolores northeast of the site of the town of Cahone, whose name perpetuates the description given by Escalante of the difficult gorge. Again crossing Dolores River, the travelers camped at La Asunción, near the mouth of Narraguinnep Creek. All through this area and beyond it there are place names that constitute an enduring monument to the beautiful Ute language. Escalante was now in the country of the tribe called Muhuaches.

That afternoon the travelers were overtaken by a *coyote* and a *genízaro* from Abiquiú, the first called Felipe and the second Juan Domingo. As their designations indicate, these men were mixed bloods of Indian and European stock. Escalante writes: "In order to wander among the heathen they had fled from that pueblo without the permission of their superiors, protesting that they wished to accompany us. We did not need them, but to prevent the mischief which either through ignorance or malice they

---
[1] August 14.

might commit by traveling alone any longer among the Yutas if we tried to send them back, we accepted them as companions." There was nothing else they could do about it.

The weather at this season was sizzling hot, but although the travelers were from the cool New Mexico plateau, no complaint on this score was recorded in Escalante's diary. Two trails led out from La Asunción. Taking the one that ran the more westward and some distance from the river, they traveled[1] west-northwest through a rough and stony canyon, turned northwest nearly a league and a half, then north-northwest more than three leagues through a chamise thicket but over good and almost level terrain, then northwest a league, and halted for siesta at an arroyo which the guides thought would have water, but to their great disappointment they found it dry. At the left of their trail for that day the town of Dove Creek now stands. It is difficult to show all these turns on a small-scale map, but Escalante's minute record of the turns and directions for this day's travel illustrate his attention to details.

Scouts now went out and found a permanent pond with enough water for the men but not sufficient for the animals. Says Escalante: "It was covered with stones and logs, apparently on purpose. Perhaps this was done by the Yutas because of some misfortune they had suffered at this place, for according to what was told us by some of the companions who have been among them, they are accustomed to do this in such cases." Escalante's party followed the scouts, traveled two and one-half leagues northwest and north and reached the pond, naming it Agua Tapada or Covered Pool. In this long and hot day's march they had traveled nine leagues and three-quarters, or some twenty-five miles, and camp was made in the vicinity of Egnar, Colorado.

August 16 was a hectic day for the travelers. That morning over half of the animals were missing. Crazed by thirst, they had stampeded, turned about on the trail, and found water half way back to the previous camp. Herdsmen, sweating and perhaps cursing when out of the padres' hearing, recovered the cattle and finally overtook the caravan, but because of the delay the forward march from Agua Tapada did not start until half-past ten in the forenoon, which was very late for these early risers and for this hot weather. Setting forth at that time, Escalante's party followed a

---

[1] August 15.

dim trail, thinking it would lead them once more to Dolores River, which they had planned to follow. But, after they had marched two leagues northwest and a league and a half west, the trail played out because the soil was loose and all the footprints had been erased by showers. So they continued northwest, and having traveled a quarter of a league they entered a wide canyon in which they found a well-beaten path. Following it a short distance, they arrived at a pool with plentiful water for both men and animals. And because the pool was concealed in a grove of piñon and juniper trees, they named the place Agua Escondida or Hidden Water.

This camp at Agua Escondida was a pivotal point in the entire Escalante expedition and on it hinged momentous consequences. Ever since leaving Santa Fé the route had led steadily northwest for some three hundred miles. The wayfarers were bound for Monterey in California. It seems reasonable to assume that from what he had learned through the Santa Fé traders and trappers who had preceded him, Escalante might have planned to swing westward here or at a point farther south, cross the mountain divide to Colorado River, or even descend to it by the McElmo and San Juan rivers, and then head for Monterey by way of the Havasupai settlements which Garcés had visited. But perhaps this is attributing to Escalante more information than he could have possessed. At Agua Escondida the trappers' trail to Gunnison River, where Rivera had carved his name on a tree, swung sharply eastward, and in that direction the guides now led Escalante and his companions. Moreover, Escalante had heard interesting news about the Sabuaganas toward the northeast, and he desired to visit them.

Miera now had another adventure, and at the same time he sorely worried his fellow travelers. While the men were examining the trail ahead, Don Bernardo set forth alone down the canyon, unobserved by his companions, and disappeared as completely as if the earth had opened and swallowed him. When his absence was discovered, one of the men went out to bring him back for fear he might get lost, and so the caravan might proceed on its way. But Don Bernardo was so far ahead that before the scout overtook him he had again reached Dolores River, and when they got back it was past midnight. But to compensate for all this trouble Miera had found a better route by which to go forward, and had an adventure to tell about for the rest of his life.

Next day[1] in the afternoon the caravan left Agua Escondida, entered Miera's tortuous labyrinth, and traveled seven leagues northeast, although by a straight line it would not have been more than five. Imposing cliffs rose high on either side of the gorge, and the farther they went the more difficult it would have been to get out if they had tried. At the end of the day's march they arrived for the third time at Dolores River. Residents in the vicinity will recognize the scene of Don Bernardo's adventure.

"On reaching the river," says Escalante—this was at San Bernardo, named for Miera's patron saint—"we saw very recent tracks of the Yutas, and for this reason we thought one of their rancherías must be nearby, and that if they had seen us and we did not seek them they might fear some harm from us and be disquieted. Moreover, since we hoped that some one of them might guide us or give us information, enabling us to continue our journey with less difficulty and toil than we were now suffering, because none of the companions knew the waterholes and the terrain ahead, we decided to seek them." From this we conclude that none of the guides had ever traveled by precisely this route.

The caution now observed by the Spaniards is indicated by Escalante's words. "As soon as we halted in a bend of the river which we called San Bernardo"—the bend, that is to say—"Father Fray Francisco Atanasio set forth, accompanied by the interpreter Andrés Muñiz and Juan Pedro Cisneros. Having followed the tracks upstream about three leagues they saw that the Indians were Yutas Tabehuaches, but they were not able to find them although they went clear to the place where the little Río de las Paralíticas[2] empties into the Dolores. They say this Río de las Paralíticas is so-called because the first of our people who saw it,"—traders from Santa Fé—"found in a ranchería on its bank three Yuta women suffering from paralysis. The stream separates the Yutas Tabehuaches from the Muhuaches, the latter living to the south, and the others to the north." This statement contains precious ethnological information.

Early the next morning[3] two men set forth to find a way out of the canyon of the river without leaving their northerly course or turning away from water and pasturage. But they could find no

---
[1]August 17.
[2]Now Disappointment Creek.
[3]August 18.

way to go forward except by the bed of the stream, which they had to cross many times, and which was so stony that there was danger of bruising the feet of the animals. So, leaving the bend of San Bernardo, the caravan traveled north downstream a league and camped. Scouts continued north, and returned at night reporting that "only by the bed of the river" would they be able "to emerge from this impassable network of mesas, and then only with difficulty." So they decided to continue next day by the canyon of the river. This was one of their shortest marches, for they had advanced only one league.

August 19 was another hectic day. They continued two leagues northward downstream, and halted at Cajón del Yeso[1] to let the animals drink. Finding the river bed impassable, a scout went ahead to seek a route northwest across a chain of high and stony mesas, but with no better luck. A passable trail to the southwest was found, but, says Escalante, "we did not dare follow it," for beyond the point now reached they saw "high mesas and deep canyons in which we might again be walled in and find ourselves forced to turn back." Moreover, they feared a lack of water by that route.

---

[1] Now Gypsum Creek.

VI

ACROSS TABEHUACHE SIERRA
AND DOWN UNCOMPAHGRE RIVER

WHEN A CONFERENCE with the guides was held, everyone very humanly expressed a different opinion. "So," says Escalante, "finding ourselves in this state of confusion, not knowing whether we should be able to follow the trail mentioned, or whether it would be better for us to go back a short distance and take the road that goes to the Yutas Sabuaganas," of whom we shall hear again, "we put our trust in God and our will in that of His Most Holy Majesty. And having implored the intercession of our Most Holy Patrons, in order that God might direct us in the way that would be most conducive to His Holy Service, we cast lots between the two roads, and drew the one leading to the Sabuaganas, which we decided to follow until we reached them." We wonder if they pulled straws. Escalante was a pious gambler. He adds, "In this place, which we called the Cajón del Yeso[1] because there was gypsum in a mesa nearby, we observed the latitude by the Sun and found it to be 39° 6'." They had traveled two leagues north that day, and this was Miera's third astronomical observation made on the expedition.

Leaving Cajón del Yeso[2] and backtracking a league southeast, Escalante and his companions again crossed Dolores River. In some hills about a quarter of a league from the trail they "saw some mines of transparent and very good gypsum." They now entered a wide valley and traveled three leagues east-northeast, by a well-beaten trail that ran along the foot of a high mesa. "Then, at the urging of Don Bernardo Miera, who did not wish to follow this road," Andrés the interpreter led the travelers up a very high and rugged acclivity having so many stones that they expected to be forced to turn back when half way up, because it was so hard on the animals that many of them left their tracks on the rocks with the blood of their feet! They climbed the ridge with tremendous difficulty, and at the end of several hours, having

---

[1]Gypsum Canyon, the name which it still bears, thus confirming the interpretation of the route.
[2]August 20.

traveled less than a mile on the ascent they reached the top, where men and animals no doubt took a breather.

Continuing a mile northwest, and looking down, they saw to their relief or their chagrin, that at the bottom of the mesa there was a good road over level country and which they had missed. Descending to it by an easy trail without stones, they traveled about two leagues, first north, then northwest through a thicket of chamise and thorny cactus. This was troublesome for the animals, so they entered the bed of an arroyo, where the footing was softer, and having traveled along it about a league to the east, in the southern end of the canyon they came unexpectedly and joyfully to a large pond of good water, and a spring which they called Fuente de San Bernabé, on the banks of the stream now called Basin Creek. Escalante remarks, "Judging from the trails and the ruins of old huts, this is a camping place of the Yutas, and the road we left to climb the impassable ridge above mentioned leads right to it." Somebody had blundered, but on this score Escalante made no comment. Here they camped on the night of August 20, having traveled six leagues that day, not counting the distance they had retraced. They were now in the drainage of San Miguel River, and the natives here apparently were Tabehuaches.

From the Spring of San Bernabé they traveled[1] in the canyon four leagues north over not very good terrain, and some really tough pulls. In the middle of the canyon they passed some pools of good water, and almost at the end of the gorge in a stretch of a quarter of a league they found as much water as would run from a fair-sized spring. Now leaving the canyon, they traveled nearly a league northward through a level chamise thicket. Then, entering another gorge, and traveling a league over a difficult trail, they arrived at Río de San Pedro,[2] and camped in a meadow which they named San Luís, having marched for the day six leagues. Camp was made northwest of Naturita. The natives here were Tabehuaches, and Tabehuache Creek joins San Miguel River north of the place where the travelers crossed it. Thus Escalante's diary makes clear the general location of two divisions of the Yuta tribe in this vicinity—Muhuaches in the south and Tabehuaches in the north.

---
[1] On August 21.
[2] Now called San Miguel River.

Leaving San Luís next morning,[1] they crossed San Miguel River, ascended a steep but not very stony grade, and reached a wide mesa "which looks like a fragment of the Sierra de los Tabehuaches," now called Uncompahgre Plateau. Traveling two leagues northeast, then more than half a league east-southeast, they descended from the mesa. Escalante writes, "it is the one which Don Juan María de Rivera in his diary describes as very difficult." From this we conclude that Escalante at the time was square on the old trappers' trail, a fact which must have given him renewed confidence.

Continuing a league northeast upstream they halted for siesta, while scouts explored a route for the afternoon march, planning to leave the river if they found water, otherwise they would leave it next day. The scouts returned late at night to Camp San Felipe on the upper waters of San Miguel River and near the base of Uncompahgre Plateau. This day's travel was four leagues toward the east. On August 23 they left Camp San Felipe, traveled along the foot of Sierra de los Tabehuaches, and continued four leagues by a winding trail which took them two leagues east of San Felipe.

The next passage in Escalante's diary is most significant, and sustains our interpretation of Escalante's route in all the region where he traveled after leaving Gypsum Canyon. He writes: "We left Río de San Pedro which rises in a spur of the Sierra de las Grullas." This great sierra is now called the Rocky Mountains and in it San Miguel River rises in the vicinity of Telluride and Ophir, where, at an elevation of 14,000 feet the headwaters of San Miguel River mingle with those of Dolores River, their main courses running almost at right angles to each other, the Dolores flowing southwest and the San Miguel northwest. Taking their separate ways down the western slope, they meet again near Paradox Valley. Escalante adds, "near here is the small range which they call Sierra de la Sal because close to it there are salt flats, where, according to what we were told, the Yutas who live hereabouts get their salt." Sierra de la Sal is a conspicuous peak in Utah just across the Colorado state line, and nearly straight west of the place where Escalante was writing.

After leaving Río de San Pedro,[2] they halted for siesta near a permanent stream that descended from the sierra to a plain

---

[1] August 22.
[2] On August 23.

covered with chamise, and on whose southern edge there was a valley in front of which there was a ruin of an ancient stone pueblo and fortification, built, it was assumed, by the Tabehuaches. The horses now had good pasturage, which, all the way from Asunción, on Dolores River in the vicinity of Cahone, had been scarce. After a shower the travelers turned northeast, ascending Sierra de los Tabehuaches by a stiff climb for two leagues. Here the Spaniards were overtaken by a Yuta Tabehuache, the first Indian they had seen since the day they left Abiquiú, when they had met two natives, of what tribe we are not told.

In order to talk with this Tabehuache they camped at a spring called La Fuente de la Guía,[1] on the edge of Uncompahgre Plateau. They gave the Indian "something to eat and to smoke," and through an interpreter "asked him various questions concerning the land ahead, the rivers, and their courses." They likewise asked him the whereabouts of the Tabehuaches, Muhuaches, and Sabuaganas. At first the Indian appeared ignorant of everything, "even of the country in which he lived," but when relieved of his fear, "he said the Sabuaganas were all in their own country," toward the northeast, "and that we would soon meet them; that the Tabehuaches were wandering dispersed through this sierra and its vicinity; that all the rivers, from the San Pedro to the San Rafael inclusive, flow into the Dolores, which in turn joins the Río de Navajó," now called the San Juan. Escalante asked this intelligent Indian if he would guide them to a village of Sabuaganas "said by our interpreter and others to be very friendly toward the Spaniards, and to know a great deal about the country." He consented on condition that the Spaniards should wait for him till next day, to which the travelers agreed. Of the Sabuaganas we shall hear again.

At the appointed time[2] the Yuta guide arrived at camp, bringing his wife, two other women, and five children, "two at the breast and three from eight to ten years old, all good looking and very friendly." This was no Nordic speaking. Thinking the Spaniards had come to trade, as Rivera and others had done in former years, the visitors brought tanned deerskins, dried manzanita berries, and other things for barter. In order that the natives might not fear he had come as a conquerer, and thinking that perhaps they had heard of the journey of Father Garcés to Oraibe,

[1] The Guide's Fountain.
[2] August 24.

Escalante told them that the lone wanderer had returned to the Cosninas. "Thereupon the Yutas calmed down and sympathized with us in our trouble." They said they had heard of the travels of Father Garcés, an example of the way news spread among the Indians. Escalante gave the visitors food from his dwindling supply, and to the new guide, whom he named Atanasio, in honor of Father Domínguez, he gave "two hunting knives and some strings of white glass beads." The fellow was now a millionaire!

Leaving the Indian families behind, the Spaniards set forth with Atanasio to find Sabuaganas to guide them on a new leg of their peregrination. They traveled eastward two leagues and camped in a deep valley called La Cañada Honda on a branch of Horsefly Creek, where there was "an ample spring of good water, plentiful firewood, and abundant pasturage for the animals." This was and is beautiful country.

The march on August 25 was a long one. Leaving Cañada Honda, the wayfarers traveled four and one-half leagues east-southeast, and started to cross Uncompahgre Plateau. Swinging northeast a league and a half they reached the crest, near Logsill Mesa, at an elevation of some nine thousand feet, where they saw ferns and beautiful groves of cottonwoods. Here also they found three trails. Taking the one that led northeast, they followed it a league and a half and halted at another spring which they called Ojo de Laín, presumably because Laín discovered it. The men were hungry, but before they had time to prepare any food a heavy rain fell, and they spent an uncomfortable night, wishing they were snugly at home in beloved Santa Fé.

Next day[1] they continued two and one-half leagues northeast, and arrived at Río de San Francisco, now Uncompahgre River, but then called by the Yuta Indians Ancapagri, meaning "red lake," because near its source far to the south in the Rocky Mountains there was a spring of red and bad tasting water. Swinging northward, they traveled a league and a half downstream and halted at a large marsh which they called La Ciénega de San Francisco, having traveled for the day five leagues. Camp was a short distance south of the city of Montrose, founded long afterward.

Here Escalante inserts in his diary a "description of the sierras thus far seen," and some others, including Sierra de la Grulla, Sierra de la Plata, Sierra de los Tabehuaches, Sierra del Venado

---

[1] August 26.

Alazán, Sierra del Almagre, Sierra Blanca, Sierra del Dátil, Sierra de la Sal, and Sierra de Abajo. He gives most space to Sierra de los Tabehuaches, across which he had just traveled. He says "it abounds in excellent pasturage, is very moist, and has good land for crops without irrigation. It produces in abundance piñon, spruce, royal pine, dwarf oak, several kinds of wild fruits, and in some places flax. In it there are stags, fallow deer, and other animals, and fowls of size and shape similar to ordinary domestic hens, from which they differ in not having combs. Their flesh is savory." Perhaps these were sage hens.

Of Uncompahgre River our newsy traveler writes: "this Río de San Francisco is medium-sized, and a little larger than the Dolores. It is fed by several small streams that flow down from the western slope of the Sierra de las Grullas, and it runs northwest. In the place where we first saw it," south of Montrose, "there is a meadow about three leagues long with excellent land for crops, opportunities for irrigation, and everything needed for the establishment of a good settlement. North of this meadow there is a chain of little hills and lead colored knolls crowned with yellow earth." Residents in the vicinity will easily recognize them.

Traveling northward from La Ciénega de San Francisco,[1] the wayfarers descended Uncompahgre River to the vicinity of Montrose, where they met a Ute Indian whom they called El Surdo,[2] with his family. Of the conference here Escalante irritably remarks, "we stopped with him a long while, but in the lengthy conversation we learned nothing new except to have suffered from the heat of the sun, which was very hot all the time the confab lasted." Continuing northward the same day, they traveled two and one-half leagues, passed the site of Montrose, crossed to the east bank of the river, entered a stony plain, and having advanced downstream three and one-half leagues to the north-northwest, near the site of Olathe they camped in another meadow which they called San Agustín el Grande.

They were now approaching the confluence of the Uncompahgre River with the Gunnison. They did not descend clear to the junction, but Escalante gave an interesting account of the region. He wrote: "farther downstream and about four leagues to the north of this meadow of San Agustin, this river[3] joins

---

[1] On August 27.
[2] The Deaf One.
[3] Uncompahgre River.

another and larger one which by our people is called the Río de San Javier and by the Yutas the Río del Tomichi." It is now called Gunnison River in honor of a celebrated Gringo pioneer of a much later date. Escalante adds, "in the year 1761 Don Juan María de Rivera reached these two streams below their junction, having crossed the same Sierra de los Tabehuaches, on whose crest, according to the description which he gives in his diary, is the place he called El Purgatorio. The meadow where he halted in order to ford the river,[1] and where he says he carved on a second-growth cottonwood a cross, the letters which spell his name, and the year of his expedition, is also found at the same junction on the south bank of the river." Apparently Escalante's men did not find the carving, for surely if they had done so the event would have been recorded in the diary as a rare discovery. But just then they had news of more immediate interest than mere history.

---

[1] Gunnison River.

VII

SILVESTRE BECOMES GUIDE

Sometime during August 27 Escalante had been told by Yuta Indians that toward the northeast in the mountains there was a settlement of Sabuaganas, and with them some Timpanogotzis, or Laguna Indians, from the valley of Utah Lake, far to the northwest, where they were said to live in pueblos or towns "like those of New Mexico." This was most interesting news, for it promised an opportunity to Christianize sedentary Indians. But more to the immediate point, Escalante saw in it a chance to get help on his way to California, to reach which he had come by a most roundabout trail to avoid the hostile Apaches of Gila River and the Hopis of western New Mexico. So it was here in Colorado, on Uncompahgre River, that Escalante decided to make a wide detour that had decisive bearings on the outcome of his expedition bound for California, and at the same time led him to another Promised Land —the Provo Valley.

On August 28 the wayfarers continued northward from San Agustín, left Uncompahgre River, crossed the area now called the Delta, and having traveled four leagues for the day arrived at San Javier River,[1] "otherwise known as Río del Tomichi."[2] In a bend of the river they halted at a place called Santa Monica, near the site of present-day Austin, planning to take a short siesta and then continue northeast up Gunnison River to find the camp of the Sabuaganas. But to avoid the long trek east to visit the Sabuagana camp, for the horses were badly worn and lame, and to avoid using up their supplies, they sent the interpreter with the guide Atanasio to bring the Sabuaganas to camp, "and to see if for pay any of them or any of the Lagunas would guide the Spaniards as far as they knew the way toward the settlement on the Lake." The messengers set forth on this errand and the Spaniards camped for the night at Santa Monica. Here, too, Miera for the fourth time observed the latitude and found it to be 39° 13′ 22″.

---
[1] Gunnison River.
[2] Tomichi Creek joins Gunnison River a short distance southwest of the town of Gunnison, far east and south of Escalante's route.

About ten o'clock next morning,[1] five Yutas Sabuaganas appeared on a hill across Gunnison River shouting loudly. The Spaniards thought they must be the people the guides had gone to seek at the Sabuagana village in the mountains toward the northeast, but soon it was discovered that this was not the case. They were a different band. Escalante writes: "We gave them something to eat and to smoke, but after a long conversation, whose subject was the dispute they had this summer with the Cumanches Yamparicas, we were unable to learn from them a single thing useful to us, because their aim was to frighten us by setting forth the danger of our being held by the Cumanches ... if we continued on our way."

But Miera and the padres were not easily scared. They had dealt with Indians before and were learning every day. And says Escalante, "we refuted the arguments by which they tried to prevent us from going forward." Resorting to a little bluff, he told them that "Our God, who is Lord of everybody, would defend us in case of encounters with these enemies with whom the Sabuaganas had tried to frighten the Spaniards." He adds, "Thus ended the debate," which had not been wholly theological. Perhaps among the Ute Indians today there is a legend, handed down from generation to generation, telling of the arrival "a long time ago" in their country near Gunnison River, of men wearing broad brimmed sombreros and long flowing robes, and inquiring the way to California, a country in the distant west ... *mas allá*.

Next morning[2] Andrés the interpreter and Atanasio the guide crossed over to the south bank of Gunnison River with five other Sabuaganas and a young Laguna Indian. After serving the visitors with food and tobacco, for both of which they had keen appetites, the Spaniards told them they now planned to go to the Laguna pueblos.

When Escalante asked for a guide to the Lagunas, promising to pay him liberally, the Sabuagana visitors raised objections. They said the only road to the Lake ran through the country of the Comanches, who would kill the Spaniards. Moreover, they said none of them knew the way to the Lake, and with violent gestures they urged the travelers to turn back. Escalante writes: "We

---
[1]August 29.
[2]August 30.

tried to convince them, now with arguments and again with flattery, in order not to displease them." More to the point, he offered the Laguna youth a woolen cloak, a hunting knife, and some white glass beads. This turned the trick. The Laguna accepted the gift and promised to guide the Spaniards to his people at the Lake, and he was now given the name Silvestre.

The Sabuaganas now had a change of heart. They said they knew the way but the Laguna boy did not. They ceased talking about difficulties and invited the Spaniards to go by way of their camp in the mountains toward the north. Escalante wrote: "We knew very well that this was a trick by which to detain us, and to enjoy for a longer time the benefits we were conferring upon them, for to all who came, and today there were many, we gave food and tobacco." However, in order not to displease them and not to lose the promised guide, the Spaniards consented to visit the Sabuagana settlement, even though it necessitated a long detour. In fact they had already planned to go there.

VIII

UP THE MOUNTAINS TO THE SABUAGANAS

This business settled, in the afternoon[1] the caravan, with its now wealthy guide and its escort of Sabuaganas, left Santa Monica, crossed Gunnison River, whose waters reached above the shoulder blades of the horses, and raised the problem of keeping provisions and gunpowder dry. Then, climbing a long hill, the wayfarers passed the site of Austin, traveled upstream east-northeast two leagues over terrain now less broken but grown with chamise and cactus and strewn with small volcanic stones,[2] passed the bend of Gunnison River where it swings west, left the site of Lazear to the south of their route and camped northwest of the site of Hotchkiss on the North Fork of Gunnison River, which they named Santa Rosa de Lima, in honor of the famous Peruvian saint. Escalante observes: "This river rises in the Sierra del Venado Alazán[3] whose slope we were ascending, and flows into the Río de San Javier." Having traveled four leagues for the day, they camped in a small meadow with good pasturage and pleasing groves of white cottonwoods and small oaks. The Sabuaganas and the Laguna guide spent the night with the Spaniards and ate ravenously of their supplies.

Next day's march[4] was one of the longest and hardest thus far undertaken. Leaving Santa Rosa de Lima, they continued northeast up the north fork of Gunnison River, passed the sites of Paonia and Orth, and of Bowie at the head of the open valley. Here they swung sharply north, climbed the Sierra del Venado Alazán, traveling gingerly along the fearsome edge of a deep valley on their right and through dense thickets of dwarf oak. Then going four more leagues north, they camped at a permanent watering place which they called San Ramón Nonnato, some fifteen miles directly east of Overland Reservoir.

Escalante tells us that one of the Sabuaganas who now accompanied the Spaniards "gorged himself so barbarously and with

---
[1] August 30.
[2] *Malpais.*
[3] Mountain of the Roan Deer.
[4] On August 31.

such brutish manners that we thought he would die of overeating. Finding himself in such distress, he said the Spaniards had caused him this trouble," poisoned him perhaps. "This foolish notion caused us great anxiety," says Escalante, "for we knew that these barbarians, if by chance they become ill after eating what another person gives them, even though it be one of their own people, think the giver has harmed them, and try to avenge a wrong they have never suffered. But God was pleased that he should be relieved by disgorging some of the great quantity of food he could not digest." Escalante was experiencing "adventure in the raw."

Leaving San Ramón next day,[1] the wayfarers continued north three leagues through small valleys with abundant pasturage and dense groves of dwarf oak. On the way they met some eighty Yutas, all on good horses, most of the Indians being from the village or camp to which the guides were now leading them. They said they were going on a hunting expedition, but the Spaniards surmised they had come out in a body "partly to make a show of their large force, and partly to learn whether any more Spaniards were following us, or if we came alone." For, says Escalante, "having known since the previous night that we were going to their village, it was not reasonable that all of the men should leave it at the same time, when they knew that we were coming, unless they were moved by the consideration we have just indicated."

Going forward now with only the Laguna Indian, Silvestre, as guide, the Spaniards descended a steep slope, entered a pretty valley in which flowed a small river fringed with straight royal pines, "intermingled with cottonwoods that seemed to emulate the straightness and the height of the pines." Swinging east, they traveled a league and arrived at the Sabuagana settlement, which consisted of about thirty skin tents. Having traveled four leagues for the day, and 199 since leaving Santa Fé, Escalante notes, they camped a mile below the village, on the bank of one of the headwaters of the North Fork of Gunnison River, naming the place San Antonio Mártir.

---
[1]September 1.

IX

DOMÍNGUEZ TALKS AT SAN ANTONIO

Here at the mountain camp a most interesting scene was enacted. As soon as the Spaniards halted, Father Domínguez went to the village with the interpreter, Andrés Muñiz. Entering the chief's tent, Domínguez embraced him and asked him to call his people together. The chief complied, and, "when as many of either sex as could come had assembled," through Muñiz as interpreter Domínguez told them about the Gospel. All listened with signs of pleasure, especially six Indians from the Lake in the far northwest, who also were present, and "amongst whom our guide and another Laguna were conspicuous."

When Domínguez began his discourse and displayed a crucifix, Silvestre interrupted him, admonishing both the Sabuaganas and the Lagunas that they must believe whatever the father might tell them, because it was all true. In the audience there was a deaf person who, not understanding, with his hand to his ear asked what the father was saying. Thereupon the other Laguna told the deaf man, "The father says that what he is showing us (it was the image of Christ crucified) is the one Lord of All, who lives in the highest part of the heavens; and that in order to please Him and go to see Him, it is necessary to be baptized and to beg His pardon." The Laguna illustrated these last words by touching his breast with his hand, "an action surprising in him, because he had never before seen either the Father or the interpreter." Witnessing the pleasure they manifested at hearing him, Father Domínguez said to the chief that if after conferring with his people they desired to accept Christianity, he would return to instruct them and to prescribe for them a mode of living to prepare them for baptism. The chief replied that he would discuss the matter with his people, but, says Escalante, "during the whole afternoon he did not return to give a report on which to base a well-founded hope of their acceptance of the proposal."

Domínguez was pleased with the disposition of the Laguna Indians in the party, and by way of conversation he asked what the second Laguna, who had imparted his knowledge to the deaf man, was called by his own people. When they told him his name was Red Bear[1] Domínguez said they should not name each other for wild animals, and that hereafter he should be called Francisco. The other Indians, hearing the new name began to pronounce it, "although with difficulty." When Domínguez dubbed the ruler of the village "Captain," the Indian modestly replied that he did not merit the title, for the real chief was a youth, a good-looking fellow who was present. He had two wives, and was a brother of a famous Sabuagana chief called Yamputzi. Domínguez hereupon admonished the men not to have more than one wife at a time. He also purchased from the Indians some dried buffalo meat, giving them glass beads in exchange, and arranged to trade some of the Spaniards' lame horses for sound ones. This done Domínguez returned to the Spanish camp.

Shortly before sunset the chief, some old men, and many other Indians visited the Spanish camp, and as professed friends they urged the travelers to turn back to Santa Fé, setting forth anew the danger that would be encountered in going forward, and declaring that the Comanches would not permit them to do so. The Spaniards reciprocated the good wishes, but confidently said that God would defend them against the Comanches or anybody else.

Seeing that their excuses were of no avail and that the Spaniards paid no attention to their warnings, the Sabuaganas told the fathers they must write to the "Great Captain," as they called the Governor of New Mexico, telling him they had passed through this region, so that if the Franciscans had any mishap and did not return to Santa Fé, the Spaniards there would not think the Sabuaganas had murdered them. Escalante, who was not easily hoodwinked, remarked that "this letter was the idea of some of our companions who desired to turn back or to remain with these Indians." But he said he would write the letter and leave it here, so that if any of the natives should go to Santa Fé they might carry it to the Governor.

The Indians replied that they could not take the letter to Santa Fé, and that Escalante must send it by some of his own men. Escalante said that none of his men could return to Santa

---

[1] Oso Colorado.

Fé nor remain here with the Indians, which someone had suggested. It is not known whether Escalante did write the letter; if so, it may turn up some day in the archives of Santa Fé, Mexico, or Spain. The Indians now said that if the Spaniards refused to turn back they would not trade sound horses for lame ones, as had been proposed. Escalante replied that he could not turn back without learning the whereabouts of Father Garcés, who had been among the Cosninas and Moquis, and might at this very moment be wandering about lost. "To this the Indians, inspired by those of our men who understood their language and were secretly conspiring against us," replied that the fathers could not get lost because the Spaniards had "all the lands and roads painted on paper." That is to say, Garcés must have carried a map. The Indians again insisted, "repeating all the foregoing arguments to persuade us to turn back. Seeing our unshakeable determination, they declared it was because they loved us that they were urging us not to go forward, but if we persisted they would not prevent it, and next morning they would exchange horses.

"After nightfall they took their leave, not without hope of overcoming our determination next day. According to what we observed, they were given that hope by Felipe of Abiquiú, the interpreter Andrés, and his brother Lucrecio, they being the ones who, either through fear, or because they did not wish to go forward, had secretly connived with the Sabuaganas ever since they learned these Indians were opposed to our plan.

"By this conduct we were caused much grief, and even more by the following discovery: Before leaving the town of Santa Fé we had warned the companions that no one who wished to go with us should carry any merchandise, and that anybody who would not agree to this must remain at home. All promised not to carry any merchandise whatsoever, nor to have any purpose other than the one that inspired us, namely, the glory of God and the salvation of souls. For this reason they were given whatever they requested for themselves and to leave for their families. But some of them had failed to keep their promise, and secretly carried some merchandise which we did not discover until we were near the Sabuaganas. Here we again charged and entreated everybody not to engage in trade, in order that the heathen might understand that another and higher motive had brought us through these lands. We had just told the Sabuaganas that we did not need weapons or soldiers, because we depended for our safety and defense on the omnipotent arm of God, when Andrés Muñiz, our interpreter, and his brother Lucrecio, showed themselves to be so obedient, loyal, and Christian that they bartered what they had kept hidden, and with great eagerness solicited weapons from the heathen, telling them they were necessary because they were going to travel through the lands of the Cumanches. By this conduct, greatly to our sorrow, they manifested their little faith or entire lack of it, and their total unfitness for such enterprises." Thus Escalante had his troubles, and likewise on occasion he could be sarcastic.

Early next morning,[1] the same Indians, and even more of them than on the previous day, assembled at the camp. They again urged the Spaniards not to go forward, raising another serious difficulty, " for they dissuaded Silvestre, the Laguna, completely from his intention to guide us, and made him return to us what we had given him to induce him to accompany us to his land." After arguing with Silvestre for more than an hour and a half without avail, the Spaniards declared they would go without a guide, and, moreover, they would no longer consider the Sabuaganas as their friends. Thereupon the Sabuaganas about-faced, and the young brother of Chief Yamputzi and another chief both prudently spoke in the Spaniards' favor. Now all the Sabuaganas chimed in, pointing out to Silvestre that he could not back out of his original agreement, and he, after some persuasion, reluctantly agreed to keep it.

The Sabuaganas now started to leave the camp. Escalante and his party set out after them but Silvestre, evidently still disgruntled with his bargain, thought of an excuse to lag behind. Pretending to look for a saddle for the horse the friars had given him, he refused to start out on the trail. Andrés Muñiz was sent back to hurry him along and Silvestre told the interpreter to bring the travelers back to where he was. Accordingly the Spaniards turned back and found Silvestre bidding farewell to the other Lagunas, who were remaining with the Sabuaganas, and receiving from them advice about the route ahead. At the last moment,

---
[1]September 2.

another young Laguna boy, whom the Spaniards named Joaquín, decided he wanted to go with them. Since he had no mount, "to avoid further delay, Don Joaquín Laín put him behind him on his horse." The travelers now set forth westward, retracing their way to the trail they had been following toward the Lake.

X

NORTHWEST TO GREEN RIVER

Having gone back a league west from San Antonio, says Escalante, "we took another trail, traveled less than a league and three-quarters northwest, then more than a quarter of a league west-northwest and camped in a small valley which we called San Atanasio," so-named in honor of Father Domínguez. That day they had traveled three winding leagues but advanced only two.

Early next morning[1] it rained, but about eleven o'clock the weather cleared and the Spaniards again set forth. Leaving San Atanasio, they traveled by a devious trail but generally northwest, through Yuta country that was dotted with huts. Having traveled seven leagues for the day, they camped on the upper waters of Buzzard Creek, near a hill by the Yutas called Nabuncari, naming the place San Silvestre, thus commemorating both the saint and the young guide who was showing the way.

On September 4 they continued westward down Buzzard Creek, through hills grown with various species of broom. At one place, says Escalante, "the beaver with logs have made such large ponds that at first they looked like a good-sized river." Swinging northwest they came upon three Yuta women and a child who were drying berries they had gathered. The Spaniards stopped to chat with them and by them were given choke-cherries, garambullo, limes, and piñon, which were among the native riches of the primitive country. Escalante remarks: "The garambullo which grows in these parts is very bitter while on the bushes, but when dried in the sun as these Yutas had done, it is bitter sweet and very savory." Farther on they saw a "rock about five palms high shaped like a washbowl," in which some of the horses of the travelers slipped. Having traveled that day six leagues, and a total of 201 since leaving Santa Fé, they halted north of the site of Collbran and northwest of Plateau City, naming their camp Santa Rosalía. Although it was early in Sep-

---

[1] September 3.

tember the night was very cold, even for these travelers from the high plateau of New Mexico.

September 5 was a still harder day. Leaving Santa Rosalía they swung sharply north-northwest, ascended Battlement Mesa by a trail that was steep and dangerous to climb, says Escalante, "because there are turns where the trail is less than a third of a yard wide. The soil is of loose and soft earth, so it is very easy for an animal to slip, and if he should lose his footing he would not be able to stop until he reached the plain below." When I read this passage from the diary to a citizen at nearby Collbran he expostulated, "Hell, if he went off on the west side he's goin' yit!" Having traveled five leagues for the day, mainly north-northwest, Escalante reached Colorado River, crossed it and halted on its bank. Camp San Rafael was near Una, below the present town of Grand Valley and some fifteen miles northeast of the site of Debeque, Colorado, a place which, like many others along the route, is proud of the lore of Escalante's historic trek through its vicinity.

Crossing the river, they camped on its west bank. Escalante says that on the west side of the stream "there is a chain of high mesas, whose upper half is of white earth and the lower half evenly streaked with yellow, white, and not very dark colored red earth." These mesas are conspicuous in the vicinity. Escalante says, "This river carries more water than the Río del Norte. It rises, according to what they told us, in a great lake which is toward the northeast near the Sierra de la Grulla." At the crossing the river was split into two channels. West of the Colorado in this latitude are the famous Book Cliffs, so-called because in shape they resemble half-open books, with their white and yellow backs to the sky. Here Miera for the fifth time observed the latitude and found it was 41° 4'. "Thinking we had not reached a point so far above Santa Monica," says Escalante, "and fearing some defect in the observation, we decided to take it by the sun tomorrow, stopping at a suitable hour in order not to remain in this place where the Sabuaganas might bother us."

Next day[1] the travelers left San Rafael, traveled downstream half a league and then zig-zagged generally westward three more leagues and "descended to a small valley" in which ran a slender

---
[1] September 6.

stream of good water. This was Roan Creek, which they reached perhaps eight miles northwest of Debeque. Here they took the latitude, finding it to be 41° 6' 53", and concluded that on the previous day they had made no error. According to modern surveys they were close to the parallel of 39° 30' north latitude.

Going forward, they overtook their companions who, having traveled two leagues, had halted. The Spaniards were displeased with their guide because, leaving the road which ran west upstream, he had led them by another trail which, entering a canyon, ran north. The Spaniards who knew the Yuta language tried to convince Escalante that Silvestre was purposely misguiding them in order to delay them or lead them into ambush by the Sabuaganas. They said they had heard many Sabuaganas in the ranchería tell Silvestre he must lead the Spaniards by a trail which did not go to the Lake, and after having delayed them eight or ten days by useless wanderings, he must turn them back toward Santa Fé. Escalante did not believe the story. He knew that if he continued north instead of northwest, the distance to the Lake would be greater, but when Silvestre said he was going north to avoid a hard climb, Escalante and Domínguez approved that plan. But all the companions except Don Joaquín Laín insisted on taking the other trail, "some because they feared the Cumanches too greatly and without foundation," and some for other reasons not stated.

While the travelers were here a Yuta Sabuagana arrived and said the road by the north "went up very high." So they continued west two leagues, crossed a smaller stream, and halted on its bank, naming the campsite La Contraguía, having traveled seven leagues for the day. By his stubbornness the guide at least got into history, which is more than most of us will accomplish. Here were three huts of Sabuaganas from which six men went to the Spanish camp. One of them had just returned from the country of the Comanches Yamparicas, whither with four other Sabuaganas he had gone to steal horses, a manly deed of which he boasted. He said the Comanches had recently moved east, perhaps to the Napeste River.[1] "With this report our companions were somewhat encouraged," says Escalante. These Sabuaganas were the last of that tribe seen by the Spaniards.

---

[1] Arkansas River.

Leaving La Contraguía on September 7, the travelers went west a league up Roan Creek to a meadow with abundant pasturage, swung northwest three leagues up the same valley, halted to water the animals, turned north-northeast without a trail, and climbed a ridge so steep and difficult that they feared they might not reach the top. The ascent was about half a league, and at the top two pack animals lost their footing in the brittle shale and rolled down more than twenty yards. "But God willed that none of the men coming behind should be trampled upon and that the mules should not be injured." The friars "climbed the mountain on foot, suffered much fatigue, and had some very bad frights," for which reason they called the place La Cuesta del Susto.[1] Escalante testifies that on the way up, the guide gave "irrefutable proof of his sincerity and his innocence" of any intention to injure the travelers. After reaching the top of the grade they continued north-northwest half a league, descended to a small valley, and camped by a very scanty spring near some fair pasturage. Having traveled a little more than five and a quarter leagues, they camped at La Natividad de Nuestra Señora.

Next day[2] they broke camp, traveled north up Roan Plateau, which forms a divide. Continuing northwest they struck the waters of Douglas Creek, and found themselves on a better trail. From a high ridge Silvestre pointed out the sierra on whose northern slope the Comanches Yamparicas dwelt, north of the Subuaganas. Toward the west at the end of the same sierra he pointed out the location of his own people at the Lake, which was a long distance ahead. Descending north from the same summit by an extremely long slope, rugged in places but without stones, and covered with groves of dwarf oak and choke-cherry, "which served to prevent the horses from slipping and rolling," they entered Douglas Canyon, traveled down it a league and a half, and halted to let the animals drink. In the afternoon they continued down the same canyon and camped at a place called Santa Delfina, having traveled five leagues for the day.

From the campsite at Santa Delfina, next day[3] they continued half a league northwest down Douglas Canyon, then swung north-northwest. Having traveled in the canyon nine leagues.

---

[1] The Hill of the Scare.
[2] September 8.
[3] September 9.

or some twenty-five miles in all, over a well-worn Indian trail with only one bad stretch, and having threaded a grove of tall chamise and rockrose,[1] they emerged into open country. And of what they had seen in Douglas Canyon they had an interesting story to tell. "Halfway down the gorge on the left side of the trail," says Escalante, "there is a very high cliff, on which we saw crudely painted three shields or *chimales* and the blade of a lance." One of the shields was still plainly to be seen high up on a cliff on the left side of the road when I explored this stretch of Escalante's trail. "Farther down, on the north side, we saw another painting which crudely represented two men fighting. For these reasons we called this valley the Cañon Pintado." Escalante remarked that this Painted Canyon was the only route by which one could go from Roan Mountain to the nearest river, because the rest of the terrain was so rough and stony, but modern highways have done much to change this situation.

On the same side of the trail in Cañon Pintado, near its northern end, the travelers saw veins of metal which Miera said "was one of those which the miners call *tepustete*, and was an indication of gold ore." Escalante remarks, "On this matter we assert nothing, nor shall we assert anything, because we are not experienced in mines, and because a more detailed examination than the one we were able to make on this occasion is always necessary." He did not wish to be held responsible for a gold rush that might prove to be disappointing, but if Miera read the diary, he could not have been flattered by Escalante's skeptical comment.

Having emerged from the canyon, the travelers arrived at Río San Clemente, now called White River. Escalante writes: "This stream is medium-sized; along here it runs westward, and the region adjacent to it does not have advantages for settlement." Because of this remark, among citizens of Rangely, which now occupies the site, Escalante may not be highly popular.

On September 10, because the guide said the next watering place was far ahead, the travelers decided to "split the journey"— that is, to start in mid-afternoon, camp for the night, and finish the

---

[1] *Jara.*

distance next morning. So, after midday they left San Clemente, or White River, traveled northwest over hills without stones, and across plains without pasturage or trees, traveled a league, swung northwest two leagues over level terrain scarred by dry ravines, advancing three leagues for the day. Before dark they camped in the bottom of a gorge called El Barranco, where there was neither water nor pasturage, making it necessary to corral the horses to prevent them from straying in the night. This region was a winter haunt for buffaloes, but none of these ponderous beasts were mentioned here by Escalante. From San Clemente the wayfarers had traveled without a trail, indicating that the region was not thickly populated by Indians.

On September 11, as soon as it was daylight, they set forth from El Barranco. With Raven Ridge at their left they traveled west-northwest across dry arroyos and deep ravines, finding in one of them a tantalizing spring which the horses could not reach because of the rugged terrain. Continuing west-northwest they climbed a ridge, and beyond it traveled three leagues. The animals were now suffering from hunger and thirst, and one mule was so worn that they had to relieve him of his cargo, for other tired animals to carry. Swinging half a league north, they camped at Arroyo del Cibolo,[1] having traveled six leagues for the day.

A short distance beyond El Barranco the explorers saw a recent buffalo trail. Farther on they saw it again, where it was fresher, and ran in the same direction as the travelers were going. By now the Spaniards were short of supplies, and here was a chance to replenish the larder with buffalo steak. Moreover, adventure beckoned. So two horsemen turned aside to follow the trail, and one of them soon came back to report that he had seen a buffalo, the first one mentioned on the whole long trek. Other men now rode out on the swiftest horses, chased the animal for some ten miles, in which direction they do not say, killed it, and at nightfall returned with a goodly supply of buffalo meat, "much more than comes from a large bull of the common variety." So, to prevent the meat from spoiling, and in order to rest the hard-ridden horses, they did not travel on the 12th, but camped and had a feast at Arroyo del Cibolo, so-named for the lone buffalo which thus got permanently into history.

---
[1]Buffalo Creek.

National Parks Service Photo, George Grant

ESCALANTE'S CROSSING OF GREEN RIVER
Six miles north of Jensen, Utah, near the upper end of thick grove of trees.

On September 13 the wayfarers left Arroyo del Cíbolo, now called Cliff Creek from the white rocks of Yampa Plateau in the north, which rises to an elevation of eight thousand feet, and by the natives then was called Sabuagari or Sabuagana, indicating that it was a range for that tribe. Having traveled two leagues and three-quarters to the west, they reached a watering-place known to the guide. It was a small spring at the foot of the cliffs of Yampa Plateau. Continuing a quarter of a league in the same direction they passed two large springs a musketshot apart, which they named Las Fuentes de Santa Clara,[1] whose name is widely scattered over the entire Western Hemisphere in a measure that can be claimed for few conquerors or rulers.

They continued northwest, skirted the white cliffs of Yampa Plateau, and having advanced six leagues for the day, they arrived at Rio de San Buenaventura, now called Green River, which then was regarded as the boundary between Yutas and Comanches, the Yutas toward the south and the Comanches toward the north. Here were fine meadows and good land for crops, though none of it was cultivated. The river entered the meadows between high cliffs, forming a natural corral for stock. The travelers halted on the eastern bank of the stream, about a mile from the ford, naming the site La Vega de Santa Cruz. Camp was a few miles north of Jensen, Utah, and about half a mile south of the now world famous Dinosaur Quarry. Here for the seventh time, the travelers took the latitude, and concluded it was in 41° 19'.

On September 14 the explorers remained in camp east of the river, in order that the weary animals might rest and feast on the fine pasturage there. Before noon the latitude was observed by the sun, and found to be in 40° 59' 24", which was lower than the record of the previous day, and Escalante surmised that the discrepancy might be due to the declination of the needle at this place. So, at night they observed the latitude by the North Star, finding it to be in 41° 19', the same as on the previous night. The two different methods gave the same result.

With regard to this historic campsite, Escalante made a precious entry in his diary: "In this place there are six large black cottonwood trees that have grown in pairs, attached to one an-

[1] The Fountains of Saint Clara.

other, and they are the ones closest to the river. Near them there is another, standing alone, on whose trunk, on the side facing the northwest, Don Joaquín Laín with an adz cleared a small space in the form of a rectangular window, and with a chisel carved in it the letters and numbers of this inscription, *The Year 1776*; and lower down in different letters the name *Laín*, with two crosses outside, the larger one above the inscription and the smaller one below it."

The six giant cottonwoods still stand at the site described by Escalante, but the inscription, perhaps covered by the growth of a century and three-quarters, is not visible. Less than a mile north of these giant cottonwoods lies the Dinosaur Quarry which, like the historic trees, is in danger of obliteration by dams proposed for the development of power and irrigation in the region. If this comes to pass, two great and irreplaceable natural monuments will be sacrificed to what we call progress.

Here Escalante's hunters brought into camp the carcass of another buffalo, killed in the vicinity. Here also Joaquín, the Laguna guide, as a prank, mounted a fiery steed. "While galloping across the meadow the horse thrust his forefeet into a hole and fell head over heels," throwing Joaquín and giving him a bad scare. "But God was pleased that the only damage done was the injury to the horse, which completely broke his neck, leaving him useless," but not dead. We shall hear of this hardy animal again, still traveling.

XI

WESTWARD TO UTAH LAKE

The camp at the six cottonwoods was another turning point in the historic trek, for the travelers now entered the borders of Comanche country. Moreover, it marked a definite change in direction. From the Sabuagana village at San Antonio some twelve days and over one hundred and fifty miles farther back the direction of travel had been northwest. Now for a similar distance it was nearly straight west. Having halted two days[1] at Vega de Santa Cruz on Green River, the travelers moved forward toward the setting sun, led by Silvestre and Joaquín, the proud Yuta guides who were now approaching their homeland.

On September 16, leaving the historic cottonwoods behind, and ascending Green River halfway to the Dinosaur Quarry, of which apparently they had no inkling, the wayfarers traveled a short distance north, crossed Green River at the ford, swung southwest and west, crossed Brush Creek, noted fertile lands along the route, passed the site of Jensen, forded Ashley Creek, crossed the neck of the great oxbow of Green River, and camped on its bank near the place where it swings sharply south, about midway between Vernal and Ouray, naming the campsite Las Llagas de Nuestro Padre San Francisco.[2]

On this day's march they discovered a fresh trail of Indians, some on horseback and some on foot, suspecting they were Sabuaganas who had followed them to steal horses, thinking the blame would be laid on Comanches, since Escalante was now in Comanche country. But Silvestre the guide was temporarily under suspicion, for the previous night he had slept outside the camp, nobody knew where. Moreover, during the whole journey until now he had not once worn the gay cloak given him by Escalante far back on Gunnison River, but today he wore it from morning till night. And, says Escalante, "we suspected that, having come to an understanding with the Sabuaganas, he now donned the cloak so that in case they attacked us he would be

---
[1]September 14 and 15.
[2]The Wounds of Our Father St. Francis.

recognized by them" and not be killed. "Our suspicions were increased when he stopped for a time before reaching the peak where we found the tracks, as if puzzled and in doubt, at first going along the banks of the river and then leading us that way." But the Spaniards gave Silvestre no hint of their mistrust, and in the course of the day's march they had emphatic proofs of his innocence, says Escalante.

Leaving Las Llagas on September 17, the Spaniards continued nearly west and traveled a league, now concluding that the Indians whose trail they had been following were Comanches going in pursuit of Yutas. Farther west the caravan climbed a high ridge from which Silvestre pointed out in the south the direction to the distant junction of San Clemente and San Buenaventura rivers.[1] Continuing west to Duchesne River, which was reached near the site of Randlett, and ascending the stream, they camped on its banks at San Cosme, east of the site of Myton. On the Duchesne they passed the ruins of a very old settlement where there were fragments of *metates*,[2] jars, and jugs made of clay. The settlement had been circular in form, judging from the ruins, which now were nearly level with the ground. Here some smokes seen in the distance were thought by the guide to have been sent up by Comanches or perhaps by Laguna Indians of Utah Valley, which they were now approaching.

Next day[3] they left Ribera de San Cosme, and the guide, wishing to ford the river,[4] led the Spaniards into a thicket of rockrose, and across marshy creeks which forced them to ford the river three times, making "many useless turns." Then, continuing upstream past the site of Myton, they traveled three leagues southwest and one league west-southwest, crossed the river a fifth time, and again turned west for three and a quarter leagues. They now ascended a mesa, which was level and stony on top, traveled three-quarters of a league including the ascent and the descent, crossed a small stream which enters the San Cosme, named the small stream Santa Catarina de Sena, and camped on its banks, having traveled nine leagues for the day, which was one of the longest marches. Camp was a mile or more northeast

---

[1] White and Green rivers which join at Ouray.
[2] Mortars.
[3] September 18.
[4] The Duchesne.

of the present town of Duchesne. Here Escalante, feeling retrospective and weary, writes: "From the ranchería of the Sabuaganas and the campsite of San Antonio Mártir to this place we counted eighty-eight leagues, and from Santa Fé two hundred and eighty-seven leagues" or nearly eight hundred miles.

Citizens of Duchesne and vicinity should think well of Escalante, for he wrote: "Along these three rivers we have crossed today there is enough good land for crops to support three good-sized settlements, with opportunities for irrigation, beautiful cottonwood groves, good pastures, with timber and firewood nearby." He adds: "from the country of the Cumanches a very long and high sierra descends, running from northeast to southwest as far as the country of the Lagunas, and which we could see for more than seventy leagues." He refers to the Uinta Mountains which, a little farther west, he climbed to a high elevation. He adds, "Toward the north of the Rio de San Buenaventura at this season its highest hills and peaks are covered with snow, for which reason we named it Sierra Blanca de los Lagunas, and tomorrow we shall begin to ascend and cross it where it is least elevated."

September 19 was a hard day. From camp at Santa Catarina they swung sharply southwest past the site of Duchesne and here turned north, following the bend of Duchesne River. Then they traveled west close to the route of the modern highway, "through almost impassable terrain, over many stones and along rocky precipices," one of which lamed a horse and forced the travelers to go down to another meadow near the stream. Now crossing the river, breaking through thickets, threading the Canyon of the Swallows[1] whose nests built of mud "looked like little pueblos," and having traveled ten hard leagues for the day, they spent the night at San Eustaquio, east of the site of Fruitland. They arrived at camp much fatigued, "partly because a very cold wind blew unceasingly from the west," and partly because they had made an unusually long march. Here at San Eustaquio died the stalwart horse that was said to have broken his neck at the camp of the six cottonwoods on Green River. How he so long had survived that accident was regarded as a miracle. Veterinary surgeons may have some opinions regarding his injury.

---

[1]Las Golondrinas.

Next day,[1] leaving San Eustaquio near south-flowing Red Creek, they continued westward with numerous turns, climbed a long but easy slope grown with chamise and cactus, passed the site of Fruitland, crossed Currant Creek, whose name in its present form of course is of modern origin, and having traveled five leagues for the day they camped at a bountiful spring which they called Ojo de Santa Lucía. Since leaving Santa Catarina near the site of Duchesne they had traveled north of and parallel with Strawberry Creek. That September night was so cold that even the water that stood in vessels close to the campfire was found frozen next morning.

On September 21 they left Ojo de Santa Lucía, by the same valley they had just ascended, through a grove of white cottonwoods, traveled west a league and three-quarters, "now through thickets of troublesome chamise, now through valleys of very soft earth, the animals sinking and stumbling every instant" in the many little holes that were hidden in the grass. Then they descended to a fair-sized river[2] in which there was an abundance of good trout, two of which Joaquín killed with an arrow, "each of which would weigh somewhat more than two pounds," but we infer that if the same arrow killed two trout there was more than one shot. This fish story is Escalante's, and we leave it with all truthful anglers. In this valley, which they named Valle de la Purísima, and where Strawberry Reservoir is now impounded by a dam, there were all the advantages necessary for a good settlement. Silvestre said that some Lagunas had once lived here, but withdrew through fear of the Comanches, who were beginning to make raids into this part of the sierra.

Having crossed the river, the wayfarers entered the floor of the valley, traveled west-southwest through a ravine with much chamise and bad terrain, crossed a tributary stream of very cold water, entered a grove of white cottonwood, dwarf oak, chokecherry and royal pine, took the south slope of a wooded ravine, and then crossed the stream. This description of the trail does not include all the turns they made by their zig-zag route.

Silvestre, anxious to reach home, went so fast that the friars could not follow him, so Escalante ordered him to slow down and

---

[1]September 20.
[2]Strawberry Creek.

remain always in sight. Emerging from the forest, they now ascended a high ridge from which Silvestre pointed out the direction to Utah Lake, where his people lived. They were now at the Wasatch Mountain divide, from which the streams flow west. Continuing southwest and west through thickets of choke-cherry and dwarf oak, they entered a grove of cottonwoods so dense that they thought the packs would not get through without being unloaded. On the way Father Domínguez got a hard blow on one of his knees by hitting it against a cottonwood tree. Finally, having traveled six and one-half leagues from Santa Lucía, they camped at San Mateo in a narrow valley with good pasturage and good water. This was one of the toughest days in the whole journey thus far.

Leaving San Mateo on September 22, they traveled through "perilous defiles and slides," without a trail, changing their direction at every step. After going five or six leagues up and down hills and high elevations, some of them rough and stony, they descended a long and passable slope with plentiful pasturage to a small plain where two creeks joined. Having traveled six leagues for the day, but advancing only three, and the animals being all worn out, they halted here for the night, naming the camp San Lino. It was on Diamond Creek at the junction of Diamond Creek and Wanrhodes Canyon.

From the top of the last ridge they crossed that day, they saw ahead of them large columns of smoke, thought by Silvestre to have been made by some of his own people who were out hunting. Says Escalante, "We replied to them with other smoke signals, so that if they had already seen us they would not take us to be enemies and flee, or welcome us with arrows." The natives "replied with larger smoke signals in the pass through which we must travel to the Lake, which caused us to believe they had already seen us, because this is the most prompt and common signal used in any extraordinary occurrence by all the people of this part of America." So Escalante warned Silvestre to be on the *qui vive* that night, to guard against trouble with any natives who might prowl around the camp. Silvestre not only kept close watch, but "about two o'clock in the morning, the hour when according to his opinion there might be one or more Indians close at hand, he made a long speech in his own language, giving them to understand that we were peaceable people, friendly and good, but we do not know whether or not anyone heard him," a circumstance discouraging for any orator.

Next day[1] Escalante wrote, "Knowing that we were now arriving at the Lake, in order that . . . Silvestre and Joaquín might enter their land feeling happier and more friendly toward us," and thus assure the Spaniards a good reception, "we again gave each one a vara of woolen cloth and another vara of red ribbon, with which they at once set about adorning themselves . . . Silvestre donned the cloak previously given him at the Sabuagana camp, wearing it like a mantle or cape, and the cloth which we now gave him he wore like a wide band around his head, leaving the two long ends hanging loose down his back. And so he paraded about on horseback, the living image of the captives whom the Father Redemptors bring out in their processions on this feast day of Nuestra Señora de la Merced. This event seemed to be a happy omen of the friendly disposition of these captives, whose liberty we desired and besought of the Redeemer of the World, through the intercession of His Immaculate Mother, who, in order to encourage us in this endeavor, wished to give the name which the Church celebrates today."

Continuing southwest from San Lino, the travelers ascended a small elevation on whose summit they found a large ant hill, "composed of very fine alum rock, pure and crystalline." Then descending to the little river of San Lino,[2] and having traveled a league through its meadows, they swung west and continued downstream. Here the river was joined by a smaller one[3] and in both there were pretty meadows and "everything else necessary for stock-raising." A quarter of a league farther down they passed three large springs of hot water, which they tasted and liked. Escalante remarks, "It is of the same sulphurous character as the spring . . . near the pueblo of San Diego de los Hemes in New Mexico." Continuing west three-quarters of a league, they entered the narrowest part of the river canyon, swung a mile north, and discovered three other hot springs like the foregoing, "all of which rise on this north bank at the foot of a very high hill close to the

---
[1]September 23.
[2]Diamond Creek.
[3]Soldier's Fork.

river into which they flow." For this reason they called the stream Río de Aguas Calientes. It is now called Spanish Fork.

Then came the great moment! Continuing northwest half a league they crossed the river, climbed a hill, "and beheld the lake and the wide valley of Nuestra Señora de los Timpanogotzis." All around the travelers the natives were sending up smoke signals, one after another, "thus spreading the news of our coming." The Spaniards continued to the plain, entered the valley and again crossed the river. Then traveling more than a league through the meadows on the north bank of the stream, they crossed to the other side and camped on one of its southern meadows, which they called Vega del Dulcísimo Nombre de Jesús.[1] Camp was south and east of the present-day town of Spanish Fork. The day's march had been five and one-half leagues or some fifteen miles.

Some of the meadows of the valley had been burned and others were still burning, the Indians perhaps thinking the approaching visitors were Comanches, "and," says Escalante, "since perhaps they had seen that we had horses, they had attempted to burn the pastures . . . so that lack of grass might force us to leave the plain more quickly."

As soon as the Spaniards camped, Domínguez went ahead with Silvestre, Joaquín and the interpreter Andrés Muñiz. In order to arrive that afternoon at the center of the settlement they pushed the horses to the point of tiring them out, traveling north-northwest six and one-half leagues (fifteen or more miles) and arrived at the Indian ranchos. They were on Provo River east of Utah Lake in the vicinity of the city of Provo.

Native men sallied forth with weapons in their hands to defend their homes, but as soon as Silvestre spoke to them "the guise of war was changed into the finest . . . expression of peace and affection" and the Indians took the visitors to their "poor little houses." Domínguez embraced each one separately and told them he came in peace. Silvestre in the Yuta tongue told the natives the story of the expedition, and, says Escalante, "it was so much in our favor that we could not have wished for a better report." Silvestre told especially of their lack of trouble with the Comanches, which surprised the Lagunas. "He concluded by saying that only the fathers told the truth, that in their company one

---

[1] Meadow of the Most Sweet Name of Jesus.

could travel through all the land without risk, and that only the Spaniards were good people." The natives were confirmed in this opinion by seeing that the boy Joaquín was so fond of the friars that he paid no attention to his own kinfolks. He even refused to leave Father Domínguez, sleeping at his side that night.

Meanwhile many natives had assembled from the nearby ranchos. Domínguez gave them something to smoke, and through Joaquín and Silvestre he explained the reason for their coming. "Of these the principal one was to seek the salvation of their souls." If the natives wished it he would instruct and baptize them, other friars would come to instruct them, and secular Spaniards to live with them, teach them how to plant crops, and to raise cattle, "then they would have food and clothing like the Spaniards." For this purpose, said Father Domínguez, "if they would consent to live as God commands and as the fathers would teach them, everything necessary would be sent by our Captain, who is very grand and rich and whom we call King. For if he saw that they wished to become Christians he would regard them as his children, and would care for them just as if they were already his people." Afterwards Father Domínguez told them that since the Spaniards must continue on their way, "in order to get news of the other padre, our brother,[1] we needed another of their people to guide us to some other tribe known to them and who might furnish us still another guide."

Escalante adds, "in all this we were aided by the good offices of Silvestre. The natives listened gladly, and replied that they were ready to do all this, thereby exhibiting their great docility." Although two chiefs were present, the head chief was absent, so Domínguez requested that they send for him. They replied that he was "at his house, which was distant, and that he would come next day." Now most of the natives went to their homes, but some of them remained talking all night with Silvestre, and listening to his tale of adventure.

Next day[2] the Spaniards sent word by Joaquín and another Laguna Indian to the rest of the Escalante party, ordering them to go forward from the camp at El Dulcísimo Nombre de Jesús, to the Yuta village where Domínguez had spent the night, and where

---

[1] Father Garcés.
[2] September 24.

the natives were assembling, and shortly before noon the Spaniards arrived.

Meanwhile the head chief and two lesser chiefs, several old men, and many other Indians assembled at the Indian village. The friars explained to them at greater length what they had already mentioned, and "all of them unanimously replied that if Franciscans should come, they would live with the Tatas" (as the Yutas called the friars) who would rule and teach them. They offered the Spaniards all their lands so they might build their houses wherever they pleased, adding that they would scout through the country and be always on the watch for the inroads of the Comanches, and if they tried to enter this valley or the vicinity of the sierra, the Spaniards would be promptly warned and they all could go forth together to punish them. Escalante here remarks: "Seeing such admirable docility, and having achieved our purpose, we told them that after finishing our journey we would return with more fathers and Spaniards to baptize them and live with them, but from now forward they must be careful what they said, so that later on they might not have to repent." The Yutas replied that they were sincere in what they were promising, and added with earnest supplication that the Franciscans must not long delay their return. Escalante writes, "We told them that although our people would believe whatever we might say about them, they must give us a token showing that they wished to be Christians, *et cetera,* so we could show it to our Great Captain," the King of Spain, "and to the rest of the Spaniards, so that by means of it they would be more convinced of their good intentions and be encouraged to come more quickly." He adds, "We did this the better to sound out their intentions, and they replied that they would gladly give us the token next morning."

The Franciscans now presented to the head chief "who was a man of good presence," a hunting knife and a string of beads, and Don Bernardo Miera gave him a hatchet. To the rank and file of the villagers they distributed some white glass beads, for which they were happy and grateful, although they could give them only a few because the Indians were so numerous. They now reminded the Yutas of their promise of a guide to California, and said they would like to have Joaquín, who desired to accompany the Spaniards. The Yutas said they had already discussed this matter, and had decided that not only Joaquín, but also a new guide should go with the Spaniards, perhaps as far as Santa Fé, and that both should return to the Lake when Domínguez and Escalante should come to found a mission for them. The Indians confessed that none of them knew much about the way toward California, but said that through Joaquín and the other guide, the Spaniards could make inquiry of Indian tribes along the way. Says Escalante, "This most sincere expression of their sentiments, so clear and satisfactory, filled us with an inexpressible joy, and assured us completely that without the least duplicity, and with spontaneous and free will, moved by the Divine Grace, they accepted the desired Christianity."

The new guide was called José María, and he too was given a suitable present. The same day a Laguna woman brought a sick child to be baptized. Since he was rather large and was recovering from his illness, the friars said they would baptize the boy on their return "which would be soon. All this being arranged," says Escalante, "we decided to continue our journey next day to the settlements and port of Monterey."

Next morning[1] the natives assembled and brought the requested token. Escalante had warned the interpreter that nobody should discuss this matter, for he wished to see what the Indians would bring of their own accord. The token consisted of a painting of men. They said the one with the most blood (red ochre) represented the head chief because in the battles with the Comanches he had received the most wounds. Two other figures which were not so bloody represented lesser chiefs, and one that had no blood represented not a war chief "but a man of authority among them." The figures were crudely pianted with clay and red ochre on a small piece of buckskin. Escalante writes: "We accepted it, saying that the Great Captain of the Spaniards would be much pleased to see it, and that when we returned here we would bring it with us so they might see how much we esteemed these things, and in order that the token itself might be a guarantee of their promises." Escalante told the natives that if while awaiting the return of the Spaniards they should have any difficulty in the way of sickness or enemies they must call upon God, saying "Oh true God, aid us! Favor us!" But when the Spaniards saw that they were unable to

---
[1]September 25.

pronounce these words clearly, they told them they should say only "Jesús María, Jesús María." With the help of Silvestre they pronounced these words with ease, greatly to Escalante's edification, "and all the time we were preparing to leave they kept repeating those holy words."

XII

PARADISE VALLEY

Escalante was charmed by Utah Valley, and although he was anxious to hurry on his way to California, he halted here two days and wrote a graphic account of what he saw. He named the valley "Our Lady of Mercy."[1] The natives called themselves Timpanogotzis, or Fish Eaters. The valley was surrounded on all sides by mountain ranges and peaks, from which flowed four medium-sized rivers that fertilized the land and ran into Lake Timpanogotzis, now in Anglicized form called Timpanogos. Escalante said the valley was sixteen leagues or some forty miles long from north to south. The land was all cleared of brush, with the exception of some marshes on the lake shore. The soil was good and suitable for raising all kinds of crops by irrigation, which to the Spaniard was the customary way.

First of these four rivers, beginning in the south, where the visitors had entered the valley, was the one with hot springs, or Aguas Calientes, now called Spanish Fork. Escalante said this stream would support two good-sized Spanish settlements. The next river toward the north, called San Nicolás, now Hobble Creek, had more water than the first, and would provide for two or even three good settlements. Before entering the lake this stream divided into two branches, and on its banks, besides the cottonwoods, there were large sycamores.

Three and one-half leagues or some ten miles toward the north, was the third stream (Provo River), the intervening country being level and having good land for crops. This river carried more water than either of the two foregoing streams, had larger cottonwood groves and meadows of good land, and with its fine opportunities for irrigation would support two or even three good settlements. The present-day city of Provo and others in the vicinity verify this prophecy. Escalante remarks: "We were close to this stream on the 24th and 25th, and we named it Río San Antonio de Padua." He adds, "We did not reach the fourth river (American Fork) although we could see its alameda or grove of trees. It

---

[1] Nuestra Señora de la Merced.

THE VALLEY OF PARADISE ALSO CALLED TIMPANOGOTZIS BY ESCALANTE
Utah Lake and Valley looking south of west. Rio San Antonio de Padua (Provo River) empties into the lake to the right of center

Photo Elden D. Beck

is northwest of Río de San Antonio and has in this direction a great deal of good and level land, judging from what we have seen. They told us that it had as much water as the other streams, and therefore some ranchos or pueblos could be established on its banks. We named it Río de Santa Ana. Besides these rivers, there are many pools of good water in the plain, and several springs running down from the sierra." Escalante said this valley alone "would provide for as many pueblos of Indians as there are in New Mexico," which was the highest praise he could think of. He adds, "The lake, which must be six leagues wide and fifteen long . . . runs northwest through a narrow passage and, according to what they told us it communicates with another much larger." The Indians apparently had told him about Great Salt Lake, farther north. But the two lakes do not communicate, one having fresh water, the other being heavily charged with salt.

Escalante added another enthusiastic paragraph about Utah Lake and the friendly people who dwelt on its shores. "This lake of Timpanogotzis abounds in several kinds of good fish, geese, beaver, and other amphibious animals which we did not have an opportunity to see. Round about it live these Indians, who subsist on the abundant fish of the lake, for which reason the Yutas Sabuaganas call them Come Pescados" or Fish Eaters. "Besides this food, they gather grass seeds in the plain from which they make *atole*,[1] supplementing this by hunting hares, rabbits, and fowls, of which there is a great abundance here. There are also buffaloes not very far to the north-northwest, but fear of the Cumanches prevents the Come Pescados from hunting them. Their habitations are *chozas* or little huts made of willow, of which they also make nice baskets and other necessary utensils. In the matter of dress they are very poor, their most decent garments being a buskskin jacket and long leggings of the same material. For cold weather they have blankets made of the skins of hares and rabbits. They speak the Yuta language, but with notable differences in the accent and in some of the words. They have good features, and most of the men have heavy beards, especially those living farther south. In all parts of this sierra to the southeast, southwest, and west, live a large number of people of the same tribe, language, and docility as these Lagunas, with whom

---

[1] Porridge.

a very populous and extensive province could be formed." Another New Mexico perhaps.

Escalante devoted a separate paragraph to Great Salt Lake, of which he heard through the Lagunas but did not see. He wrote: "The other lake with which this one communicates,[1] according to what they told us, covers many leagues and its waters are noxious and extremely salty, for the Timpanois (Timpanogos) assure us that a person who moistens any part of his body with the water of the lake immediately feels much itching."

Miera greatly supplemented Escalante's account of the Yuta country in his report to the king, and his map of it contains important data. He gave a glowing description of a Spanish settlement that he envisioned on the shores of Lake Timpanogos, on one of the rivers flowing into it. This he proposed as the chief and principal colony of a "New Empire" to be carved from the vast area between the lake and Gila River; "for," he said, "this is the most pleasing, beautiful, and fertile site in all New Spain. It alone is capable of maintaining a settlement with as many people as Mexico City, and of affording its inhabitants many conveniences, for it has everything necessary for the support of human life. This lake and the rivers that flow into it abound in many varieties of savory fish, very large white geese, many kinds of ducks, and other exquisite birds never seen elsewhere, besides beavers, otters, seals and some strange animals which are or appear to be ermines, judging by the softness and whiteness of their fur. The meadows of these rivers produce abundant hemp and flax without cultivation."

There were other assets in the Yuta country. "The sierra or mountains toward the east are likewise very fertile, having many rivers and springs, good pastures for raising all kinds of cattle and horses, timber, including royal and other pines, and lands for the planting of all kinds of grain in their valleys. The veins that are seen in the sierra appear at a distance to have minerals, and to the south of this sierra there are some hills of very fine mineral salt."

He urged that one hundred Spanish families, as well as persons skilled in all kinds of trades, be sent to colonize this valley paradise. He suggested especially two carpenters capable of building boats to be used on the lake for fishing, transporting supplies,

---

[1] It does not.

and for exploring the extent of the lake and visiting the surrounding tribes.

The Lagunas had told Miera of a broad and navigable river flowing westward from Great Salt Lake, and Don Bernardo assumed that this was the same river that Juan de Oñate had called Rio del Tizon. This, of course, was Colorado River which Oñate had reached near its mouth in southwestern Arizona in 1605. Oñate had heard reports of large tribes of "civilized" Indians living beyond the river, and Miera apparently held high hopes of planting Spanish settlements among them. Moreover, he must have dreamed of sailing down the river to California, for in urging the establishment of the Utah Valley settlement, he pointed out that it would soon be in a position to supply the far away ports of the California coast. He well knew that a proposed colony which might conceivably aid California would acquire additional merit in the eyes of the King of Spain.

Miera tells also of the rise of the Comanche scourge of the Spanish settlements. On his map he notes east of Great Salt Lake, "The Cumanche nation reaches as far as here. Preventing their expansion are the very numerous rivers and lakes on the east, north, and northeast of their habitations." He adds, "The Cumanche nation was first brought by the Yutas a few years ago" to the Spanish settlements of New Mexico. "They say they left their lands on the northern border, breaking through several tribes, and other Yutas took them [to New Mexico] to barter with the Spaniards, bringing a multitude of dogs loaded with their hides and tents. They acquired [from the Spaniards] horses and weapons, and they have had so much practice in the management of horses and arms, that they excel all other tribes in dexterity and courage. And they have become lords and masters of all the buffalo country, wresting it from the Apaches, who formerly were the most numerous tribe known in America. The Cumanches have destroyed many tribes, and those still remaining have been pushed to the frontiers of our Majesty's provinces. In this way they have suffered so many losses that, lacking their chief means of support, necessity compels them to maintain themselves by eating horses and mules," either raised by themselves or stolen from the Spaniards. This paragraph by Miera is one of the best ever written on the subject. From his long career in New Mexico, he knew what he was talking about.

XIII

FORWARD TO MONTEREY

On September 25, about one o'clock in the afternoon, the Spaniards said goodbye to the friendly Lagunas, left Silvestre behind with his own people, and continued on their way toward California, accompanied by Joaquín and a new guide called José María, whom they had obtained at the Lake. Is it possible that Silvestre was still living at Provo some seventy years later when Brigham Young arrived there with his Mormons in 1849? He then would have been perhaps ninety years old. Having traveled a little more than three and one-half leagues or some ten miles, they camped for the night on Río de San Nicolás, now called Hobble Creek, northwest of present-day Springville.

Next day[1] they left Hobble Creek, continued south, crossed Spanish Fork, marched two more leagues in the same direction and halted, still in the valley, at a creek with good water called Arroyo de San Andrés, near the site of Payson. Escalante remarks, "It appears to flow continuously and therefore is rather a small river or creek than an arroyo. On its banks Escalante noted a species of medium-sized trees on whose foliage lived "a vast number of little insects, as strange to us as the trees." Some scientist perhaps can tell us what they were.

On the 27th they continued south a league, still in the plain, then crossed a small stream running through "good land for crops." A league and a half farther south they left the Timpanogos basin through a pass which they called Puerto de San Pedro, and entered another large valley. Because the salt flats from which the Laguna Indians got their salt were close by toward the east, they called the place Valle de las Salinas. The valley was fourteen leagues long from north to south, five leagues wide from east to west and well watered by a small river. Continuing four more leagues southward, they camped at a large spring which they called Ojo de San Pablo in honor of Saint Paul. Camp was in the vicinity of the town of Starr, and just east of Mona Reservoir. As soon as the travelers halted, the guides José María and Joaquín brought five Indians

---

[1] September 26.

from the nearby ranchos. Escalante says: "We gave them something to eat and to smoke, and told them the same things we had told the others at the Lake, in-so-far as was appropriate to the circumstances." He adds, "We found them as docile as the others. Manifesting great joy on hearing that more fathers and Spaniards were coming to live with them, they remained with us until nearly midnight." This day's march was six and one-half leagues or some twenty miles to the south, generally along the present-day highway.

Next day[1] they continued south four leagues to a west-flowing stream[2] said by the natives to descend from the salt flats in the eastern sierra. The weather was hot, men and horses were sweaty, and, says Escalante, "We stopped here a short time in the shade of the cottonwoods on the bank to get some relief from the great heat." They had scarcely sat down to rest, "when from some thickets of willows eight Indians very fearfully approached us, most of them naked except for a piece of buckskin around their loins. We spoke to them and they to us, but neither of us understood the other, because the two Lagunas and the interpreter had gone ahead. By signs we gave them to understand that we were peaceful and friendly." Continuing south three leagues, Escalante then swung southeast half a league and camped in the same valley near a spring called San Bernardino, near the site of present-day Levan, having traveled eight leagues for the day, still along Highway 91.

Leaving San Bernardino next day,[3] they started south-southwest and immediately met six Indians. Says Escalante, "We talked to them a long while and preached to them through the interpreter and the Lagunas, and they listened with great docility." Going forward two and one-half leagues they swung southwest, now leaving Valle de las Salinas, which continued south. "Here," says Escalante, "we met an old Indian of venerable appearance. He was alone in a little hut, and his beard was so thick and long that he looked like one of the hermits of Europe. He told us about a river nearby, and about some of the country we still had to traverse," and there was more of it than Escalante had imagined. They continued southwest half a league, and west-northwest through some small valleys and dry hills for another half a league. Then travel-

---

[1]September 28.
[2]Probably Salt Creek.
[3]September 29.

ing a league and a half, they came to a river which they did not see until they were "on its very bank." It was Sevier River. Here they camped in a meadow which they called Santa Ysabel, close to the site of the town of Mills, and observed the latitude by the North Star, finding it to be in 39° and 4'.

Here occurred another interesting conference. Soon after the Spaniards halted, four Indians appeared on the opposite bank, and Escalante invited them to cross over to the camp. They did so and remained all the afternoon, consuming Escalante's scanty rations and telling about the neighboring country and the watering place to which the travelers must go next day. Escalante says, "This river, according to the name the Indians gave it, appears to be the San Buenaventura, but we doubt whether this is the case, because it carries much less water than where we crossed that stream in 41° 19'," far to the east. Escalante's skepticism was justified. He adds, "Moreover, it seems likely that where we crossed it in that latitude, Silvestre would have told us that river ran near his homeland, as he told us other things about the sierra and the other rivers and lakes, which we found to agree with his account, and in it I include this river which passes through Santa Monica." His faith in Silvestre was complete, but his geography here was faulty. The San Clemente was White River, which they had crossed far to the east, three days before reaching the six cottonwoods near the Dinosaur Quarry. It flows west into Green River, which in turn runs south a long distance and empties into the Colorado. But it is not surprising that in one reconnaissance Escalante did not get a correct perspective of every detail of the vast wilderness over which he was traveling.

THE BEARDED UTES

XIV

Next day[1] early in the morning "twenty Indians arrived in camp, together with those who were here yesterday afternoon, wrapped in blankets made of the skins of rabbits and hares. They remained conversing with us very happily until nine in the morning, as docile and affable as the preceding ones." Escalante adds, "These people have much heavier beards than the Lagunas. They have holes bored through the cartilage of their noses, and they wear as an ornament a little polished bone of deer, fowl or some other animal, thrust through the hole. In features they look more like Spaniards than like the rest of the Indians hitherto known in America, from whom they are different in the foregoing respects. They speak the same language as the Timpanogotzis. At this river and place of Santa Ysabel this tribe of bearded Indians begins." This is another precious ethnological item. He adds, "It is they, perhaps, who gave rise to the report of the Spaniards that they live on the other side of the Río del Tizón, which according to several coinciding reports is the Río Grande, formed from the Río de Dolores and the others and which joins the Navajó." We shall hear more of the Río del Tizón before our story is finished. Here at Santa Ysabel near the site of Mills, Miera sketched the heavily bearded Utes. Auerbach enlarged and described the picture. "The men wear shirts of almost knee length, and moccasins. They carry quivers made of animal skin which sheath their supply of arrows. One of the Indians is holding a rabbit in his hand and a net used for snaring hares and rabbits. In the preparation of their rabbit nets the Indians use soapweed, sagebrush, or hemp dogbane bark, stripping the outer fibres from these plants, and twisting them into cords and ropes. The rabbit net fences made of these cords were three or four feet high and strung on willow posts, set to form a crescent-shaped enclosure into which the rabbits were driven, trapped and slaughtered."[2]

At nine o'clock the same morning the travelers set forth from

---
[1] September 30.
[2] *Utah Historical Quarterly*, XI (1943).

Santa Ysabel, crossed Sevier River, and continued south. Having traveled three and one-half leagues or some ten miles along the river, over a plain covered with troublesome chamise, they passed west of Sevier Bridge Reservoir, entered a small canyon, then reached a plain with good pasturage but without water. Continuing south a league and a half, near the site of the town of Scipio they camped beside a spring which they called Ojo de Cisneros. The two small trees which then marked the place have probably disappeared, otherwise they may be very sizeable now. That day they had traveled five leagues south.

Next day's march[1] was one of the longest and hardest, and one of the most difficult to show on a small-scale map. But it took the travelers to another settlement of these interesting Bearded Utes, where they had new and exciting experiences. Retracing their previous day's trek a short distance north, they traveled by a circuitous route but generally west, over rough and stony country and along a dry arroyo. Having traveled fourteen leagues or nearly forty miles for the day, they found what they had thought was a lake to be a vast salt flat or marsh, just northeast of Clear Lake, on the Union Pacific Railroad.

From here the desperate search for water was continued. Two of the men returned from a long scouting trip and reported that they had seen some water about a league beyond the campsite. Thereupon it was decided that as soon as the moon came up the horses should be taken a few at a time to drink, and that water should be brought to camp for the rest of the men. Since the scouts were not certain about the water they thought they had seen, two men were left in camp with the horses, and three went to look for water in the direction of Río de Santa Ysabel, apparently Sevier River, but they did not return that night. Nothing is said here about cattle, and we conclude that none were left, for none are mentioned hereafter.

When morning dawned,[2] nothing had been heard from the men who had gone with the horses to look for water. About six o'clock one of them returned to camp but was unable to tell the whereabouts of the horse herd, or any of the rest of the men, because he and his companion had fallen asleep at their post. Mean-

---
[1] On October 1.
[2] October 2.

YUTA INDIAN GIRLS
Typical of those seen by Escalante's party.

A BEARDED INDIAN
Typical of those met by Escalante in present Juab and Millard counties.

while the animals, driven by thirst, had strayed away, and the two sleepy watchers, awakening at different times, went by different routes to look for them. Don Juan Pedro Cisneros then set forth on the trail, riding bareback, and overtook the horses seven leagues back, that is midway in the previous day's horrible march toward Ojo de Cisneros, arriving in camp shortly before noon.

Soon afterward the men who had gone to scout for water arrived, accompanied by some Indians whose camps they had discovered on the bank of Sevier River. These Indians were another group of the Barbones, or Longbeards, whose tribe or band were called Tirangapui. "The five who first came with their chief had such long beards that they looked like Capuchin or Bethlemite fathers," says Escalante. "Their chief was an attractive man of mature years but not aged. They remained . . . happily talking to us, and in a short time they became very fond of us." When the chief learned that one of the Spaniards was missing, he sent four of his men out on the trail to look for him, each one going in a different direction. Says Escalante, "This was a deed worthy of the greatest gratitude toward and admiration for people so wild that they had never before seen people like us. While the chief was giving these orders, he saw that the absentee was already coming, and very gladly he told us the news."

Escalante did not neglect this opportunity to exercise his priestly calling. He says, "We preached the Gospel to them as well as the interpreter could explain it, telling them of the one God, the punishment which He has in store for the bad and the reward for the good, the necessity of holy baptism and of the knowledge and the observance of the divine law." Meanwhile three of the Long Beards were approaching. The chief told the Spaniards they were some of his people, and that the conversation should be suspended till the others arrived, "in order that they also might hear what we were saying for their benefit." When all were assembled the chief told them the Spanish visitors were priests, and were telling them what they must do in order to go to Heaven, and that they must pay close attention. "He said this so forcefully that although we understood only now and then a word of the Yuta language, we gathered what he was telling them before the interpreter had translated it for us, solely by the gestures with which he was expressing himself."

Escalante told the vistors that if they wished to accept Christianity he and Domínguez would return with more fathers, so that all of the Yutas might be instructed, "like the Lagunas who were already awaiting religious teachers," but in that case "they must live together in a pueblo, and not scattered about" as they were at present. Escalante says "They all replied very joyfully that we must return with other fathers, and that they would then do whatever we might teach them and command them." Hereupon the chief said that "if we wished, and thought it better, they would go to live with the Lagunas, which we had already proposed to him." Whether or not they did so we have no means of knowing.

The Spaniards now said goodbye to these Long Beards, "and all of them, especially the chief, took our hands with great fondness and affection. But the time when they most emphatically expressed themselves was when we were leaving the place. They scarcely saw us depart when all of them, imitating their chief, who set the example, burst out weeping copious tears, so that even after we were a long distance away we still heard the tender lamentations of these poor little lambs of Christ who were unhappy only for lack of The Light. They so moved us that some of our companions could not restrain their tears."

This place was called Llano Salado, the name which it still bears, and because of some white shells he found there Escalante surmised that the lake[1] had once been much larger than at the time when he saw it. Here, almost in the middle of the plain Miera observed the latitude by the sun, and found it to be 39° 34' 36", which like the rest of his findings, was too high. Escalante said the plain must extend nearly thirty leagues from north to south and fourteen from east to west. He added: "In most places it is very short of pasturage, and although two rivers enter it, the Santa Ysabel from the north, and a medium-sized one whose waters are very salty from east to west, we saw no place whatever that was suitable for a settlement."

---
[1] Salt Lake.

XV

A GUIDE DESERTS

In the afternoon of October 2, Escalante and his caravan set forth toward the south-southeast, because the marshes and lakes would not permit them to travel south, "which was the direct route to the pass through which we were to leave the plain." Having traveled three leagues they halted at El Cerrillo, a small hill surrounded by marshes, with plentiful pasturage but only salty water. Camp was east-southeast of the site of Clear Lake.

Now for three days the route ran east of and parallel to Cricket Mountains, and converged with the line of the Union Pacific Railroad. Leaving El Cerrillo on October 3, they made many turns because they were surrounded by marshes, so they crossed a river which apparently disappeared in bogs and lakes. The ford was miry, and in it the horse which Andrés the interpreter was riding, stumbled and threw him head over heels into the water, "giving him a hard blow on his cheek" not to mention the scare.

From here they traveled six leagues south by west over good and level terrain, and arrived at an arroyo which at a distance appeared to have plenty of water, but they found only some pools in which it was difficult for the animals to drink. However, because of the good pasturage they camped there for the night. Escalante says, "All along the arroyo there was a sort of white, dry, and narrow bank which from a distance looked like a stretched canvas," and for this reason they named the stream Arroyo del Tejedor.[1] Escalante or somebody else in the party had a lively imagination. Camp was about twenty-five miles due west of the town of Fillmore and in the vicinity of Borden on the Union Pacific Railroad. Sevier Lake, beyond Cricket Mountains, was west of their line of march that day.

On October 4 they traveled south upstream a quarter of a league, swung south-southwest, passed near the site of Bloom, their route converging with the line of the Union Pacific Railroad; and having traveled nearly five leagues they arrived at "the South

---

[1] The Arroyo of the Weaver.

Pass," where the elevation is nearly seven thousand feet. Now, having left the salt flat, they found in an arroyo more and better water, and beautiful meadows with fine pasturage for the animals, which were badly worn and ill from the salty water of previous days. The campsite called Las Vegas del Puerto[1] was on Beaver River, east of Cricket Mountains, and a few miles northeast of the site of Black Rock.

That night there was dissension in camp. This may mean that the men were getting on each other's nerves, which under the circumstances was almost inevitable. Cisneros sent for his servant, Simón Lucero, to join the rest in saying the Rosary. For some unknown reason Lucero did not respond, so Cisneros reprimanded him for his laziness and his lack of Christian devotion. Thereupon Lucero attacked Cisneros and they had a rough and tumble fight. Hearing the hullabaloo, the rest of the men ran to the scene, but not in time to prevent José María, one of the Laguna guides, from getting a bad scare and a feeling of disgust at the fracas.

The men tried to convince José María that Cisneros did not mean to harm Lucero, but was only correcting him, saying that although a father might correct his son, or a master his servant, he would not kill him. But José María was not convinced. Next morning,[2] before the travelers set forth on the march, he left the Spanish camp and turned back on the trail without saying goodbye to anybody, and Escalante said nothing to him, "wishing to leave him in complete liberty." The interpreter said that apart from the quarrel in camp, José María was homesick, and "disconsolate at their departure from his country." On two counts Escalante regretted the loss of his guide. He wrote: "José María turned back from here, leaving us without anybody who knew the trail ahead, even from hearsay." Moreover, "we felt very sorry about this incident because we desired to hasten his salvation, which now he would not be able to obtain so quickly."

Now without the Laguna guide, Escalante left Las Vegas del Puerto, traveled south two leagues on the banks of the arroyo, swung southwest three leagues, and halted for the night in another meadow of the same stream, naming the campsite San Atenógenes, having advanced five leagues for the day. Camp was southwest of the site of Black Rock.

---
[1] The Meadows of the Pass.
[2] October 5.

As soon as they halted, two men went to see if the western part of the sierra and a valley which they saw in it were passable, "and if they gave any hope of finding in them pasturage for the animals." After dark the men returned to report that they had found "no pass whatever by which to cross the sierra, that it was very rough and high in this direction, and that in front of it there was a wide plain without any pasturage or water whatsoever. Therefore we were unable to take this direction, which was the best one for reaching Monterey, that place being our objective. So we decided to continue south until we emerged from this sierra through a very wide valley beginning at this campsite of San Atenógenes, which we named Valle de Nuestra Señora de la Luz. Through it continues the Arroyo del Tejedor, with adequate wells and pools of good water, and very spacious meadows abundant with pasturage, both of which in the valley are very scarce." Escalante adds: "On the preceding days a very cold head wind from the south had blown fiercely and without ceasing, followed by a snowfall so heavy that not only the peaks of the sierra but likewise all the plains were covered with snow tonight." All this was most discouraging to Escalante and his men.

Next day[1] it was still snowing, "and it continued all day without stopping," says Escalante, "so we were unable to travel. Night came, and seeing that it still did not stop, we implored the intercession of Our Mother and Patroness, repeating in chorus the three parts of her rosary and of all the saints, and saying the litanies. And God willed that at nine o'clock at night it should cease to snow, hail and rain." Next day[2] says Escalante, "although we were greatly inconvenienced by the lack of firewood and the excessive cold, we were unable to leave San Atenógenes today either, because with so much snow and water, the land, which here is very soft, was impassable."

On October 8, they left San Atenógenes through the plain toward the south, but traveled only three and one-half leagues, and that with great difficulty because the ground everywhere was so soft and miry that many pack animals and saddle horses, and even the loose herd, either fell down or mired in the mud. So they camped about a mile west of the arroyo, naming the

---
[1]October 6.
[2]October 7.

campsite Santa Brígida. Here they observed the latitude by the North Star, finding themselves in 38° 3' 30" north latitude.

At this camp they suffered greatly from cold because all day a sharp north wind had been blowing, and here they made a momentous decision. "Hitherto," says Escalante, "we had intended to go to the presidio and the new establishments of Monterey, but thinking them still distant because, although we had descended 1° 23½' to this place of Santa Brígida, we had not advanced toward the west, according to the daily directions, more than 136½ leagues. According to the opinion which we had formed, partly on account of not having heard among all these last people any report of the Spaniards and fathers of Monterey, partly because of the great difference in longitude between that port and the town of Santa Fé, as shown on the maps, there were still many more leagues westward to be traveled." Moreover, "Winter had already begun with great severity, for all the sierras we were able to see in all directions were covered with snow. The weather was very unsettled, and we feared that long before we arrived at our destination the passes would be closed, and we would be delayed for two or three months in some sierra, where there might be no people nor any means of obtaining necessary sustenance, for our provisions were already very low, and so we would expose ourselves to death from hunger if not from cold.

"Moreover, we reflected that even granting that we might arrive at Monterey this winter, we should not be able to reach the Villa of Santa Fé before the month of June next year. This delay, together with the one that would arise in the regular and necessary pursuit of such an interesting undertaking as the one now in hand, might be very harmful to the souls who, according to what has been said before, desired their eternal salvation through holy baptism. Seeing such delay in fulfilling what we had promised them, they would consider their hopes frustrated, or would conclude that we had intentionally deceived them, whereby their conversion and the extension of the Dominions of His Majesty in this direction would be more difficult in the future." He here referred to his promise to the natives of Provo Valley to send missionaries to convert them. He continued: "To this it might be added that the Laguna Joaquín, terrified, and weary of so many hardships and privations, might stray away from us and return to his country, or to other people of whom he might have heard, as was done by the other Laguna.[1]

"To offset these considerations there was the possibility that by continuing south from Santa Brígida we might discover a shorter and better road than the one by way of the Sabuaganas by which to go from Santa Fé to the Laguna de Timpanois and to these other Indians, the Long Beards, and perhaps to some other nation hitherto unknown, who may have always dwelt on the north bank of the Río Grande.

"Therefore, we decided to continue south, if the terrain would permit it, as far as the Río Colorado, and from there proceed toward Cosnina, Moqui, and Zuñi." From this last sentence it is evident that Escalante, in spite of his long peregrination, was still pretty well oriented as to the position of the vast country he had explored in relation to New Mexico, from which he had started and to which he now decided to return.

---

[1] He was referring to José María.

XVI

BACKTRACK TOWARD SANTA FÉ

ALTHOUGH ESCALANTE did not succeed in his dream of reaching California, nevertheless for a long distance he still was a discoverer of new lands; and he added yet another chapter to the history of North American exploration and especially to the history of Utah, Arizona, and New Mexico. To the next segment of his Diary he gave a separate title, calling it "New Itinerary, and the Beginning of Our Return from 38° 3′ and 30 Seconds of North Latitude." It is of little consequence, historically speaking, that his astronomical reckoning was no more accurate here than formerly. It merely emphasizes the shortcomings of his instruments.

On October 9 Escalante left Santa Brígida, where he had decided not to continue to California, and traveled south six leagues with less difficulty than he had experienced the previous day, "because the ground was not so soft nor so wet." They camped at San Rústico, south of the site of Milford, where they "found everything convenient, it being unnecessary for us to go to the arroyo for water or to its meadows for pasturage."

Next day[1] they continued south a league, then traveled south-southwest to a small hill "to view the extent of this valley and plain of La Luz," and saw that it extended southwest more than thirty-five or forty leagues, for, says Escalante, "we could scarcely see the sierras where it ends in this direction, although they are very high, as we afterward discovered." On the way they saw also three springs of hot sulphurous water on top of and on the eastern slope of these hills, near to and below which there were small patches of ground covered with what they called saltpeter. Continuing south two leagues, making six for the day, they camped, fearing that if they went any farther they might not find water for the night. At the campsite, called San Eleuterio, there was melted snow "in a kind of lake" and near it good pasturage. Escalante adds this precious comment: "The Long

[1]October 10.

Bearded Yutas[1] extend this far south, and here apparently their territory ends." So we may conclude that these people reached from the site of Mills where Escalante first saw them, past Milford to San Eleuterio.

We now learn that the decision not to continue to Monterey was resented by some of the companions, and gave Escalante a subject for conversation. On October 11, he says, "We set out from San Eleuterio, letting the companions go ahead so that we two might discuss between ourselves the means we ought to adopt to relieve the companions, especially Don Bernardo Miera, Don Joaquín Laín, and the interpreter Andrés Muñiz, of the great dissatisfaction with which they were leaving that route to Monterey and taking this one. We thought the latter route was now desirable and harmonious with the most holy Will of God, in accord with which alone we desired to travel, and to obey which we were disposed to suffer and if necessary to die.

"We had already told them at Santa Brígida the reasons for our decision, but instead of listening to the force of our arguments, they opposed our views and from then on they were very insubordinate. Everything now was obnoxious to them and everything insufferably difficult. They talked of nothing but how useless so long a journey would be. For to them it was of no importance to have already discovered so great an extent of country, and people so willing to attach themselves to the Vineyard of the Lord and the Dominions of His Majesty, God spare him; nor to have become acquainted with such extensive regions hitherto unknown; nor finally to bring one soul, now almost assured, to the fold of the Church, an achievement more than notable and worth even a longer journey of greater difficulties and fatigues. Moreover, we had already made much progress toward reaching Monterey at some later time." Apparently he meant by the same route. "But to all this they paid no attention, for the first of the persons here mentioned,"—Don Bernardo Miera—"without any cause whatsoever, at least on our part, had conceived great hopes of profit by merely reaching Monterey, and had communicated these hopes to the others, building castles in the air. And now he assured them that we were robbing them of these blessings which they imagined would be so great, with

---

[1] Yutas Barbones.

the result that even the servants greatly tried our patience. Shortly before this decision was made, Don Bernardo said we had advanced but little toward the west, and that it was still a long distance to Monterey, but now even the servants frequently maintained that we would have arrived there within a week."

Escalante continued: "Many times, before leaving the Villa de Santa Fé, we had told each and every one of our companions that in this journey we had no other destination than the one which God might give us, and that we were not inspired by any temporal aim whatsoever; and that any one of them who might attempt to trade with the heathen, or to follow their personal desires instead of devoting themselves to the one purpose of this enterprise, which had been and is the greater honor of God and the spread of the Faith, had better not go with us. On the way we repeatedly admonished them to purge themselves of any other intentions they might have, because otherwise we should suffer trouble and misfortunes, and should fail to achieve all our aims, a thing which in part they now saw happen under circumstances which, unless they close their eyes to the light, they will never be able to attribute to accident.

"With all this we were more mortified each day, and we were disconsolate to see that instead of the interests of Heaven, those of the earth were first and principally sought. And so, in order that the cause of God might be better served, and to make them see more clearly that not through fear nor by our own will, we had decided to abandon entirely the heavy responsibility of the foregoing reflections." That is he would again gamble.

Escalante continues: "Having implored the divine clemency and the intercession of our patron saints, we decided to inquire anew the will of God by means of casting lots," a practice with which God apparently was familiar, "putting in one the word 'Monterey' and in the other 'Cosnina,' and to follow the route which might turn up." Their private conference ended, the friars overtook their companions and had them dismount. When all were assembled, Father Atanasio set forth the difficulties that would be encountered by continuing toward Monterey; what they might accomplish by returning by way of Cosnina, "and finally the mistakes and setbacks they would have suffered with some of their projects. He pointed out to them all the evil that might result from continuing now to Monterey," reminding them of the threatened desertion by Joaquín, the Laguna Indian. He warned them that if the lot fell to Monterey there would be no other guide than Don Bernardo Miera, for he was the one who thought that place was so close at hand, and that "all this dissatisfaction was the result of his ideas." Father Atanasio now made a brief talk, exhorting the men to subject themselves to the will of God. The men all submitted in a Christian spirit and said the Rosary while the friars repeated the penitential Psalms, the litanies, and prayers. With the men thus prepared for the outcome of the gamble, they cast the lot, "and it was decided in favor of Cosnina." Escalante adds, "Now, thank God, we all agreeably and gladly accepted this result." But we suspect that Miera swore under his breath. Apparently the lots were drawn at a point about east of Lund, Utah.

The travelers now quickened their pace, and having advanced ten leagues from San Eleuterio by a zigzag trail, generally south, they camped after dark on the banks of Coal Creek, some ten miles north of Cedar City, at a place where there was an abundance of pasturage. They named the campsite the Meadows of the Valley of Señor San José. If Miera was a little glum that night it would be no cause for surprise. Here they turned from mundane to heavenly interests, and by the polar star they observed the latitude of the campsite of San José, finding it to be in 37° and 33′ of north latitude.

XVII

TO THE VIRGIN RIVER

NEXT DAY[1] Escalante began a new chapter in his narrative, labeling it *The Itinerary and Diary Continues from 37° Thirty-three Minutes of Latitude; and from the Small River of Señor San José it is Directed Toward the Río Colorado and the Cosninas.* He may have regarded the new heading as a memorandum of his triumph over Miera.

The secular members of the party had gone ahead, possibly to sulk and talk about the previous day's debate over the question of going to Monterey, a conjecture which is idle and, we hope, harmless gossip. In their wake the two friars left Señor San José, crossed a large and miry marsh and a plain with plentiful water and pasturage, and through which ran a little stream the size of an irrigation ditch. They then turned south down the west side of the meadows, over good terrain, and traveled four and one-half leagues or some ten or more miles.

As they neared the men who had gone ahead, the friars saw them hurriedly leave the trail. Curious to learn the cause of this commotion, Escalante and Domínguez quickened their pace and found the men talking with some twenty native women who were gathering grass seeds, and who had tried to run away but were detained by the Spaniards. Escalante says, "We were sorry to see them so frightened, for they could not even speak, and through Joaquín the Laguna we tried to relieve them of their fear and timidity." Probably they never before had seen a European. "When they had somewhat recovered their composure, they told us that in this vicinity," not far from the site of Cedar City, "there were many of their people, that they had heard it said that toward the south there were people who wore blue clothes, and that the great river (the Colorado) was not very far from here. We were unable to learn from them with certainty from what tribe they had obtained these blue garments or rags, nor from what they said could we form any opinion regarding this matter. But we knew that the Payuchis traded

---
[1] October 12.

only for red garments, and it immediately occurred to us that the Cosninas purchase their blue woolen cloth in Moqui, so we concluded that it was of these people they were talking, and from this we inferred that this place was near the Río Colorado and the Río Cosnina." Escalante was getting near to country with which he was familiar, at least through hearsay.

He continues: "These Indian women were so poorly dressed that they wore only some pieces of buckskin hanging from their waists, which hardly covered what can not be looked at without peril. We bade them good-bye, telling them they must notify their people that we were coming in peace, that we harmed nobody and loved everybody, and that their men who were able to do so should come without fear to the place where we were going to camp."

Continuing across the Plain and Valley of Señor San José, passing near the site of Cedar City, and having traveled three more leagues to the south, the Spaniards saw other Indians running away. So they sent the interpreter with Joaquín the Laguna and another companion, to try to bring one of the natives to the camp they were soon to make, to inquire whether the Río Grande de Cosnina[1] was as nearby as the Indian women had said, and to see if one of the Indians would guide them as far as the Cosnina settlement on the Colorado River, which Father Garcés had recently visited on his way to and from Hopi Land. The natives ran so fast that the Spaniards were barely able to overtake and detain one of them. Don Joaquín Laín put him up behind him on his horse, and carried him to the place where the Spaniards, having meanwhile traveled another half league south, had camped near a stream called Nuestra Señora del Pilar de Zaragoza, "where, as in all the valley," there was plentiful and good pasturage. Camp was in Cedar Valley in the vicinity of Kanarraville, on one of the tributaries of Ash Creek, presumably Kanarra Creek, and for the day they had traveled eight leagues, or more than twenty miles south.

The Indian whom the Spaniards brought to camp was very much excited, and so terror-stricken that he acted like a crazy man. He looked about in every direction, watched everybody, was frightened by every action or movement on the part of the Span-

---

[1]Colorado River.

iards, "and tried to escape what his timidity had led him to fear." When the Spaniards talked to him he gave close attention, and responded so quickly that he appeared rather to guess than to understand the questions asked him. After a while he quieted down a little and the Spaniards gave him something to eat and pinned a ribbon on him, a simple form of knighthood perhaps. He carried a large net well made of hemp, which he said he used to catch hares and rabbits. Apparently it was similar to the one Miera had sketched among the Long Beards farther north. When they asked him where the net came from he said it was from other Indians who lived down the Colorado River, whence also, the Spaniards learned later, these people obtained colored shells. And, says Escalante, according to the distance and directions which he gave, "they appear to be the Cocomaricopas," who lived far away on Colorado River north of the Yuma junction. "With respect to the distance to the Río Grande and the blue clothing, he said the same as the Indian women, adding that some colored woolen yarn which he possessed, he had purchased this summer from two of those people who wear the blue clothing and who had crossed the river." Was he referring to Spaniards on their way to California? This was about the time of Anza's first expedition to Monterey.

Escalante questioned the timid Indian "in various ways" about the Cosninas, but he gave no information concerning them, "either because he knew them by another name, or perhaps because he feared that if he said he knew them we would take him by force, in order that he might guide us to them, or, finally because he really did not know them." When asked if he had heard it said that toward the west or northwest there were priests and other Spaniards he again said "No, for although many people lived in that direction, they were of the same tribe and language as himself." The Spaniards now showed the Indian a kernel of maize, and he said he had seen how it was raised, adding that next day the travelers would arrive at a place where there was a little of this grain, which had been brought from some place where it was grown. Escalante adds, "We made great efforts to get him to tell us the name of these people who were now planting maize, and to clarify other things about which he was giving a confused account, but we were able to learn only that they lived on this side of the large river on another and smaller one." The Indian spent the night voluntarily at the Spanish camp, and promised to lead the strangers next day to the people of whom he had told them.

Next day[1] the Spaniards left Nuestra Señora del Pilar, accompanied by their overnight guest, who had very little baggage, and to whom they had promised a hunting knife if he would guide them to other Indians. Traveling south two and one-half leagues, or some six or more miles, they arrived at the rancho where the new guide lived, about east of New Harmony. There the wayfarers found an old Indian, a young man, several children and three women, "all of them very good looking," says Escalante. Among their possessions there were piñon nuts, dates, and some little sacks of maize. The Spaniards talked a long time with the old man, but he told them nothing new. They gave the promised hunting knife to the Indian who had guided them to this place, and told the inhabitants that if one of the men would lead them to the people who planted maize they would pay him well. From the cool response Escalante saw that the natives were suspicious and afraid, but "at the suggestion of our companions we placed before them a hunting knife and some glass beads." These riches brought the desired result. "The old man seized them, and impelled by his great fear, he offered to guide us, in order to get us away from there, as later became evident to us, and to give his family time to reach a place of safety by withdrawing to a nearby sierra."

The Spaniards continued on their way, accompanied by this old man and the timid Indian who had spent the previous night with them. They traveled a league and a half or some four miles south, descended to Río del Pilar, now called Ash Creek, crossed it, left the valley of Señor San José, and entered a stony pass of black slag between the two high sierras. In the roughest part of the pass the two guides disappeared, and says Escalante, "we never saw them again. We admired their cleverness in having led us through a place so well suited to the sure and unhindered execution of their plan, which we had already suspected, not only because of their timidity, but also from the manner in which they had consented to guide us." They were suspiciously willing. The Spaniards now continued south over a rocky trail strewn with

---
[1]October 13.

black slag, descended a second time to the Río del Pilar, and camped on its bank in a pretty cottonwood grove, naming the place San Daniel. Camp was on Ash Creek just over the ridge from the valley they had traversed and some five miles north of the town of Pintura. They had put behind them another long and hard day's march.

Escalante now gives a description of the Ash Creek region on whose eastern border lie Zion National Monument and Park. "The Valley of Señor San José, through which we have just passed, in its most northern part is in 37° 33' of latitude. From north to south it is about twelve leagues long,[1] and from east to west in some places it is more than three leagues wide, in others two leagues, and in still others less. It has very abundant pasturage, large meadows, fair-sized marshes, and plenty of good land for a settlement with seasonal crops, because, although there is not enough water in the two small rivers of Señor San José and Pilar to irrigate more than a few small areas, nevertheless the great moisture of the land may supply this lack, so that the irrigation will not be missed, because the moisture in all the valley is so great that not only the meadows and the flats, but even the highlands at this time had green and fresh pasturage, like the most fertile meadows of rivers in the months of June and July. Roundabout the valley and very near at hand there is plentiful timber, firewood of spruce and piñon, and good sites for raising large and small stock.

"The Indians who live in the valley and its vicinity to the west, north, and east, are called in their language Huascari. They dress very poorly, and eat grass seeds, rabbits, piñon nuts in season, and dates. They do not plant the dates, and judging from what we saw, they obtain very few of them. These people are extremely timid, and in this respect they are different from the Lagunas and the Bearded Utes. On the northwest and north they border on the latter, and they speak the same language, although with some differences. The Sierra de los Lagunas ends in this place of San Daniel, having run directly south from the Valley of Las Salinas to this place. From here to the Río Grande (Colorado) all the land is poor, although it appears to be rich in minerals."

---
[1]Some thirty miles.

A TYPICAL SCENE IN SOUTHWESTERN UTAH THROUGH WHICH ESCALANTE PASSED

Photo Hal Rumel

On October 14, leaving San Daniel, Escalante and his party traveled along the west side of the stream, swung away from it, traveled two leagues over hills of very white sand, very stony in places, passed two springs of good water, traveled over *malpais*, like slag although heavier and less porous, but not difficult, then over sandy stretches, and having marched four leagues for the day they descended for a third time to the stream now called Ash Creek, and camped at San Hugolino, about midway between the towns of Toquerville and Pintura. At San Hugolino Escalante wrote: "Here the climate is very mild, for although yesterday we felt great heat, last night and today the cottonwoods of the river were so green and leafy, the roses and other flowers which grow here so flaming and fresh, that they showed that through here they had not yet been frozen nor frosted. We also saw mesquite trees, which do not grow in very cold lands."

Next day[1] Escalante continued to sing the praises of the area now affectionately referred to in Utah as "Dixie." Leaving San Hugolino, he and his companions traveled on the west bank of Ash Creek. Having advanced two and one-half leagues, meanwhile having left the stream, the wayfarers returned to its bank, near the site of La Verkin, where there were pleasant groves. Here they found a well-made mat, and on it a large supply of ears of green corn. Nearby in the plain and along the river bank the small fields of maize had very well-made irrigation ditches. "For this reason," says Escalante, "we felt especially pleased, partly because it gave us hopes that we should be able to provide ourselves farther on with assured supplies, but principally because it was evidence of the application of these people to the cultivation of the soil, and because of finding this preparation for reducing them to civilized life and to the Faith when the Most High may so will, for it is well known what it costs to induce other Indians to do this, and how much their conversion is impeded by their dislike for this labor, which is so necessary for a civilized life, especially in pueblos. From here downstream and on the mesas on either side for a long distance, according to what was learned, live Indians who sustain themselves by planting maize and calabashes, and who in their language are called Parussi." This was a promising region.

---

[1] October 15.

The travelers continued downstream toward the south, and having traveled a league and a half they swung southwest, leaving the river, but a high cliff from which there was no way to descend forced them to backtrack more than a quarter of a league and return to the river, which there ran southwest. On this part of the day's march they had passed near the site of Toquerville. In the stretch of the river where they retraced their steps there were ash heaps, veins and signs of minerals, and many stones of reddish mica. Near the site of La Verkin the stream was joined by two others, one coming from the north-northeast, La Verkin Creek, and the other from the east, the main Virgin River. The latter had hot and sulphurous water, so the travelers named it Río Sulfúreo. This river was named later by Spaniards for the Virgin Mary, not for Thomas Virgin, the American fur trader, as some persons have thought. Here Escalante was charmed by "a beautiful grove of large black cottonwoods, willows, and wild grapevines."

The Spaniards now crossed Ash Creek and the Virgin River near their junction, then going south past the site of Hurricane, they ascended a low mesa between crags of black rock. Having reached the top of the mesa they found open country, crossed a small plain, which toward the east had a chain of very high mesas and toward the west some hills covered with chamise, "the plant which in Spain is called *brezo*," and also red sand. Escalante says "we might have gone to the edge of the mesas and finished our day's march over good and level country, but the men who went ahead changed their direction in order to follow some fresh tracks of Indians, and led us over these hills and sand flats, where our animals now became very much fatigued." Having traveled by the mesa and the plain two leagues south, the main party turned southwest and marched three leagues through the same hills. They then traveled south more than two leagues, and "descried a small valley surrounded by mesas, from one of which we found it impossible to descend to the valley." They were now unable to go forward, and forced to descend from a high, rugged and very stony ridge. Then, having traveled three-fourths of a league to the south, making ten for the day, they halted at sunset at an arroyo near some pools of good water and good pasturage for the animals. Camp was apparently near the site of Old Fort Pierce, southwest of the town of Hurricane on Fort Pierce Creek, and close to the

Arizona line. They named the camp San Dónulo, or Arroyo del Taray, "because here there were some tamarisk trees or *palo taray.*"

XVIII

ALONG THE BASE OF HURRICANE CLIFF

Leaving San Dónulo on October 16, the wayfarers marched southward, planning to continue in that direction as far as the Colorado River, which they thought could not be far ahead. Having traveled a short distance, and passed some hills abounding in what they called transparent gypsum and mica, they heard people behind them shouting. While the companions continued on their way, Escalante and Domínguez turned back to learn who had caused the hullabaloo, and saw eight Indians on a hill near the campsite they had just left. Escalante invited them to come down, saying the Spaniards were visiting them as friends. Thereupon the natives descended from their refuge and offered the Spaniards for barter some strings of green stone called *chalchihuite,* each string having in it one red shell. "This gave us something to think about," says Escalante, "for from below, the strings of stones looked like rosaries and medals of saints." The Spaniards remained with the natives a short time, but because the Indians spoke the Yuta tongue so differently from the others they had encountered farther north, neither the interpreter nor Joaquín the Laguna could make the Indians understand clearly nor could they understand much of what the Indians said. So they sent for the interpreter to return.

Escalante now understood the Indians to say they were all Parusis, except one who spoke a language more like Arabic than Yuta, and which he thought was Jamajab, that is, Mojave. He also gathered that they lived on the Río del Pilar. He adds, "We took them to be Cosninas, but learned afterward that this was not the case." The natives offered *chalchihuites* for barter. Escalante replied that at the moment he had nothing to trade, but if they would go with him to overtake the rest of the Spaniards he would give them what they requested, and would talk with them at length. He adds, "All came very cheerfully, although with great fear and suspicion on the part of those who appeared to be the most intelligent." Having overtaken the companions, they talked with the natives "more than two and a half or three hours." The

Indians told the Spaniards they could reach the Colorado River in two days, but would not be able to go the way they desired "because there was no watering place, nor would we be able to cross the river in this region because it ran through a tremendous gorge [the Grand Canyon], and was very deep, and had on both sides extremely high cliffs and rocks, and finally, that from here to the river the terrain was very bad."

The travelers now gave the Indians two hunting knives and to each one a string of glass beads, and asked for a guide to the Colorado River, saying he would be liberally rewarded. The Indians refused to escort the Spaniards to the great river, but offered to lead them south some distance along the foot of Hurricane Fault, and to put them on a trail leading eastward to the Cosninas. Escalante was obliged to take their advice. So he offered the Indians some soles of satchel leather if they would guide him over the rough trail, and two of them consented, as Escalante wrote, "to go with us until they had put us on a good and straight road." So the Spaniards continued along the base of the Hurricane Fault toward the trail leading eastward up the cliff. They entered a canyon, traveled through it a league and a half over a difficult trail. This stretch was followed by a rocky cliff so rough that even on foot it would have been difficult to ascend it. The Indian guides now fled, so the Spaniards had to continue south. They retraced the canyon, and having advanced half a league, still below the cliffs, they camped without water for either men or animals, apparently at the southern end of Black Rock Canyon. They were now so short of food that they decided to kill a horse to satisfy their hunger, but because there was no water available they changed their minds. No name is given in the diary for the camp.

On October 17 the travelers threaded a pass along an arroyo where they found good water for men and animals. Continuing south two leagues and southwest two more they reached an arroyo with good rainwater, and found some herbs called *quelites,* but gathered only a few and remained hungry. Then traveling southeast, and having advanced four and one-half leagues over good country for the day, they halted, partly to look for water "and partly to give Don Bernardo Miera some of these ripe herbs as food, because since yesterday morning we had not had a thing to eat, and he was now so weak that he scarcely was able to talk." Miera the soldier was not as hardy as the friars. "We ordered the bags and other containers ... ransacked, to see if there were any leftovers, but found only some pieces of calabash which the servants had obtained yesterday from the Parusis Indians, and which they had hidden to avoid having to share them with the rest of the men. With this and a little sugar, which we also found, we made a stew for everybody and took a little nourishment." Finding no water here the travelers decided to continue south. Meanwhile some of the men climbed the ridge and examined the eastern mesa and the country beyond. They reported the ascent to the mesa good and the plateau level, with many arroyos in which there could not fail to be water, and that apparently there was a river in a plain.

Everybody now voted for a change of direction, but, says Escalante, "we knew very well how they had been deceived on other occasions, and that in so short a time they could not have seen so much; and we were of the opposite opinion because toward the south we had much good and level land in sight, and had found so much water today, contrary to the story told by the Indians, and had traveled all day over good land. All these facts increased our suspicion," says Escalante. "But since now we were without food, and water might be far away, and so that the adoption of our plan should not make more intolerable for them the thirst and hunger which for our sake they might endure, we told them to take the route they thought best calculated to lead us southeast toward the mesa." So they ascended a ridge by a rough and stony wash or arroyo. They had just finished climbing the mesa by a very rough black stone slope when night fell. So they camped on the mesa near good pasturage but without water, naming the camp San Ángel. Their trail that day was later called the Old Temple Road, because by it the Mormons ascended the Hurricane Ridge and thence to Mount Trumbull to get timber for building the Temple at St. George.

Here at San Ángel Escalante writes: "We were very sorry to have changed our direction because, according to the latitude in which we found ourselves, by continuing south we would very soon have arrived at the [Colorado] River." As soon as they halted some of the men who had previously been on the mesa told Escalante that a short distance from here they thought they had seen water. Two of them now went to bring some of the precious fluid but did not return that night, and Escalante concluded they had been looking for Indian camps where they might relieve their hunger. And since there was no water at San Ángel, it was decided to go forward without awaiting the absentees.

So next morning[1] the adventurers set forth from San Ángel toward the east-southeast, traveled half a league, then swung east by south for two leagues over hills and extensive valleys with plentiful but stony pasturage. Then, not finding water, they swung east by north for two more leagues, ascending and descending stony hills that were very hard on the feet of the animals.

On the way the travelers saw five Indians spying upon them from the top of a small but high mesa. The friars were now following behind the rest of the men, and as they passed the foot of the mesa the Indians spoke to them. When the friars turned toward them four of the Indians hid, only one remaining. Escalante wrote: "We saw how terrified he was, but could not persuade him to come down, so we both ascended on foot with great difficulty. At each step we took toward the Indian he tried to run away. We gave him to understand that he must not be afraid, that we loved him like a son, and desired to talk with him. So he waited for us, making a thousand gestures which showed that he was greatly afraid of us. As soon as we had ascended to where he was, we embraced him and, seating ourselves beside him, we had the interpreter and the Laguna come up. Having now recovered his composure, the Indian told us that the others were hiding nearby and, that if we so desired he would bring them, in order that we might see them. When we answered in the affirmative he laid his bow and arrows on the ground, took the interpreter by the hand and went with him to bring the other Indians." They came, and the Franciscans remained about an hour in conversation with them, in the course of which the Indians said there was water nearby.

Escalante asked the Indians to guide the Spaniards to the water, promising them a piece of woolen cloth as a reward, and after much urging three natives consented to lead them to the water. At first they were excited and afraid, but when they questioned Joaquín the Laguna, they quieted down. "Greatly

---

[1] October 18.

surprised at his valor, they asked him . . . how he had dared to come with us. Wishing to relieve them of their fears, and himself from the privation he was suffering, he answered them as best he could, and they were reassured. Doubtless it was because of this that they did not desert us before arriving at the watering place." So, continuing a league to the southeast and another to the south, over a bad and stony road, the Spaniards arrived at a grove of cedar and an arroyo where some deep holes contained large pools of good water. They took a supply for themselves and sent for the horses, which were so thirsty that they drained the pools. Apparently they were at Cooper's Pockets, some twenty miles north of Mt. Trumbull. Having traveled six leagues for the day, here the travelers spent the night, naming the place San Samuel.

As soon as the Spaniards camped they gave the guides the promised woolen cloth, with which they were greatly pleased. Learning that the travelers were short of provisions, the Indians told them to send a Spaniard with one of the natives to their huts, which were some distance away, and they would bring some food, the rest remaining at the Spanish camp. Escalante sent on this errand one of the genizaros with Joaquín the Laguna, provided with goods to barter for the supplies, and pack animals on which to bring them. They left the other Indians at the campsite, and after midnight returned with a small supply of "wild sheep, dried tuna made into cakes, and grass seeds," a statement which tells us what these natives lived on. They also brought news of the two men of Escalante's party who the preceding night had gone to look for water. The other had already arrived at the camp about ten o'clock this night. Such was the scene that transpired in the cedar breaks at San Samuel.

Here Escalante got acquainted with the natives of the region, and gave a good account of some of their cultural traits and assets. Next day[1] twenty Indians of the vicinity visited the Spanish camp with cakes or loaves of tuna, and bags containing the seeds of various herbs to sell to the strangers. If there had been a botanist in Escalante's party he might have made comments of interest to science. The Spaniards paid the natives for what they had brought, and told them that if they had "meat, piñon nuts or more tunas, they should bring them" and they would buy

---

[1] October 19.

them all, "especially the meat." The natives said they would do so but "that we must wait for them until midday." Escalante agreed and the Indian departed. One of them promised to accompany the Spaniards as far as the Colorado River if they would wait till afternoon, and Escalante agreed to this also. "After midday many more Indians came to camp . . . , among them being one who was said to be a Mescalero Apache [from the east] and to have come with two others from his country to this one, crossing the river a few days previously. His features were not very pleasing, and he was distinguished from the rest of the Indians by the disgust he showed at seeing us here, and by the greater display of animosity which we noticed he was purposely making." The natives here said these Apaches were their friends. They did not bring meat, but many bags of the seeds mentioned and some fresh tunas.

Escalante talked a long while concerning the distance to the Colorado River,[1] the road to it, the number of these people, their mode of living, the neighboring tribes, and the guide for whom he was asking. They showed him the direction he must take to the river, giving confused reports of the ford, and saying that in two or three days the Spaniards would arrive there. They said they were Yubuincariris and that they did not plant maize; that their foods were seeds, tunas, piñon nuts, of which they gathered very few, judging from the small quantity they gave Escalante, and what hares, rabbits, and wild sheep they hunted, adding that on this side of the river only the Parusis planted maize and calabashes; that on the other side, just across the river were the Ancamuchis (who Escalante understood were Cosninas) and that they planted much maize. Besides these, they gave Escalante the names of other people, their neighbors to the south-southwest, on this bank of the river, saying the latter were the Payatammumis. They also told of the Huascaris, whom Escalante had already seen in the Valley of Señor San José.

Concerning the Spaniards of Monterey the Indians did not give the least indication that they had ever heard them mentioned. One of the Indians who had spent the preceding night with the Spaniards gave Escalante to understand that he had already

---

[1] Escalante was now inquiring about the Colorado River east of here and not south.

heard of the journey of Father Garcés. "This," says Escalante, "together with the denial by all these people that they knew the Cosninas (unless they know them by the above name of Ancamuchi) seems to verify what we have already said we suspected."

Having finished this long conversation, the natives began to leave the camp, and in spite of their promise the Spaniards were unable to get any of them to accompany them as far as the Colorado River. "Today," says Escalante, "Don Bernardo Miera was sick at his stomach," making it impossible for the Spaniards to continue their journey. A short distance from the camp of San Samuel the Spaniards found pools of water for the night.

Next day[1] the travelers left San Samuel and turned northeast, directing their way "toward the ford of the Colorado River, avoiding a low wooded sierra with many stones on this side of it." This was the northern edge of Kanab Plateau. Having traveled a little more than two leagues, they found in an arroyo several pools of good water. Then, going a league east-northeast, and having traveled seven leagues for the day, they camped on the bank of an arroyo between two small hills, where there was a large supply of water and pasturage, on one of the western branches of Kanab Creek. They named the place Santa Gertrudis. Here they observed the latitude by the North Star, finding themselves in 36° 30'. If their record had been correct they would have been on a western extension of what later became the famous Missouri Compromise Line.

Leaving Santa Gertrudis[2] they traveled northeast. Several times they crossed Arroyo de Santa Gertrudis, a branch of Kanab Creek, in which there were many pools of water. The details of the crossings of the Arroyo of Santa Gertrudis confirm our interpretation of the route through this region. Then they wound their way by twists and turns for five and one-half leagues east-northeast, through chamise thickets and over good soil, and camped after nightfall at Santa Bárbara near a little valley with plentiful pasturage, "but without water even for the men." Camp was in Kimball Valley near Johnson Creek, and some eight miles southeast of Fredonia. Some persons feel certain that Escalante

---

[1]October 20.
[2]October 21.

on this day's march must have stopped at the now famous Pipe Spring, but the diary does not sustain such an interpretation of the route. Pipe Spring is several miles north of Escalante's route.

As soon as camp was made, Lorenzo de Olivares, "driven by thirst because he had eaten too many of the seeds, piñon nuts and tunas" which they had purchased from the Indians, "went to look for water in the nearby arroyos" and was absent all night, causing his companions much worry.

Next day[1] the caravan left Santa Bárbara and traveled northeast, looking for Olivares, and after going some two leagues they found him near a pool with a small amount of water, "there being only enough for the men to drink and to fill a little barrel which we carried in case we should find no water tonight." This gives us another detail regarding their equipment. The thirsty horses had to wait for water.

Escalante and his men continued through the plain, and having traveled four more leagues northeast, they saw a trail running southward, and, says Escalante, "when the interpreter said the Yubuincariris had told him this was the one we ought to take to go to the Colorado River, we took it. But having traveled along it a league to the south, we found that the interpreter was uncertain about the signs, because, after going a short distance the trail turned back. And so, going east, we ascended the low sierra that we were trying to avoid. It runs from north to south the whole length of the eastern side of the plain." They crossed the sierra with great hardship for the animals, "for, besides having many canyons, it is very stony and full of pebbles."

Night overtook the travelers when they were crossing a high ridge, from which they saw several fires on the far side of a small plain. They thought that Andrés the interpreter and Joaquín the Laguna, who had gone ahead to look for water, had made the fires to guide the men who were following behind. Having finished the descent, and traveled five leagues, or some twelve or more miles, from the place where they had left the trail, they arrived at the fire, where there were three little huts, and where they found Andrés and Joaquín awaiting them. There was a joyful reunion. Here they spent the night, naming the place San Juan Capistrano. This campsite was apparently on Utah soil

---

[1]October 22.

near the state line on a branch of Paria River. That day they had traveled twelve hard leagues or more than thirty miles.

Since it was night when the Spaniards arrived at the camp, the Indians could not see how many visitors there were, and they were so frightened that in spite of some coaxing by the interpreter and Joaquín, most of the natives fled, leaving only three men and two women, who also were much disturbed. One of them said to the Laguna guide, "Little brother, you are of the same race as ourselves. Do not permit these people with whom you came to kill us." The Spaniards embraced the Indians, and tried by every conceivable means to allay their fears. So the natives quieted down, and to please their uninvited guests they gave them two roasted hares and some piñon nuts. The hares were probably jackrabbits. Moreover, two of the natives went fearfully to show the Spaniards where to find water for the horses.

Escalante writes: "This campsite is east of the northern point of the small sierra mentioned, near several hills of red earth, to the south of which, very close by on some rocky hills having some piñon and juniper trees, there are two good pools of rainwater. Nearer to them in a small arroyo there are some other pools of water, but they are small and not very good. To the west-southwest of the same little hills, at the foot of the sierra, there is also a small permanent spring." This entry illustrates the great care taken by Escalante in recording the details of his route. Camp was on a small western branch of Paria River, near longitude 112°.

After Escalante and Domínguez had retired and presumably were alseep, Miera and some others of the Spanish party went to a hut to chat with the Indians. When they told the natives that Don Bernardo was ill, one of their medicine men proceeded to doctor him, "with songs and ceremonies which, if not openly idolatrous (for such they might be) were at least superstitious." And, writes scandalized Escalante, "All of our people permitted them willingly, and among them the sick man, and they applauded them as harmless compliments, when they ought to have stopped them as contrary to both the Evangelical and the Divine Law which they profess, or at least they should have withdrawn." Escalante admits that both he and Domínguez "listened to the songs of the Indian but did not know what their purpose was."

Such an action on their part might be excused as anthropological research.

Early next morning someone told the friars what had taken place, and says Escalante, "we reprimanded the men, telling them that next time they must not sanction such errors by their voluntary presence, nor in any other way. This conduct is one of the reasons why the heathen who deal most with the Spaniards and Christians of these regions, more stubbornly resist the Gospel Truth, making their conversion more difficult each day."

Escalante now became reminiscent. "When we were preaching to the first Sabuaganas we saw[1] regarding the necessity of holy baptism, the interpreter, either in order not to displease them nor to lose the ancient friendship which they maintain with them through the vile commerce in furs, even in violation of justifiable prohibitions by the governor of this kingdom, by whom it has been ordered repeatedly that no Indian, genízaro, or citizen shall enter the lands of the heathen without having obtained a license for it from the governor of his province, translated for them in these very words: 'The Father says that the Apaches, Navajos and Cumanches who do not become baptized cannot enter Heaven, but go to Hell, where God punishes them and where they will burn forever like wood in the fire.' The Sabuaganas were greatly pleased at hearing themselves thus exempted from and their enemies included in the inescapable necessity of either being lost or suffering eternally. The interpreter was reprimanded and seeing that his foolish infidelity had been discovered, he reformed." We are not told just how this reformation was manifested.

Escalante adds, "We might give other examples from the lips of these same persons who have been among the Yutas," on this expedition we assume, "and who perhaps applauded and even cooperated in many idolatrous actions, but the two referred to above, of which obviously we are certain, will suffice. For if in our company, after having many times heard these idolatries and superstitions refuted and condemned, they witness them, encourage them, and applaud them, what will they not do when they wander two, three, or four months among the heathen Yutas and Navajos with nobody to correct or restrain them? Besides

---

[1]This was at the Sabuagana camp in the mountains north of Gunnison River.

this incident, some of them have given us sufficient cause in this journey to suspect that while some go to the Yutas and remain so long among them because of their greed for peltry, others go and remain with them for that of the flesh, obtaining there its brutal satisfaction. And so in every way they blaspheme the name of Christ, and prevent, or rather oppose, the extension of His faith. Oh, with what severity ought such evils be met. May God in His infinite goodness inspire the best and most suitable means!" Escalante here was talking about an Indian problem that had confronted Europeans everywhere in the Western Hemisphere—the mingling of white men with the natives and its effect on one or both races.

Next day[1] the caravan remained in camp in order to give the natives here time to quiet down, and to enable others of the vicinity to assemble. Meanwhile, the grass seeds and other native foods they had purchased here, says Escalante, "made us very sick, weakening instead of nourishing us. We were not able to induce these people to sell us any ordinary meat, so we now had a horse killed"— the first time on the expedition —"and the flesh prepared so that it could be carried." It would be interesting to know just how they did this. Perhaps the meat was partly cooked, or par-boiled. "Today Father Atanasio was very ill from a pain in the rectum so severe that he was not able even to move."

All day the Indians kept coming to the Spanish camp from the nearby ranchos, and all were duly embraced and entertained. These people gave the Spaniards a clear account of the Cosninas and Moquinos, "calling them by these very names." They also told the travelers how to reach the Colorado River, which they said was not more than twelve leagues or some thirty miles distant, and gave them a description of the ford. The Spaniards here purchased about a fanega of piñon nuts, and the natives gave them a present of more than half a fanega of grass seeds, for food of course.

Early next morning[2] twenty-six Indians assembled from the nearby ranchos, among them being some who had been there the previous afternoon, and some whom the Spaniards had never

---
[1] October 23.
[2] October 24.

before seen. The friars preached a sermon, telling the natives about the Gospel, denouncing idleness and sin, "especially in the superstitious doctoring of the sick" by the native medicine men. They "admonished them to rely in their troubles upon the true and only God, because He alone has at His command health and sickness, life and death, and He alone is able to help everybody." Escalante comments: "And although our interpreter could not explain this to them clearly, one of them, who doubtless had dealt extensively with the Yutas Payuchis, understood it well, and explained to the others what he had heard. Since we saw they had listened with pleasure, we told them that if they wished to become Christians, fathers and other Spaniards would come to instruct and live with them. They replied that this would please them, and when we asked them where we would find them when we should come, they said they would be in this little sierra and on the nearby mesas. Then, to increase their affection for us, we distributed thirteen varas of red ribbon, giving to each one half a vara, with which they were much pleased and grateful." This was one of the most interesting of the conferences with the natives since leaving Utah Lake.

XIX

THE CROSSING OF THE FATHERS

THIS SAME DAY,[1] about nine o'clock in the morning, "or a little later," the Spaniards left San Juan Capistrano, traveling southward. An Indian at the last camp had agreed to show them the way to a ford of Colorado River, which they were now approaching, but after he had accompanied them half a league he became frightened and refused to go any farther. The Spaniards continued without him, crossed the Arizona line, and having traveled four leagues southward through a valley they found at the foot of the eastern mesa three pools of very good water, with enough for the men but not sufficient to supply the horses. From the campsite to here they had traveled over good country, but even now little populated. Having advanced two more leagues southward, they swung east-southeast for about three leagues over sandy and difficult terrain, and although they did not find water for the animals they did find pasturage. So they halted here because the horses were exhausted and it was already nightfall. The camp called San Bartolomé was on the southwestern edge of Paria Plateau near House Rock. Escalante said, "Here is an extensive valley, but the land is poor, for the part which is not sandy is a kind of soil which on the surface has about four fingers of gravel and beneath it loose soil of a different color. There are many deposits of transparent gypsum, some of mica, and apparently there are also some metals." He adds, "Through this region [south of his present location] the Rio Colorado flows from north-northeast to south-southwest and runs through a deep canyon so that although the land might be good, the river banks are of no use for planting. This afternoon we thought we saw the canyon and cliffs of the river bed which, seen from the west side, looked like a long row of houses, but we concluded it was the canyon of one of the many arroyos which are in the plain." In House Rock Valley in recent years a buffalo herd has been pastured. Theodore Roosevelt once visited the place, but the

---
[1] October 24.

widely spread story that he established the buffalo herd apparently is erroneous.

Next day[1] they left San Bartolomé, traveling east-southeast, and then less than a league and a half to the east, swinging around Paria Plateau with beautiful Vermilion Cliffs at their left. Escalante writes: "We did not try to reach the canyon which, we afterward learned, was really the channel of the Río Grande [Colorado], because we had crossed several arroyos which had canyons as large as that one. So we concluded that the river did not run there but in some other channel." It is true that in this flat plain one may not recognize the gorge of the Colorado River until he is close to it. So they swung north-northeast to avoid some mesas. Seeking water for the animals, they followed the bed of an arroyo for two leagues northeast, and to get out of the gorge they were forced to climb up a very difficult bank. Swinging north-northeast two leagues, they went to some cottonwoods at the foot of a great mesa and found there a good spring of water. Around the edge of the spring there was a white deposit resembling saltpeter, but the water was fresh and good. Here they camped, naming the place San Fructo. The site was probably at the place now called Jacob's Pools. The day's march was five leagues. In the afternoon Don Juan Pedro Cisneros, accompanied by others no doubt, explored the northern corner of the valley to see if there was a pass, and if he could get a glimpse of Colorado River and the ford. He returned after midnight and reported that he had reached the river [apparently at Marble Canyon], but said he did not know whether they would be able to cross some mesas and high crests that were on the other bank. Nevertheless, says Escalante, "because he said the river appeared to him to be all right and to have a ford here, we decided to go to it."

Next day[2] the explorers left San Fructo, traveled northeast three and one-half leagues, and reached the place which they previously had thought was the northern exit from the valley. "It is a bend completely surrounded by very high cliffs and crests of red earth of various formations," says Escalante, "and since the intervening plain below is of the same color, it has an agreeably variegated appearance. We continued in the same direction

---
[1] October 25.
[2] October 26.

with excessive difficulty because the animals, breaking through the surface gravel, sank in the ground clear to their knees, and having traveled a league and a half we arrived at the Rio Grande de Cosninas. Here it is joined by a small river which we named Santa Teresa," now called Paria River. "We crossed the latter stream and camped on the banks of the Rio Grande, near a high gray rock, naming the campsite San Benito Salsipuedes,"—Get out if you can! The tall gray rock still is conspicuous at the spot Escalante describes. He adds: "All the terrain from San Fructo to here is very difficult, and in places where a little moisture has been left from snow or rain, it is entirely impassable." That day the wayfarers had traveled five leagues northeast, and camp was near the site of Lees Ferry, established about a century later by John D. Lee of Utah.

In telling the story of the Crossing of the Colorado, writers have given most of their space to the last and most spectacular day, but there were eleven hard days before the historic feat was accomplished. The travelers wasted no time in setting about the solution of their difficult problem. Escalante says: "We decided to reconnoiter this afternoon to learn whether, having crossed the river, we might continue from here to the east or southeast," toward Santa Fé. "On all sides we were surrounded by mesas and inaccessible heights. Therefore, two men who were good swimmers entered the river naked, carrying their clothing on their heads. It was so deep and so wide that the swimmers, in spite of their prowess, were scarcely able to reach the opposite shore, and they lost their clothing in the middle of the river, never seeing it again." So the travelers had a wardrobe shower for the unfortunates. Since the swimmers arrived very tired, naked, and barefoot they were unable to walk the distance necessary for the reconnaissance, "and returned after having eaten something."

After a day spent in reconnoitering, Escalante says, on the 28th, "We returned to the same undertaking but all in vain. In a short time a raft of logs was constructed and with it Father Fray Silvestre, accompanied by his servants, attempted to cross the river. But since the poles which served for propelling the raft, although they were five varas long, failed to touch the bottom a short distance from the shore, the waves caused by the contrary wind drove it back. So the raft returned three times to the shore it had left, but was unable to reach even the middle of the river. Aside from being so deep and so wide, the stream here has on both banks such deep and miry places that in them we might lose all or the greater part of the animals."

They had been assured by the Yubuincariri and Pagampachi Indians farther back on the trail that the river everywhere else was very deep, but not at the ford, for when they crossed it the water reached only a little above their waists. "For this reason and on account of other landmarks they gave us, we conjectured that the ford must be higher up the stream, so we dispatched Andrés Muñiz and his brother Lucrecio with orders to travel until they found a place where we might cross the mesa mentioned above, and that when they arrived at the river they should seek a good ford, or at least some place where we could cross on a raft and the animals could swim without danger." Andrés and Lucrecio had a hard and responsible job on their hands.

Next day,[1] not knowing when they might leave this place where they were so completely stalled, and having consumed all the flesh of a horse they had killed, and the piñon nuts and other supplies they had purchased, they ordered another horse killed. Three days were spent here[2] awaiting the men who had gone to find a way up the mountains and a ford. On November 1 they returned in the afternoon saying they had found a way up the mountain, although a difficult one, and also a ford. The pass over the mesa was an acclivity which Cisneros had seen, and since it was very high and rugged they decided to approach it the same afternoon. So, leaving the west bank of the Colorado River and the unfortunate campsite of San Benito Salsipuedes, they followed the Paria River, traveled a league northwest, and camped on its bank at the foot of the acclivity. Camp was on the Paria some three miles upstream from its junction with the Colorado. That night, from sunset until seven o'clock next morning, they suffered greatly from cold.

Next morning[3] they left the Paria and climbed the acclivity, which they called Cuesta de las Ánimas. It was only half a league long (less than a mile and a half), but it cost them more than three hours to climb it, because at first it was rough and sandy,

---
[1]October 29.
[2]October 29, 30, and 31.
[3]November 2.

and afterward had steep stretches and perilous rock ledges, and finally became impassable. Having finished the climb toward the east they descended the other side through difficult rocky gorges. Then after swinging north for a league, they turned northwest half a league through a stretch of red sand which was hard on the horses. They ascended another short acclivity, traveled two and one-half leagues northeast, and descended to an arroyo which in places had running water that was salty but fit to drink. Here too they found pasturage, so they halted for the night, naming the place San Diego. Apparently it was on Wahweap Creek, some distance above the point where it enters Colorado River. Escalante says the campsite was about three leagues directly northeast of San Benito Salsipuedes, near a multitude of narrow valleys, little mesas, and peaks of red earth "which at first look like the ruins of a fortress."

There were even more difficult hurdles ahead. Next day[1] they set out from San Diego toward the east-southeast, traveled two leagues, and arrived a second time at the river, "that is to say, at the edge of the canyon which here serves it as its channel, and whose descent to the river is very long, high, rough, and rocky, and has such bad ledges of rock that two pack animals that went down to the first ledge were unable to climb up it in return, even without the pack saddles. The men who had come here previously [that is the scouts sent out before the ascent was undertaken by the whole party] had not told us of this precipice, and we now learned that they had neither found the ford, nor in so many days had they even made the necessary reconnaissance of this short stretch of country, because they spent the time seeking some of the Indians who live hereabouts, and accomplished nothing" that they saw fit to report. Escalante had human as well as topographical troubles. "The river here was very deep, although not as deep as at Salsipuedes, but for a long distance it was necessary for the animals to swim. The good thing about it was that they did not mire, either going into the water or getting out."

The men now insisted that they should descend from the cliffs to the Colorado River, but, says Escalante, "on the other side there was no way to go forward after crossing the river,

---

[1]November 3.

except by the deep and narrow canyon of another little river" which here joined the Colorado. "And not having learned whether or not this canyon could be traveled, we feared that if we descended and crossed the river" at this point, "we should find ourselves forced to go back, which on the cliff would be extremely difficult." So, in order not to expose themselves to this predicament, they halted above the river and sent the genízaro Juan Domingo to cross the river to see if the side canyon had an outlet. If he did not find a way out he was to return, in order that the caravan might continue along the bank of the Colorado until they reached the ford said to be used by the Indians. Lucrecio Muñiz now said that with permission he would go also, riding bareback and carrying equipment for making a fire, so that if he found an exit he could send up a smoke signal for the caravan to attempt the descent. Since Juan Domingo and Lucrecio did not return, the rest of the men spent the night here, not being able to water the horses, although the river was so close by. They named this campsite El Vado de los Cosninas, or San Carlos. That day they had traveled two leagues east-southeast, and camp was on Glen Canyon.

Next day[1] Escalante wrote, "Day broke without our getting any news of the two we sent yesterday to make the reconnaissance. We had used up the flesh of the second horse, and today we had not taken any nourishment whatsoever. So we broke our fast with toasted leaves of small cactus plants and a sauce made of a berry they brought from the banks of the river. This berry is by itself very pleasant to taste, but crushed and boiled in water as we ate it today it is insipid." Escalante adds: "Since it was already late, and the two emissaries had not appeared, we ordered that an attempt should be made to get the animals down to the river, and that on its banks another horse should be killed." With great difficulty they got the animals down, some of them being injured because, "losing their footing on the rocks, they rolled down long distances." Shortly before dark the genízaro Juan Domingo returned to report that he had not found an exit, and that Muñiz, leaving his horse in the middle of the canyon, had followed some fresh Indian tracks. So the travelers decided to continue upstream until they should find a good ford and passable terrain

---

[1] November 4.

on both sides. They camped on the river bank in Glen Canyon below the campsite of the previous night.

Next morning[1] Lucrecio had not returned. So, leaving his brother Andrés at camp to await him till afternoon if necessary, the rest of the men set forth and continued along the high cliffs on the west bank of the mighty Colorado River. They traveled north over ridges and gorges for a league and a half, then descended into a deep canyon where they reported a large amount of copperas. Then leaving the canyon by a little-used Indian trail, they crossed a difficult bench of white rock. Having traveled a league and a quarter north-northeast, they found sufficient pasturage and a little water, and camped for the night near a high mesa at Santa Francisca Romana, near Warm Creek Canyon, having traveled for the day three short leagues, or some six or seven miles.

That night it rained heavily at the campsite and in some places nearby it snowed. At daybreak on November 6 it was still raining and continued for several hours. About six o'clock Andrés Muñiz arrived in camp saying his brother Lucrecio had not yet appeared. This caused Escalante and the rest of the men great anxiety, because by now he had been absent three days without food, "and with no more shelter than a shirt, for he had not even worn trousers." Andrés now decided to look for his brother. Escalante says, "We sent him off, giving him meat from our supply and instructing him that if the horse could not get out of the canyon he should leave it and continue on foot; that if he found Lucrecio on the other bank, from that side they should look for signs of us and follow us; and if on this side, they should try to join us as soon as possible." Escalante was taking careful precautions against the danger that his party might become permanently separated.

Next day[2] the rain having ceased, Escalante and the main party left Santa Francisca Romana, traveled northeast close to the river bank, and having advanced three crooked leagues, they were forced to halt for a long time because of a furious storm and a torrent of rain and large hailstones, "with terrible thunder and lightning. We chanted the litany of the Virgin," says Esca-

---
[1] November 5.
[2] November 6.

lante, "in order that she might find relief for us, and God was pleased that the storm should cease." So they continued half a league east and camped near the river because the way was blocked by immense boulders. Having traveled three and one-half winding leagues for the day, they made camp at San Vicente Ferrer, on the cliffs above the Colorado.

Don Juan Pedro Cisneros now went to inspect a nearby ford reported by the guide. Returning to the camp he said the river here was very wide, and judging from the current it did not appear to be deep, but that they would be able to reach it only through a deep canyon nearby. To make assurance doubly sure they sent two men, not named, to examine the descent and to ford the river, and they returned saying that the crossing would be difficult. Escalante adds, "But we did not give much credence to their report, and decided to examine everything ourselves next day in company with Don Juan Pedro Cisneros." From this we conclude that Cisneros was the most dependable secular in the party. Before dark, Lucrecio and his brother arrived in camp.

Early next morning[1] Escalante and Domínguez went to inspect both the descent and the ford, taking with them the two genízaros, Felipe and Juan Domingo, so they might cross the river without horses, since they were good swimmers. In order to lead the horses down the side of the canyon, the men "cut steps in a rock with axes for the distance of three varas or a little less" —some ten feet. These steps are still plainly to be seen. "The rest of the way the animals were able to get down, although without pack or rider." Escalante adds, "We went down to the canyon, and having traveled a mile, we descended to the river and went along it downstream about two musket shots, sometimes in the water, sometimes on the bank, until we reached the widest part of its current, where the ford appeared to be. One of the men waded in and found it good, not having to swim at any place. We followed him on horseback a little lower down, and when halfway across, two horses that went ahead lost their footing and swam a short distance. We waited, although in some peril until the first wader returned from the other side to guide us, and then we crossed with ease, the horses on which we rode

---
[1]November 7.

not having to swim at all." The padres were across the great river.

Part of the company, meanwhile, had remained on the cliff at San Vicente. Escalante now instructed them "that with lassos and ropes they should let the pack saddles and other effects down a not very high cliff to the bend of the ford, and that they should bring the rest of the animals by the route over which we had come. They did so and about five o'clock in the afternoon they finished the crossing of the river, praising God our Lord and firing off a few muskets as a sign of the great joy we felt at having overcome so great a difficulty and which had cost us so much labor and delay." The friars were very human and young in spirit. Their adventure at the *Crossing of the Fathers* will resound through centuries!

After tremendous difficulties and eight days of hard travel to the crossing, Escalante now indulges briefly in reminiscences and hindsight. He says, "the principal cause of suffering so much since we had reached the first Parusis, was our lack of someone to direct us over such bad terrain. For, through lack of an experienced guide we went by such a circuitous route, spent so many days in so small an area, and endured such hunger and thirst. And now, after suffering all this, we learned of the best and most direct route, where there were waterholes adjusted to an ordinary day's travel. Most of this we heard as we traveled, especially after we left our southerly direction on the day we set out from San Dónulo or Arroyo del Taray. From that place we might have gone to the large waterhole that we found in the next plain. From here we might conveniently have reached another waterhole that is about three leagues north of San Ángel. From this latter place we might have reached Santa Gertrudis. From here we might have continued three leagues and stopped in the same arroyo with good water and sufficient pasturage, going on in the afternoon as far as possible to the northeast, . . . avoiding the sierra entirely, and arriving next day at Río de Santa Teresa, three or four leagues north of San Juan Capistrano. From this river we could have gone east-southeast to San Diego and from there to the ford without any special inconvenience, and avoiding many windings, acclivities, and bad stretches. But doubtless God disposed that we could not obtain a guide, perhaps as a benign pun-

THE CROSSING OF THE FATHERS ON THE COLORADO RIVER

Photo Hal Rumel

ishment for our sins, or perhaps in order that we might acquire some knowledge of the people who live in these parts. May His holy will be done in all things and His holy name glorified." Ethnologists, a hard-hearted fraternity, are more grateful for Escalante's wandering astray than sorry for his troubles.

Escalante adds: "The ford of the river is very good here, and it must be a mile wide, or a little more." What he means is not clear, for the river channel at the same place now in ordinary times is more nearly one hundred yards wide. He continues: "Before reaching this place the Navajo [San Juan] and Dolores rivers have united, together with all those we have mentioned in this diary as entering one or the other. And in no place that we have seen along here is it possible to establish on its banks any settlement whatsoever, or even to travel on either bank a good day's journey either downstream or upstream with the hope that its water might serve for men or animals, because, aside from the bad terrain, the river runs in a very deep gorge. All the region nearest to the ford has very high cliffs and peaks. Eight or ten leagues to the northeast of the ford there is a high, rounded peak which the Payuchis, whose country begins here, call Tucané[1] which means Black Peak, and it is the only one hereabouts which can be seen close at hand from the river crossing.

"On this eastern bank, at the very ford which we call La Purísima Concepción de la Virgen Santísima, there is a fair-sized valley of good pasturage. In it we spent the night and observed the latitude by the North Star, and it is in 36° and 55′."

Escalante included in his diary an account of the Indians they saw and heard of on the return route from Utah Lake to the crossing of Colorado River. They were all of one race and spoke the same language with minor differences, and might be called a "kingdom divided into five provinces, known by the common name of Yutas." The divisions were Muhuachis, Payuchis, Tabehuachis, Sabuaganas, and Cobardes. Of these last there were Huascaris, Parusis, Yubuincariris, Ytimpabichis, Pagampachis. One band they heard of but did not see were the Payatammumis. Still other bands were heard of but Escalante does not give their names.

---

[1]Navajo Mountain.

XX

TO THE HOPIS AND SANTA FÉ

LEAVING La Purísima Concepción at the now famous ford of Colorado River,[1] the wayfarers continued their return march toward Santa Fé. The first stretch of the backtrack was southward nearly to the Hopi Towns. They ascended the mesa above the river by a long but not very difficult ridge. Then they turned south-southeast over a well-beaten trail and traveled through sandy soil with some rugged spots. Now swinging more eastward and having advanced six leagues, they halted near the last cliff of the ridge they had followed from the river to the campsite,[2] which they named San Miguel, and where they found good pasturage and plentiful rain water in pools. On the march that day they saw Indian footprints but no Indians. Escalante wrote: "Through here wild sheep live in such abundance that their tracks are like those of great flocks of domestic sheep. They are larger than the domestic breed, are of the same form, but much swifter. Today we finished the horse meat we had brought, so we ordered another horse killed. Tonight we felt much colder than on the other bank."

Next day[3] the Spaniards lost the trail and were unable to find a way by which to descend to Navajo Canyon which lay immediately southeast of them. So they swung eastward, along the northern edge of the canyon for two leagues over rough terrain, when they were obliged to halt on the mesa, not being able to take a step forward.

Near this mesa they found some tents of Yutas Payuchis, neighbors and friends of the Cosninas. The Spaniards made great efforts through the Laguna and other members of the party, to induce the Indians to visit them, but, says Escalante, "either because they suspected that we were friends of the Moquinos, toward whom they are very hostile, or because they had never before seen Spaniards and greatly feared us, we were unable to induce them to come to us."

---
[1]November 8.
[2]On the mesa north of Navajo Creek.
[3]November 9.

Next day,[1] very early in the morning Domínguez and Escalante went with the interpreter and the Laguna Indian to the ranchos, "but were unable even on foot to get to the place where they were," because they were so timid. Escalante sent the Laguna and the interpreter away, the friars remaining on an elevation "in order that, seeing us alone the Indians might approach with greater willingness and less fear. After the interpreter had urged them for more than two hours, five of them advanced toward us, but when they were about to reach us they turned and fled, and we were unable to stop them." The interpreter went back to see if the Indians would sell the Spaniards some provisions, but they said they had none. They told him the Cosninas lived in the vicinity, but at present were wandering about in the woods, gathering piñon nuts, and that nearby the Spaniards would find two roads, one leading to the Cosninas, in the west, and the other to the Pueblo of Oraibi, in the province of Moqui. They also gave him instructions for finding the trail the Spaniards had lost, saying that to reach it Escalante and his companions would have to turn back to San Miguel and then take the route described. Escalante writes, "In this way we spent most of the day, and during the remainder we returned toward the campsite of San Miguel, going half a league closer to the arroyo or canyon to which we had been unable to descend." They camped at the beginning of the descent, where a stairway of logs, built and used by the Navajo Indians, leads down to the canyon.

Early next morning[2] the descent from the cliff was examined, the lost trail was found, and the travelers went forward. They descended to the canyon with great difficulty because in some places the trail led down dangerous cliffs. Escalante says, "The Indians have repaired it with loose rocks and logs, and in the last bad place they have a stairway of the same materials, more than three varas long and two wide." The same old stairway was still in use a few years ago, and probably still is. "Here two small streams come together, entering the Río Grande near San Carlos," the site where a week previously they had attempted a crossing of furious Colorado River. He refers to the forks of

---
[1]November 10.
[2]November 11.

Kaibito and Navajo creeks, which join amid huge boulders as large as massive skyscrapers of a metropolitan city. One of my camps on the Escalante trail, with a galaxy of supermen and unbeatable companions, was precisely at this memorable site. And I am sure they will recognize themselves by this description. Now continuing south, Escalante's party ascended a long steep stretch of "slick rock" on which horses can scarcely find footing and down which they slide. Having traveled for the day five leagues southward, they camped at San Proto near a dry arroyo that joins Kaibito Creek. There was plentiful firewood to withstand the severely cold weather.

On November 12 the wayfarers continued southward over a good trail for three leagues. Then, "right on the road" they found a spring of good water from which, after they broke the ice, all the men and animals drank. Judging from the vestiges, Escalante thought it was a campsite of the Cosninas when they went to the Payuchis. Continuing south, experiencing excessive cold, and having traveled four leagues, they swung more southward on a trail used by Cosninas. On the way Miera nearly froze, and some of the men were forced to stop, make a fire, and massage him. Farther south the travelers passed some uninhabited houses where horses and cattle had been pastured by Hopi Indians. Having traveled nine leagues for the day, the wayfarers camped at San Jacinto on Kaibito Plateau, north and west of Preston Mesa.

Leaving San Jacinto[1] they traveled south-southwest along the same road, over good land with timber and abundant pasturage. After traveling two leagues they swung south a league and a half, and found in some rocks plenty of water for the men and almost enough for all the animals. Then, continuing south two leagues across a sandy plain, and another half league southeast, they camped a league beyond another pool containing bad water, midway between Whitmore Pools and Tuba City. They named the campsite El Espino because here they caught a porcupine, tried its flesh and found it very appetizing. Escalante says, "We were all greatly in need of food, for since the night before we had not tasted anything except a piece of toasted hide, so the porcupine, distributed among so many persons, served only to

---

[1] November 13.

—Photo Milton Snow U. S. Indian Service

FATHER ESCALANTE STAYED HERE
The three Hopi Indian villages, First Mesa. Tewa Village is first, Sichomovi in middle and Walpi (Gualpi) village on end of mesa.

stimulate the appetite. For this reason we ordered another horse killed, which we had not done sooner because we expected to find food in some of the ranchos of the Cosninas, but we have not seen even recent vestiges of them." On this day they had traveled six leagues.

From El Espino[1] the travelers continued southward, traveled more than six leagues, passed the site of later founded Moenkopi pueblo, and camped at La Cuesta de los Llanos on Moenkopi Plateau. On the 15th they swung a little more eastward, traveled nine leagues to camp at La Cañada de los Chizos, near Dennebito Spring. On the 16th they swung eastward, then northeastward, traveled seven leagues for the day, and arrived at the foot of the high mesa on which the Pueblo of Oraibe stood and still stands.

Here an interesting conference was held. Halting at the foot of the mesa, Escalante and Domínguez, with Cisneros as interpreter, climbed the steep high cliff to the town. At first the natives were hostile, but they soon quieted down, became friendly, and sold provisions to the travelers. Next day the friars explained Christianity to the inhabitants as best they could, but made little impression upon them.

In the afternoon of November 17, the Spaniards continued two and a quarter leagues to the pueblo of Xongopabi on Second Mesa, arrived there at sunset, and were given lodgings. Next day[2] the headmen of the three towns of Oraibe, Xipaolabi, and Mossonganabi assembled. The friars preached to them "partly by signs and partly in the Navajó tongue," but made no converts. They gave a Pueblo woman a woolen cloak, but her brother took it from her and threw it back to the friars. Having made neither converts nor friends, Escalante and his party moved forward and camped for the night at Gualpi.

Here on the 19th the chiefs of several pueblos assembled with the travelers in a kiva, where there was a competent interpreter. The Pueblo people now asked for Spanish aid against the Navajo Apaches. In reply they were assured that if they would accept Christianity the desired help would be given them. "Three times we urged them, exhorting them to enter the fold of the Holy Church," says Escalante. "After a long conference

---
[1] November 14.
[2] November 18.

among themselves the natives replied that they wished only our friendship, but by no means to become Christians." In this respect they have changed but little in the century and three quarters since that historic event.

So, on November 20, Escalante and his weary companions continued east over the old trail to Santa Fé. That day they traveled four leagues east by southeast, and camped at a watering place called El Ojito del Cañutillo, or Ojito de Moqui. Camp may have been south of Keams Canyon at Jadito Springs on North Jadito Wash. Next day[1] they traveled three leagues northeast and east-southeast two leagues, then a little more than two additional leagues to the east, and camped more than half a league before reaching a small watering place called the Estiladero, or Ojito del Peñasco, on Pueblo Colorado Wash, having traveled seven leagues for the day. Camp may have been at Senatoa Spring, south of Salahkai Mesa.

On November 22, leaving at the campsite most of the animals, which were now tired out, to follow slowly to Zuñi, Escalante, Domínguez and three companions set forth in light order, traveled nine leagues southeastward, reached the place called Cumaá, rested there awhile, then traveled two more leagues and camped, because the animals were exhausted. Having traveled eleven leagues for the day they camped southwest of a place now called Cornfields.

On November 23, although it snowed all day, Domínguez and Escalante "traveled on the gallop for twelve leagues"—thirty miles—and camped at a place called Kianatuna or Ojo de San José, in the vicinity of present-day Allantown.

Next morning[2] at daylight those hardy men were again in the saddle. Leaving Ojo de San José they traveled two leagues southeast, then halted to make a fire to warm their chilled bodies, "because it was so cold in this valley that we feared we should freeze," writes Escalante. Continuing southeast more than three leagues, then two east northeast, they halted at the watering place by the Zuñis called Okiappá. Then riding five more leagues southeast they "arrived after nightfall and greatly fatigued at the pueblo and mission of Nuestra Señora de Guadalupe de Zuñi,"

---
[1] November 21.
[2] November 24.

Escalante's own headquarters. That day they had traveled twelve leagues or some thirty miles.

"Not having sufficient strength to continue immediately to the Villa de Santa Fé," says Escalante, "we reported to the Señor Governor our happy arrival at this mission, together with a brief account of the contents of the Diary." Two days later,[1] "in the afternoon the rest of the companions arrived."

Remaining at Zuñi "on account of various incidents" until December 13, the friars set forth for Santa Fé, "and having traveled thirty leagues eastward, on December 16 they arrived at the mission of San Estéban, perched high up on the peñol or Cliff of Ácoma. Because of a heavy snow storm they remained there four days.

Setting forth on December 20, they traveled four leagues to the mission of San José de la Laguna; on December 22, six leagues to El Alamo, due west of Albuquerque; on December 23, five leagues to Isleta. Here they spent five nights, including the Christmas season. Then on December 28, they continued north to the mission of San Francisco Javier de Alburquerque, where they spent the night. Leaving that place on December 30, they continued upstream four leagues to the mission of Nuestra Señora de los Dolores de Sandía, where they spent the night. Seven leagues next day took them to the Mission of Nuestro Padre Santo Domingo. They spent a day and two nights there, and "on January 2 of this year of '77, arrived at the Villa de Santa Fé." Finally, next day, says Escalante, "We presented this diary, the token of the Lagunas of which mention is made, and the Laguna Indian. And because everything stated in this diary is true and faithful to what happened and was observed in our journey we signed it in this mission on the third of January of the year 1777."

Thus ended one of the great exploring expeditions of North American history, made without noise of arms and without giving offense to the natives through whose country they had traveled.

---

[1] November 26.

XXI

THE SEQUEL

AFTER HIS RETURN to Santa Fé, Miera went to the city of Chihuahua, then capital of the Northern Province of New Spain, as Mexico was then called. There he wrote a long report of his expedition with Domínguez and Escalante, drew his now famous maps, and proposed two Spanish settlements in the far north, one at Lake Timpanogos and one on San Juan River, as already has been set forth in these pages.

Then he turned to the southern border of New Mexico. The crux of his proposal here was the establishment of a presidio at Yuma, near the junction of the Gila and Colorado rivers, with himself as commander. The presidio, he said, would be a base for defending New Mexico from the ravages of Apaches and Comanches, and a way-station between Mexico and California, where San Diego and Monterey had recently been established. By the soldiers at Yuma, he said, the Apaches could be driven eastward to the Buffalo Plains, home of "the two most obnoxious tribes," the Comanches and the Apaches, "who by their fighting would destroy each other."

Miera's proposals, so far as he was concerned, were not adopted. But with the cooperation of the powerful Yuma chief Ollyquotequiebe, called Salvador Palma by the Spaniards, Captain Juan Bautista de Anza led from Mexico and across the Colorado River at Yuma, the colonists who founded San Francisco in 1776, year of the expedition by which Domínguez and Escalante had hoped to reach Monterey. Their satisfaction when they heard the news of Anza's colony, can be imagined.

The sequel to the founding of a Spanish settlement at Yuma was tragic, and in it one of the principals in the Escalante story met his fate. In 1776 Chief Salvador Palma went with Anza to Mexico City to ask for a Spanish mission and presidio of Spanish soldiers for his tribe, and there in the great cathedral he was baptized and named Salvador Palma. Delays ensued and Palma became impatient. In 1779 Fathers Garcés and Díaz were sent with a small garrison of soldiers to Palma's village at the Yuma junction. But their slender store of presents and supplies was disappointing, and the Yumas were unhappy with the presence of the Spanish intruders. Next year at the viceroy's order two missions were founded near the Yuma junction on the west bank of Colorado River. At the same time ten Spanish families were settled at each mission, to serve as a protection to the Franciscan friars and as an example to the neophytes.

Trouble quickly ensued, and in July 1781 the Yumas, led by Chief Salvador Palma, massacred Father Garcés and a number of Spanish colonists who were passing through Yuma on their way to found Los Angeles. At Palma's order the Spanish women and children were spared. Next year Captain Pedro Fages, famous California soldier, went to Yuma and ransomed some seventy-five Spanish captives, but the project for a mission there was abandoned.

So our story which began with the long journey of Father Garcés to the Hopi pueblo of Oraibe, ends with his death at Yuma some five years later; and Fathers Domínguez and Escalante, in spite of their long journey with that objective, never reached Monterey. By the same token, Captain Miera's ambition to command an army on the border of Gila River was never realized. But only a short-sighted historian would call the expedition of Domínguez and Escalante a failure. They made one of the most notable explorations in North American history, and their fame is as secure as that of De Soto, Cabrillo, Zebulon Pike, or Lewis and Clark. They explored more unknown territory than Daniel Boone, George Rogers Clark or even Lewis and Clark. For the opening of new vistas they belong with Coronado and the splendid wayfarers of Mexico and South America. For their relations with the strange peoples encountered they stand in a class almost by themselves.

By way of a post-lude it may be noted that the Escalante Expedition entered into the story of North American diplomacy. Pichardo, who wrote an official Spanish treatise on the famous Louisiana Boundary Question, cites Escalante's diary and Miera's maps at numerous points, in their bearing on the watershed of the Mississippi River, which was the main issue in the boundary dispute.

MIERA'S MAPS

While he was in Chihuahua Miera made a now famous map of the region he had explored, including the region from the Gila River border to Great Salt Lake. It is called *Plano Geographico de la tierra decubierta nuebamente á los Rumbos Norte, Noroeste, y Oeste, del Nuebo Mexico, demarcada por mi Don Bernardo de Miera y Pacheco, á que entro á hacer su descubrimiento en compañia de los RR.^{s} PP.^{s} fr. francisco Atanasio Doming.^{s} y fr. Silbestre Veles, segun consta en el Diario y Derrotero que se hizo y se remitió á S. M.^{d} por mano de su Virrei, con otro Plano á la letra: el que se dedica Al Sor Dn Theodoro de la Crois, del Insigne Orden Teutonica, Comandante General en Gefe de la Linea y provincia de esta America Septentrional, por su Mag^d, Hecho en S.^{n} Ph.^{e} el Real de Chiguagua, Año de 1778.*

This map is decorated in the upper right corner with a coat of arms, and a regal personage riding in a coach drawn by two lions whose significance can be interpreted by someone versed in heraldry. The map shows a picture of the Bearded Indians seen by Escalante's party on their return from Lake Timpanogos, and contains annotations regarding Great Salt Lake, the Indian country, and Oñate's supposed expedition to that area in 1605. Of his map Miera made a colored draft in two parts, one of the northern country and one of New Mexico; the former which covers the territory traversed by Escalante we reproduce here.

ASTRONOMICAL OBSERVATIONS

August 5	Nuestra Señora de las Nieves	37° 51'
August 13	Dolores	38° 13½'
August 19	Cajón del Yeso	39° 6'
August 28	Santa Monica	39° 13' 22"
September 5	San Rafael	41° 4'
September 6	Roan Creek	41° 6' 53"
September 13	La Vega de Santa Cruz	41° 19'
September 14	La Vega de Santa Cruz	40° 59' 24"
September 14	La Vega de Santa Cruz	41° 19'
September 29	Santa Ysabel	39° 4'
October 2	Llano Salado	39° 34' 36"
October 8	Santa Brígida	38° 3' 30"
October 11	Valle de Señor San José	37° 33'
October 15	San Dónulo	36° 52' 30"
October 20	Santa Gertrudis	36° 30'
November 7	La Purísima Concepción	36° 55'

DIARY AND ITINERARY

DIARY AND ITINERARY

On the 29th day of July of the year 1776, under the patronage of the Virgin Mary, Our Lady of the Immaculate Conception, and of the most holy patriarch Joseph her most happy spouse, we, Fray Francisco Atanasio Domínguez, present commissary visitor of this Custodia of the Conversion of San Pablo of New Mexico, and Fray Francisco Silvestre Vélez de Escalante, minister and teacher of the Christian doctrine at the Mission of Nuestra Señora de Guadalupe de Zuñi, accompanied voluntarily by Don Juan Pedro Cisneros, alcalde mayor of the said pueblo of Zuñi; Don Bernardo Miera y Pacheco, retired militia captain and citizen of the town of Santa Fé; Don Joaquín Laín, citizen of the same town; Lorenzo Olivares, citizen of the town of El Paso; Lucrecio Muñiz; Andrés Muñiz; Juan de Aguilar; and Simón Lucero; having implored the protection of our most holy patrons and received the Holy Eucharist, we the persons named set out from the town of Santa Fé capital of this Kingdom of New Mexico; and having traveled nine leagues we arrived at the pueblo of Santa Clara, where we spent the night.[1] — Today nine leagues.

July 30. We traveled nine leagues, more or less, and arrived at the pueblo of Santa Rosa de Abiquiú,[2] where because of various circumstances we remained on the 31st without traveling, and where by means of a Solemn Mass we again implored the aid of our most holy patrons.

August 1. After having celebrated the holy sacrifice of the Mass, we set forth from the pueblo of Santa Rosa de Abiquiú toward the west along the bed of the Chama River and traveled in it a little less than two leagues. We then turned northwest, and having gone about three and a half leagues over a bad road, for in it there are some small and very stony mesas, we halted for siesta on the north side of the valley of La Piedra Alumbre, near Arroyo Seco. They say that on some mesas to the east and northeast of this valley, alum rock and transparent gypsum are found. In the afternoon we set out from Arroyo Seco toward the north. After going a short distance we turned northeast along a

---
[1] Santa Clara Pueblo, north of Santa Fé.
[2] Abiquiú still occupies the same site on the Chama River.

wooded canyon, and having traveled two leagues over a very bad road we camped on the banks of the same arroyo.[3] Today a good shower fell upon us, and we traveled seven leagues.

August 2. We set forth up the same canyon toward the northeast. After going a little more than four leagues we turned north, and entered a wooded canyon in which for the distance of a quarter of a league there is a grove of small oaks so dense that while passing through it we lost track of four animals and had to stop to hunt for them, but they were soon found. Although we lost the trail in this grove because it was little used, we afterward saw that it ran on the east side of the arroyo which runs through the middle of the grove, the same stream which lower down they call Arroyo del Canjilón, or Arroyo Seco. Having passed through the grove, we came to a small plain of abundant pasturage which is very pleasing to the sight, because it produces some flowers whose color is between purple and white and which, if they are not carnations, are very much like carnations of that color. Here there are also groves of small limes, a red fruit the size of the blackthorn. In freshness and taste it is very similar to the lemon, so that in this country it is used as a substitute for lemons in making refreshing drinks. Besides these fruits there is the chokecherry, much smaller than the Mexican variety, and another berry which they call manzanita, whose tree resembles the lime though the leaf is more like that of celery and the size of the berry is that of ordinary chickpeas. Some are white and others black, the taste being bitter-sweet and piquant but agreeable. Where these flowers begin the canyon is divided into two by a high mesa which enters it. In each branch there is a road, one of which runs north and the other west. At the beginning of the latter and under the southern point of the mesa there is a little spring of good permanent water, but to enable the horses to drink even a little, it will be necessary to dig wells. When the animals had been found, we continued our march by the western canyon and road and traveled a league and a quarter to the north. Then, after going less than half a league to the west, we turned northwest, and having traveled a little more than three leagues over good terrain we arrived at a small stream called Río de la Cebolla, where, turning aside a short distance from the road, we took a

---

[3] South of Canjilón.

siesta. In the bed of the stream we found plenty of water in pools, although according to appearances it seldom flows. From here we went forward in the afternoon, turning north about a quarter of a league to get back to the road which we had left. We swung northwest, and having traveled a little more than three leagues over good terrain we halted in a small plain on the bank of another arroyo,[4] which is called Río de las Nutrias, because, although it is of permanent and running water, apparently during all or most of the year it stands in pools where they say beavers breed. — Today eight leagues.

August 3. We went northwest from Arroyo de las Nutrias, entered a small grove of pines, and having traveled a little less than three leagues we descended to the Río de Chama. Then, along its pretty meadow we went up to the north about a mile, crossed it, and halted for a siesta on the opposite bank. The ford of the river is good, but on the banks near it there are large hidden sinks, with small stones on the surface, in one of which Don Juan Pedro Cisneros' horse was completely submerged. The meadow of the river is about a league long from north to south, and is of good land for crops with opportunities for irrigation. It produces much flax and good and abundant pasturage, and there are also the other advantages necessary for the founding and maintenance of a settlement. Here also there is a good grove of white cottonwoods.

In the afternoon we went forward, and after climbing the western bank of the river we entered a small valley which we called Santo Domingo. Three large mesas covered with pines, beginning with three small hills almost north of here, curve around it from north to south to form a semi-circle reaching to the river. They[*] told us that to the west of these mesas there are two lakes. The first and more southerly one is west of the pass which from this bank can be seen between the first and second mesas, and the second is to the west of the next opening, which likewise can be seen between the second and the third mesas. These lakes, as well as the valley, are very suitable for raising large and small stock. We continued through the valley toward the northwest and entered a small grove of pines where a loaded mule strayed

---

[4]Near Cebolla on Nutrias Creek.
[*]The companions who had been here previously.

away and did not reappear until sunset. For this reason we had to camp on rough ground near the three small hills already mentioned and which we named the Santísima Trinidad,⁵ having traveled from the river only two leagues to the northwest. In this place there was no permanent water, although we found a little in an arroyo near the broken ground to the east-southeast. At the place where we crossed the Río de Chama today it runs from north to south, and a little before reaching the Cerro del Pedernal, it runs from west to east until it passes the pueblo of Abiquiú. — Today five leagues.

August 4. Setting out toward the north from the camp of Santísima Trinidad, we traveled two leagues through the same forest, which consists of pines, some piñon trees, and dwarf oaks. It abounds also in pasturage and in very tall flax. Two large mesas surround it, each forming a semi-circle, the north end of one almost meeting the south end of the other, the two being separated by a narrow gateway or pass. We traveled about a quarter of a league to the northwest and went through the pass where begins another lake which we called Laguna de Olivares. It must be about a quarter of a league long and two hundred varas* wide, more or less. Although its water has not a very pleasant taste it is fit to drink. From the lake and little pass we continued north half a league, then turned northeast, leaving the road which goes to the Piedra Parada** (a place known to those of us who have traveled through here). The guides directed us through a chamise thicket without any trail or path whatsoever, saying that on the road we were now leaving there were three very bad hills, and that it was less direct than the route they were taking. We traveled a little more than a league and in the same chamise thicket again turned west-northwest, entered the forest (which continues), and after half a league swung northwest. We then traveled three and a half leagues through a valley with very luxuriant pasturage and came to a large meadow of the arroyo which on the Piedra Parada road they call Arroyo del Belduque.***
In the meadow we swung west and having traveled down the arroyo two leagues we camped in a canyon⁶ which, on account

---

⁵About five miles northwest of Park View.
⁶Near Dulce.
*A vara is 33 inches.
**Standing Rock, still so-called.
***This name obviously commemorates some event involving a large knife.

of a certain incident, we called Cañon del Engaño.* — Today nine and a quarter leagues. Here there is plentiful pasturage and water in pools.

August 5. We set out from camp in the Cañon del Engaño toward the southwest and having traveled half a league arrived at Río de Navajó, which rises in the Sierra de la Grulla and runs from northeast to southwest to this point, where it turns back toward the north for a little more than three leagues, and then joins another river which they call the San Juan. Here this Navajó River has less water than the Chama. Having crossed the river we continued with difficulty toward the south in the same canyon, and after going about a league we turned to the southwest for a quarter of a league, then three quarters of a league to the west through canyons, over hills, and through very difficult brush. The guides lost the trail and even seemed to have forgotten the very slight knowledge which they had appeared to have of this country. And so, in order not to go any farther south we turned northwest, traveled about three leagues without a trail, climbing a hill (monte),** high but with no very difficult grade, and saw the bed of the same river nearby. We descended to it down slopes which were somewhat rugged but nevertheless passable, and having traveled a little more than three leagues westnorthwest, we crossed it at a good ford and camped on the north bank. Here it has already united with the San Juan River. The guides told us that a little higher up these two rivers joined, so we decided to observe the latitude of this campsite and for this purpose to stay here until the afternoon of the next day. The observation was made by the meridian of the sun, and we found the campsite, which we named Nuestra Señora de las Nieves,[7] to be in latitude 37° 51'. Fray Silvestre went to examine the place where the two rivers, the Navajó and the San Juan, join and found it was three leagues as the crow flies almost due east of Las Nieves, and that on the banks of both rivers, right at the junction, there were good advantages for a fair-sized settlement. The San Juan River carries more water than the Navajó, and they say that farther north it has good and large meadows because it runs

---
[7]Camp was on the San Juan River near Carracas, just across the Colorado state line.
*Canyon of Deceit. Evidently someone had been deceived or misled here.
**Monte generally means forest or brush, but here it clearly means hill.

through more open country. Now joined, the two streams form a river as large as the Río del Norte in the month of July. This stream is called Río Grande de Navajó because it separates the province of this name from the Yuta nation. Downstream from the meadow and campsite of Nuestra Señora de las Nieves there is good land, with facilities for irrigation and everything else necessary for three or four settlements, even though they might be large ones. This statement refers only to what we saw. On either bank of the river there are dense and shady groves of white cottonwood, dwarf oak, chokecherry, manzanita, lime, and garambullo. There is also some sarsaparilla, and a tree which looked to us like the walnut. — Today eight leagues.

August 6. In the afternoon we left the camp of Nuestra Señora de las Nieves, going downstream toward the west, and having traveled two and one-half leagues over bad terrain, we camped on the bank of the river.[8] Don Bernardo Miera had been having stomach trouble, and this afternoon he became much worse, but God willed that before day-break next morning he should be improved, so that we might continue on our way. — Today two leagues and a half.

August 7. We continued a little more than a league to the west along the bank of the river and on the slopes of the adjacent mesas, climbed a somewhat difficult hill, swung northwest, and after going one more league arrived at another river which they call Río de la Piedra Parada, at a point very close to its junction with the Navajó. Here there is a large meadow which we called San Antonio. It has very good land for crops, with opportunities for irrigation and everything else necessary for a settlement— firewood, stone, timber, and pasturage, all close at hand. This river rises to the north of the San Juan in the same Sierra de la Grulla, runs from north to south, and is a little smaller than the Chama River where it passes through the pueblo of Abiquiú. Having crossed this river we traveled west two leagues and somewhat over two more leagues to the west-northwest, and arrived at the east bank of the river which they call Río de los Pinos, because some pines grow on its banks. It has very good water, is a little smaller than the Río del Norte, runs through here from north to south, enters the Navajó River, and rises in the

---

[8]About four miles east of Árboles.

Sierra de la Grulla near its western extremity, where they call it Sierra de la Plata. Here there is a large meadow with very abundant pasturage, especially of grama-grass, extensive and good lands for raising crops by irrigation, and everything else that might be desired for a good settlement. We camped in the meadow, naming it the Vega de San Cayetano.[9] — Today a little more than six leagues.

August 8. We set out from the Río de los Pinos and the Vega de San Cayetano toward the west-northwest, and having traveled four leagues we arrived at the Río Florido, which is medium-sized and smaller than the Río de los Pinos. It rises in the same sierra but farther west. It flows in the same direction, from north to south, and where we crossed it there is a large meadow of good land for crops with facilities for irrigation. The pastures in the meadow were good, but not those in the immediate vicinity, although it evidently has them in wet years. Having crossed the Río Florido we traveled west two leagues and west-northwest somewhat over two leagues more. We then descended a stony but not very long slope and arrived at Río de las Ánimas near the western point of the Sierra de la Plata, in which it rises. Crossing it, we camped on the opposite bank.[10] This river is as large as the Río del Norte, carries somewhat more water at this point, and is more rapid because here the current has a greater fall. It runs from north to south, and like the foregoing rivers it enters the Navajó. Along here it runs in a canyon, but farther down they say it has good meadows. — Today eight leagues or a little more. Here there is no good pasturage, but there is some a little farther on.

August 9. We left the Río de las Ánimas, climbed the west bank of the river which, although it is not very high, is quite difficult because it is very stony and in places very rugged. We went through the small forest at the top, which must extend a little more than a quarter of a league. Then we entered a valley with abundant pasturage, traveled through it a league to the west, turned west by northwest, and after going three leagues through a leafy forest and good pastures, we arrived at the Río de San Joaquín, otherwise called Río de la Plata, which is small, about

---
[9] On Los Pinos River just south of Ignacio.
[10] Five miles south of Durango on Ánimas River and near Moving Mountain.

like the river which runs through the pueblo of San Gerónimo de los Taos.* It rises in the same west end of the Sierra de la Plata and flows through the canyon in which they say there are veins and outcroppings of metal. But, although years ago several persons came from New Mexico to examine them by order of the Governor, who then was Don Tomás Vélez Cachupín, and carried away ore, it was not learned with certainty what metal it was. The opinion formed previously by some persons from the accounts of various Indians and of some citizens of this kingdom that they were silver mines, caused the mountain to be called Sierra de la Plata. From the bank of Río de las Ánimas to this Río de San Joaquín the land is very moist, for, because of the nearness of the sierra it rains very frequently. For this reason, in the forest, which consists of very tall straight pines, small oaks and several kinds of wild fruits, as well as in its valleys, there are the finest of pastures. The climate here is excessively cold even in the months of July and August. Among the fruits there is a little one, black in color, of agreeable taste and very much like the medlar, although not so sweet. We did not go forward today because, since the animals did not eat well last night they were somewhat weak when they arrived, and also because a heavy and prolonged shower forced us to halt.[11] — Today four and a quarter leagues, almost all to the west.

August 10. Father Fray Francisco Atanasio awoke troubled by a rheumatic fever which he had felt in his face and head since the day before, and it was desirable that we make camp here until he should be better, but the continuous rains, the inclemency of the weather, and the great dampness of the place forced us to leave it. Going north, and having traveled a little more than half a league, we turned to the northwest, went on a league and then swung west through valleys of very beautiful timber and abundant pasturage, roses, and various other flowers. After going two leagues we were again caught in a very heavy rain, Father Fray Francisco Atanasio became worse and the road impassable, and so, having traveled with great difficulty two more leagues to the west, we had to camp on the bank of the first of the two little rivers which form the San Lázaro, otherwise called

---
[11]Near the site of Hesperus.
*In New Mexico.

Río de los Mancos.[12] The pasturage continues in great abundance. — Today four and a half leagues.

August 11. Notwithstanding the severe cold and the dampness from which we suffered, we were not able to move our camp because Father Fray Francisco Atanasio awoke very weak from the trouble mentioned and with some fever. For this reason we were not able to go to see the veins and metallic stones of the sierra, although they were nearby, as we were assured by a companion who had seen them on another occasion.

August 12. Father Fray Francisco Atanasio awoke somewhat improved, and in order to change terrain and climate rather than to make progress, we set out from the camp and Río de San Lázaro toward the northwest. We traveled a little more than a league, swung west by west-northwest, and went five leagues through leafy forests and good pastures. Then we turned west, traveled two and a half leagues through a chamise thicket with little pasturage, went a quarter of a league to the north, crossed Río de Nuestra Señora de los Dolores, and camped on its north bank.[13] This river rises on the north slope of the Sierra de la Plata, and runs southwest to this place, where it makes a sharp turn. It is a little smaller than the Río del Norte in this season. — Today a little more than eight and a half leagues.

August 13. We remained in camp, partly so that the Father might improve a little and be able to go forward, and partly to observe the latitude of this site and meadow of the Río de los Dolores where we were. An observation was made by the sun and we found we were in 38° and 13½′ north latitude. Here there is everything needed for the establishment and maintenance of a good settlement in the way of irrigable lands, pastures, timber and firewood. On an elevation on the south bank of the river in ancient times there was a small settlement of the same form as those of the Indians of New Mexico, as is shown by the ruins which we purposely examined. Father Fray Francisco Atanasio felt better, and we decided to continue our journey next day.

August 14. We set out from the meadow and river of Dolores toward the north, and having traveled a quarter of a league we turned northwest for a league, and northwest by west five

---
[12]Near the site of Mancos.
[13]They camped on the north bank of Dolores River after crossing that stream near its junction with Lost Canyon Creek.

leagues through a somewhat difficult chamise thicket. We then entered a deep and broken canyon, and having traveled in it two leagues to the north, we arrived a second time at the Río de los Dolores, which here runs northwest. We crossed it twice within a short distance and camped on the west bank, naming the place, which is a small meadow of good pasturage, La Asunción de Nuestra Señora.[14] This afternoon we were overtaken by a coyote and a genízaro of Abiquiú,* the first named Felipe and the second Juan Domingo. In order to wander among the heathen, they had fled from that pueblo without the permission of their superiors, protesting that they wished to accompany us. We did not need them, but to prevent the mischief which either through ignorance or malice they might commit by traveling alone any longer among the Yutas if we tried to send them back, we accepted them as companions. — Today eight and a quarter leagues.

August 15. We left the camp of La Asunción (on the Río de los Dolores) through a somewhat rough and stony canyon, along which we traveled a fourth of a league to the west-northwest. We then turned northwest, and having traveled a little less than a league and a half, we swung north-northwest and went a little more than three leagues through a chamise thicket on good and almost level land. We then turned northwest a league, and having traveled two and a half more to the west, by the trail which is farthest from the river of the two trails into which the one we followed from La Asunción is divided, we halted for siesta at an arroyo which the guides thought had water, though we found it entirely dry. Since we did not know whether by this route there would be another adequate water hole at a suitable distance for reaching it today, we sent men to explore the ground we would have to cover this afternoon. A water hole was found, but with so little water that although it sufficed for the men, it would not provide for the animals. It is permanent water but not very palatable. It was covered with stones and logs, apparently on purpose. Perhaps this was done by the Yutas because of some misfortune they had suffered at this place, for, according to what was told us by some of the companions who have been among them, they are accustomed to do this in such cases. In the after-

---

[14]Camp was on the west bank of the Dolores, northeast of Cahone (Cajón).

*Coyote and genízaro as used here were designations of persons of certain racial mixtures.

noon we went on, and having traveled two leagues northwest and half a league north we arrived at this water hole, which we called the Agua Tapada [Covered Pool].[15] — Today nine and three quarter leagues.

August 16. More than half of our animals were missing for, since they had not had any water, they strayed away looking for it, and found it near the road in the middle of yesterday's march. Finally they appeared, arriving when it was already late, and for this reason we did not leave Agua Tapada until half past ten in the morning. We took a little-used trail which we thought would take us once more to the Río de los Dolores, which we planned to follow. But, having traveled along it two leagues northwest and a league and a half west it played out, because the soil was very loose and the trail had been washed out by the rains. From here we proceeded northwest. After going a quarter of a league we entered a canyon which at first was wide and in which we found a much-used trail. We followed it, and having traveled another fourth of a league to the north, we found a water hole which to us appeared to be sufficient for both men and animals; and because it was on the east side of the trail and hidden in a dense grove of piñon and juniper, we called it Agua Escondida.[16] More specific directions to this water hole are not given because the trail goes right to it. Two wells were made so the animals might drink, and all did so, although not with very great satisfaction. While we reconnoitered the terrain on both sides in order to continue this afternoon, Don Bernardo Miera went on alone through this canyon without our seeing him. Because of the impossibility of continuing the journey we stopped and sent another companion to tell him to return before he got lost. But he got so far ahead that they did not return until after midnight to the place where the rest of us were waiting, greatly worried on account of their tardiness. They said that going through the canyon they had reached the Río de los Dolores, and that on the way there was only one short stretch that was difficult to get through, and that it could be improved. Therefore we decided to continue through it next day. — Today four leagues.

August 17. We set out from Agua Escondida, and about half

---

[15] Near the site of Egnar.

[16] Camp was near the Utah state line at the head of a side canyon of Dolores River, possibly Summit Canyon.

past three in the afternoon came for a third time to the Río de los Dolores, having traveled all the way through the canyon and its many turns, and going seven leagues to the north, although, by a straight line it would be four or five at most. Because of the varied and agreeable appearance of the rocks on either side which, being so high and rugged at the turns, make it appear that the farther one goes the more difficult it is to get out, and because Don Bernardo Miera was the first one who traveled it, we called this canyon Laberinto de Miera [Miera's Labyrinth]. It is everywhere passable and not very difficult for the animals, excepting one place which can be easily improved. On reaching the river we saw very recent tracks of Yutas. For this reason we thought one of their rancherías must be nearby, and that if they had seen us and we did not seek them they might fear some harm from us and be alarmed. Moreover, since we hoped that some one of them might guide us or give us information, enabling us to continue our journey with less difficulty and labor than we were now suffering because none of the companions knew the water holes and the terrain ahead, we decided to seek them. As soon as we halted in a bend of the river which we called San Bernardo,[17] Father Fray Francisco Atanasio set forth, accompanied by the interpreter Andrés Muñiz and Don Juan Pedro Cisneros. Following the tracks upstream about three leagues, they learned that the Indians were Yutas Tabehuaches, but they were not able to find them, although they went clear to the place where the little Río de las Paralíticas empties into the Dolores. They say this Río de las Paralíticas is so called because the first of our people who saw it found in a ranchería on its bank three Yuta women suffering from paralysis. It divides the Yutas Tabehuaches from the Muhuaches, the latter living to the south, and the others to the north. — Today seven leagues, which by a direct line would be four to the north.

August 18. Very early in the morning two companions went to find a way by which we could leave the bed of the river, which here has high and very stony mesas on both sides, and which would neither take us off our northerly course nor out of the way for lack of water and pasturage. But it was impossible to learn

---

[17]On Dolores River a short distance below its junction with Disappointment Creek.

where we might proceed except by the bed of the river in which, on account of the many stones and because it was necessary to cross it many times, we feared the animals would bruise their feet. Leaving the bend of San Bernardo we traveled downstream a league to the north and camped,[18] in order that the companions might go to explore farther than they had gone this morning. About eight o'clock at night they returned saying that only by the bed of the river would we be able to emerge from this impassable network of mesas and that only with difficulty. Therefore we decided to continue by the bed of the river. — Today a league to the north.

August 19. We continued downstream and having traveled, with no little difficulty, a league to the northeast and another to the northwest, we halted at another bend of the river in order that, after letting the animals drink, we might be able to leave the stream and follow a trail which ran to the northeast, from here following the river toward the north if perchance the roughness of the terrain would permit us to do so. Meanwhile one of the companions went to find out if the trail were passable as far as the chain of high and stony mesas by which we hoped to cross, because the bed of the river was now impassable. He found that the trail did not run through passable terrain in the mentioned direction of northwest. Another trail or path was found going southwest but, although it was examined for a long distance, in the course of which it had no obstacles, we did not dare follow it because beyond the part of it examined we could see high mesas and deep canyons in which we might again be surrounded and find ourselves forced to turn back. Moreover, the great aridity of the surrounding district we had seen caused us to believe that the pools of rain-water and even the springs of running water which hereabouts might be encountered would be totally dry. We conferred with the companions who had traveled through this region as to what direction we might take to avoid these obstacles, and everyone had a different opinion. So, finding ourselves in this state of confusion, not knowing whether we should be able to follow the trail mentioned, or whether it would be better for us to go back a short distance and take the road that goes to the

---

[18]About two and one-half miles downstream from the previous camp, in the neighborhood of McIntyre Canyon.

Yutas Sabuaganas, we put our trust in God and our will in that of His Most Holy Majesty. And, having implored the intercession of our Most Holy Patrons in order that God might direct us in the way that would be most conducive to His Holy Service, we cast lots between the two roads and drew the one leading to the Sabuaganas, which we decided to follow until we reached them. In this place, which we called the Cajón del Yeso[19] because there was gypsum in a mesa nearby, we observed the latitude by the sun and found it to be 39° 6'. — Today two leagues.

August 20. We left the Cajón del Yeso, going back a league to the southeast, and again crossed the river to the east-northeast of which, in some hills about a quarter of a league away, we saw mines of transparent and very good gypsum. Having crossed the river, we entered a wide valley and traveled three leagues to the east-northeast* by a very well beaten trail which runs along the foot of a high mesa. Then, at the urging of Don Bernardo Miera, who did not wish to follow this road, the interpreter, Andrés, led us up a very high and rugged hill having so many stones that we expected to be forced to go back when half-way up, because it was so hard on the animals that many of them left their tracks on the stones with the blood from their feet. We climbed it with tremendous difficulty, and at the end of several hours, had traveled north about a quarter of a league in the ascent. On the top we now traveled a mile to the northwest, and from here we saw that the road ran along the bottom of this mesa over good and entirely level terrain. In the descent, which is gradual and without stones, we traveled more than three-quarters of a league to the north, then continued a little more than a league northeast through a chamise thicket where there was much small cactus. In order to avoid the hardship which this caused the animals we entered the bed of an arroyo, and having traveled along it a league to the east we came unexpectedly to a large pond of good water. This pond is formed by rainwater and the flow of a small spring which we called Fuente de San Bernabé. Judging from the trails and the ruins of huts, this is a camping place of the Yutas, and the road which we left to climb the impassable hill mentioned leads right

---

[19]They camped again on Dolores River near the spot where Little Gypsum Creek enters it.

*The Seville copy reads east-northeast. Doc. Hist. Mex. reads east-northwest, obviously a mistake.

DIARY AND ITINERARY 147

to it. Here we camped,[20] although the pasturage is not very abundant, having traveled six leagues today (not counting the distance we retraced).

August 21. We set out from the water-hole of San Bernabé along the canyon, in the southern end of which it is situated, and traveled four leagues to the north over not very good terrain which had some difficult stretches. In the middle of the canyon there are some good pools of water, and almost at the end of it for a fourth of a league there is as much water as would run from a fair-sized spring. Having left this canyon we went a league or a little less to the northwest through a level chamise thicket. We entered another canyon with as bad a road as the previous one, and having traveled on it a long league to the north we arrived at the Río de San Pedro and camped in a small meadow which is here,[21] naming the campsite San Luís. — Today six leagues.

August 22. We left the camp of San Luís, crossed the river, ascended a very high and rugged but not very stony slope and reached a wide mesa which looks like a remnant of the Sierra de los Tabehuaches. We traveled along it to the northeast for two leagues, east-northeast more than half a league, east-southeast another half league, and then went down from the mesa by another rugged but short slope. It is the one which Don Juan María de Rivera in his diary describes as being very difficult. Then along the banks of the Río de San Pedro we traveled (upstream) a league toward the northeast. We halted for a siesta and went to reconnoiter the route which we must travel in the afternoon, planning to leave the river now if there were a water hole nearby, and if not, the next day. Those who went on this reconnaissance returned late, so we spent the night at this place, which we called San Felipe.[22] — Today four leagues.

August 23. We left the camp of San Felipe (on the Río de San Pedro), ascended a hill and along the foot of the Sierra de los Tabehuaches (so-called because it is inhabited by the Yutas of this name) we traveled four leagues which, because of the many turns we made would equal two leagues to the east of San Felipe. We now left the Río de San Pedro which rises in a spur of the

---

[20]At the place where two small arroyos unite to form a dry creek.
[21]Apparently northwest of Naturita, and about fifteen miles above the junction of the San Miguel River with the Dolores.
[22]Near San Miguel River, about five or six miles west of Nucla.

Sierra de las Grullas, which, beyond the one they call Sierra de la Plata, continues north. It then runs northwest and west until it joins the Río de los Dolores, near the small range which they call Sierra de la Sal because close to it there are salt beds where, according to what we were told, the Yutas who live hereabouts get their salt. The river is medium sized. We halted for a siesta near a permanent stream that comes down from the sierra to a plain covered with chamise, toward the southern end of which there is a valley of good pasturage. In front of it there is a sort of ledge upon which there are ruins of a small and ancient pueblo whose houses appear to have been of stone, with which the Yutas Tabehuaches have made a weak and crude fortification. By now we again had found good pasturage for the animals, which had been very scarce from the camp of La Asunción on the Río de los Dolores until today, because the country was so scorched and dry that it appeared not to have rained during this whole summer. In the afternoon it began to rain, but at the end of a little more than an hour and a half it ceased and we continued our journey, ascending the Sierra de los Tabehuaches by a high hill which was rugged in places. Having traveled a league to the northeast and another to the east we were overtaken by a Yuta Tabehuache, who is the first Indian we have seen in all the distance traveled to here since the first day's march from the pueblo of Abiquiú, when we met two others. In order to talk at leisure here, we camped near the source of the stream where we had taken our siesta, naming the campsite La Fuente de la Guía.[23] We gave the Indian something to eat and to smoke, and afterward through an interpreter we asked him various questions concerning the land ahead, the rivers, and their courses. We likewise asked him the whereabouts of the Tabehuaches, Muhuaches, and Sabuaganas. At first he appeared ignorant of everything, even of the country in which he lived, but after he had recovered somewhat from the fear and suspicion with which he talked to us, he said the Sabuaganas were all in their own country, and that we would soon encounter them; that the Tabehuaches were wandering dispersed through this sierra and its vicinity; that all the rivers from the San Pedro to the San Rafael inclusive, flow into the Dolores which, in turn, joins the Río de Navajó. We asked him if he would guide us to the ranchería of a Sabuagana chief said by our interpreter and others

---

[23] On one of the creeks which flow into San Miguel River.

to be very friendly toward the Spaniards and to know a great deal about the country. He consented on condition that we should wait for him until the afternoon of the next day. We agreed to this, partly so that he might guide us, and partly that he might not suspect us of anything which might disturb him and the rest. — Today six leagues.

August 24. Before twelve o'clock the Yuta reached the place where we were awaiting him, accompanied by his family, two other women and five children, two at the breast and three from eight to ten years old, all good looking and very agreeable. They thought we had come to trade, and therefore they had brought tanned deerskins and other articles for barter. Among other things, they brought dried berries of the black manzanita, about which we have already spoken at the beginning of this diary, and which are very savory and similar to those of the little grape. We informed them, although they were not fully convinced, that we did not come for the reason they thought, and that we did not bring goods to trade. In order that they might not regard us as explorers whose purpose was to conquer their land after seeing it, nor impede our progress, and, thinking that from the Cosninas a report of the journey of the Reverend Father Fray Francisco Garcés might have spread to the Yutas Payuchis and from these to the rest, we told them that a Padre, our brother, had come to Cosnina and Moqui and from the latter place had returned to Cosnina. Thereupon they were entirely quieted, sympathized with us in our trouble, and said they had not heard anything about the Padre. We gave food to all of them, and the wife of our guide presented us with a little dried venison and two plates of dried manzanita berries, which we paid for with flour. After midday we gave the Yuta what he requested for guiding us; that is to say, two hunting knives and sixteen strings of white glass beads. He gave these to his wife who with the others went to their ranchos when we left the Fuente de la Guía with him (whom we now began to call Atanasio). We traveled along the edge of the sierra for half a league to the east, another half league to the east-southeast and a quarter league southeast. Then we turned east, leaving a trail which runs southeast, which was the one we had been following, and having traveled three quarters of a league, one southeast, and two east, we camped in a valley[24] whose descent and ascent though not difficult are very steep. For this reason we called it La Cañada Honda. In it there is a large spring of good water, much firewood, and abundant pasturage for the animals. — Today two leagues.

August 25. We set out from Cañada Honda toward the east and traveled half a league through dense thickets of dwarf oak, then turned southeast through more open country, and by the same trail went three and a half leagues. Then, having traveled another half league to the east, we started to cross the sierra toward the northeast, and went a league and a half over good open country without any difficult slopes. We arrived at the crest which is a hill with very good pasturage, and of agreeable appearance on account of the brakes and the beautiful groves of cottonwood which here grow close together. Here there are three trails, and we took the one which runs to the northeast, and having traveled in this direction a league and a half we camped,[25] still on the north slope of the sierra, at a large spring of good water which rises about six ordinary paces to the east of the trail and which we called Ojo de Laín. Before it was possible to prepare any food, of which we were in great need, a heavy shower fell. — Today seven and one-half leagues.

August 26. From Ojo de Laín we set out toward the northeast and traveled one league. Here the trail we were following divided, one branch going east-northeast and the other northeast. We took the latter and having traveled two and a half leagues to the northeast, we finished our descent from the sierra and reached the banks and meadows of the Río de San Francisco, by the Yutas called Ancapagari* (which according to the interpreter, means Laguna Colorado) because near its source there is a spring of red water, hot and bad tasting. In the meadow of this river, which is large and very level, there is a very wide and well-beaten trail. We traveled downstream a league and a half to the northwest and camped near a large marsh with very abundant pasturage which we called La Ciénega de San Francisco.[26] — Today five leagues.

[24]Apparently on a branch of Horsefly Creek.
[25]On the north slope of the southeastern end of Uncompahgre Plateau.
[26]On Uncompahgre River a short distance south of Montrose.
*Now called Uncompahgre.

DESCRIPTION OF THE SIERRAS THUS FAR SEEN

The Sierra de la Grulla or de la Plata begins near the campsite called El Cobre [The Copper] and also near the deserted pueblo. From its beginning this sierra runs almost northwest, and about seventy leagues from Santa Fé it forms a point toward the west-southwest, which is the one they call Sierra de la Plata. From here it runs north-northeast (turning toward the north just before the Sierra de los Tabehuaches) to another small range named Sierra del Venado Alazán, where it ends on the north. At the east end, according to reports, it joins Sierra del Almagre and Sierra Blanca. About thirty leagues to the west-southwest by west from the point of Sierra de la Plata another small range called Sierra del Dátil can be seen. This Sierra del Dátil is drained on the west side by all the rivers which we have crossed up to now and those from here forward to the San Rafael inclusive. The Sierra de los Tabehuaches, which we have just crossed, runs northwest. It must be about thirty leagues long, and in the place where we crossed it is eight or ten leagues wide. It abounds in good pasturage, is very moist, and has good lands for crops without irrigation. It produces in abundance piñon, spruce (pinabete), royal pine, dwarf oak, several kinds of wild fruits and, in some places, flax. In it there are stags, fallow-deer and other animals, and some fowls of a size and form similar to ordinary domestic hens, from which they differ in not having combs. Their flesh is very savory. About twenty leagues to the west of this range is the Sierra de la Sal, which likewise looks small, and to the west-southwest about four leagues is seen another range which they call Sierra de Abajo.

This Río de San Francisco is medium-sized and a little larger than the Dolores. It is composed of several small streams which flow down the western slope of the Sierra de las Grullas and runs to the northwest. In the place where we saw it there is a meadow about three leagues long, of good land for crops and with facilities for irrigation and everything else needed for the establishment of a good settlement. North of this meadow there is a chain of little hills and lead-colored knolls crowned with yellow earth.

August 27. We set out from the Sierra de San Francisco downstream toward the northwest, and after going a short distance we met a Yuta called El Surdo [The Deaf One] with his family. We stopped with him a long time, and in a lengthy conversation we learned nothing useful except to have suffered from the heat of the sun, which was very hot all the time the conversation lasted. We continued on our way along the meadow, and having traveled two leagues and a half to the northwest we crossed the river and traveled through the dense and shady grove of cottonwoods and other trees which grow on its banks. Then we ascended a small hill, entered a plain without pasturage but with some small stones, and having traveled downstream altogether three and a half leagues to the northwest we camped in another meadow of the same river which we called San Agustín el Grande,[27] and where on both sides of the river there are abundant pastures and many black cottonwoods. — Today six leagues.

Farther downstream and about four leagues to the north of this meadow of San Agustín, this river joins another and larger one which is called by our people Río de San Javier and by the Yutas, Río del Tomichi. In the year '61 Don Juan María de Rivera reached these two rivers below their junction, having crossed the same Sierra de Los Tabehuaches, on whose crest according to the description which he gives in his diary, is the place he called El Purgatorio. The meadow where he halted in order to ford the river, and in which he says he carved on a second growth cottonwood a cross, the characters which spell his name, and the year of his expedition, is also found at the same junction on the south bank, as we are assured by our interpreter Andrés Muñiz. The latter said that although at that time he had stopped three days' journey before reaching the river, he again came past here along its bank in 1775 with Pedro Mora and Gregorio Sandoval who had accompanied Don Juan María on that entire expedition. They said that they had gone clear to the river then and from it had begun their return. Those two were the only ones who crossed it, having been sent by the said Don Juan María to look for Yutas on the bank opposite the meadow where they were camped and from which they turned back. And so this was the river they then thought was the great Río del Tizón.*

August 28. We set out toward the north from the meadow of

---
[27]Some three miles north of Olathe.
*The Colorado River.

San Agustín, leaving the Río de San Francisco and having traveled half a league we continued three and a half leagues to the north-northeast, over land which was not stony and arrived at the already mentioned Río de San Francisco Javier (commonly called San Javier), otherwise known as Río del Tomichi. It is formed by four small rivers that descend from the northernmost point of the Sierra de la Grulla. It carries as much water as the Río del Norte, runs west, and at the western point of the Sierra del Venado Alazán forms a junction, as we have already said, with the San Francisco. Its banks along here are very short of pasturage. In a bend of the river in which we found some pasturage for the animals, and which we named Santa Monica, we halted today[28] with the intention of taking a short siesta and continuing upstream until we should find some rancherías of Sabuaganas, for yesterday we learned they were near here and that in them were some of the Timpanagotzi or Laguna Indians, to whose country we now planned to go. But, considering the detour which we would have to make in going up the river in this direction; that the animals would be badly injured, for they were already lame; and that it would be necessary for us to consume many supplies in going to their habitations, we decided to send the interpreter with the guide Atanasio to summon them and to see if any of them or any of the Lagunas would guide us for pay as far as he knew the way. They set forth and the rest of us waited for them at Santa Monica. — Today four leagues. We observed the latitude of this campsite by the meridian of the sun and found it to be in 39° 13' 22".

August 29. About ten o'clock in the morning we saw five Yutas Sabuaganas on a hill on the other side shouting loudly. We thought they were those whom the guides had gone to seek, but as soon as they reached us we saw they were not the ones we had sent for. We gave them something to eat and to smoke, but after a long conversation, whose subject was the disputes which they had this summer with the Cumanches Yamparicas, we were unable to get out of them a single thing useful to us, because their aim was to frighten us by setting forth the danger of being killed by the Cumanches to which we would expose ourselves if we continued on our way. We refuted the force of the arguments with

---
[28]Near Austin on Gunnison River.

which they tried to prevent us from going forward, by telling them that our God, who is the God of everybody, would defend us in case of encounters with these enemies.

August 30. In the morning the interpreter Andrés and the guide Atanasio arrived with five other Sabuaganas and one Laguna. After we had served them with plenty of food and tobacco we informed them of our purpose, which was to go to the pueblo or pueblos of the Lagunas (the Yutas had told us that the Lagunas lived in pueblos like those of New Mexico) telling them that since they were our friends they should give us a good guide to conduct us to those people, and that we would pay him to his satisfaction. They replied that to go to the place we desired to reach, there was no other road than the one that passes through the midst of the Cumanches, who would prevent us from passing or would even kill us, and finally that none of them knew the country between here and the Lagunas. They repeated this many times, insisting that we should turn back from here. We tried to convince them, first with arguments, then with flattery, in order not to displease them. Then we presented to the Laguna a woolen cloak, a hunting knife, and some white glass beads, telling him we were giving these things to him so he would accompany us and continue as our guide to his country. He agreed and we gave him the present. Seeing this, the Sabuaganas quit raising objections, and now some of them confessed that they knew the road. After all this, they insisted that we should go to their ranchería, saying that the Laguna Indian did not know the way. We knew very well that this was a new excuse to detain us and to enjoy for a longer time the favors we were conferring upon them, for to all who came, and today there were many, we gave food and tobacco. But in order not to give them any occasion to be displeased, and not to lose so good a guide as the one we had obtained, we consented to go.

This afternoon we set out from Santa Monica, crossed the Río de San Javier, in which the water reached above the shoulder blades of the horses, climbed a hill, and traveled over rough but loose soil without stones, upstream toward the east-northeast for two leagues. Then we went two more leagues to the northeast over land less broken but with some chamise, much small cactus and small volcanic stones [malpaís], and camped on the bank of a little river which we called Santa Rosa.[29] It rises in the Sierra del Venado Alazán, on whose southern slope we now were, and enters the Río de San Javier. Here there is a small meadow with good pasturage and a pleasing grove of white cottonwood and small oaks. — Today four leagues. The Sabuaganas and the Lagunas spent the night with us.

August 31. We set out from Río de Santa Rosa de Lima toward the northeast, traveled a league and a half through good country, and arrived at another medium-sized river which flows down from the same sierra as the previous one, and with it joins the Río de San Javier. We named this river Santa Monica, in whose meadows and bends there is everything necessary for the founding and subsistence of two settlements. We continued upstream through these meadows and through the groves of trees which are in it, going four leagues and a half to the northeast, and crossing the river once. Then we swung north, again crossed the river, and entered a stony juniper grove which lasted for about three miles. Then we continued climbing the Sierra del Venado Alazán along the slope of a very deep valley, breaking through dense thickets of dwarf oak; and having traveled four leagues also to the north, we camped at a permanent watering place which we called San Ramón Nonnato.[30] One of the Yutas Sabuaganas who came with us from Santa Monica today gorged himself so barbarously and with such brutish manners that we thought he would die of over-eating. Finding himself so sick, he said that the Spaniards had done him an injury. This foolish notion caused us great anxiety, because we knew that these barbarians, if by chance they become ill after eating what another person gives them, even though it may be one of their own people, think this person has done them harm, and try to avenge an injury they have never received. But God was pleased that he should be relieved by vomiting some of the great quantity he could not digest. — Today nine leagues.

September 1. We set out from San Ramón toward the north, and having traveled three leagues through small valleys with abundant pasturage and thick groves of dwarf oak, we met about eighty Yutas all on good horses, most of them being from the

---

[29] On the North Fork of the Gunnison River in the vicinity of Hotchkiss.
[30] They swung north from Bowie, entered Grand Mesa National Forest, and camped east of Overland Reservoir.

ranchería to which we were going. They told us they were going to hunt, but we concluded that they traveled together in this way partly to make a show of their large force and partly to find out whether any more Spanish people were following us, or if we came alone. Having known since the previous night that we were going to their ranchería, it was not natural that all of those men would leave it at the same time when they knew that we were coming, unless they were moved by the considerations we have just indicated.

We continued with only the Laguna and descended a very steep slope. We entered a very pretty valley in which there is a small river having all along its banks an extensive grove of very tall and straight royal pines, among them being some cottonwoods which seemed to emulate the straightness and height of the pines. Through this valley we traveled a league to the east and arrived at the ranchería, which was populous and must have consisted of about thirty tents. We camped a mile below it on the bank of the river mentioned, naming the campsite San Antonio Mártir.[31] — Today four leagues (total 199 leagues).

As soon as we halted Father Fray Francisco Atanasio went to the ranchería with the interpreter, Andrés Muñiz, to see the chief and the rest of those who had remained. He entered the chief's tent, and having greeted him and embraced him and his sons, he begged him to assemble the people who were there. He did so, and when as many of either sex as could come had assembled, he told them of the Gospel through the interpreter. [All listened with pleasure, especially six Lagunas who also assembled],* amongst whom our guide and another Laguna were conspicuous. As soon as the Father began to instruct them, the new guide interrupted him, warning the Sabuaganas as well as his own compatriots "that they must believe whatever the Father told them because it was all true." The other Laguna indicated the pleasure and attention with which he heard the announcement of his eternal salvation in this way. Among the listeners there was a deaf person who, not understanding what was being talked about, asked what it was the Father was saying. Thereupon this Laguna told him, "the Father says that what he is showing us (it

---
[31]Camp was apparently on Muddy Creek.
*The Seville edition adds these words.

was an image of Christ crucified) is the one Lord of all, who lives in the highest part of the heavens, and that in order to please Him and go to see Him, it is necessary to be baptized and to beg His pardon." He illustrated these last words by touching his breast with his hand, an action admirable in him, because he had never before seen either the Father or the interpreter. Seeing the pleasure they manifested at hearing him, the Father proposed to the chief who at this time ruled the ranchería, that if on conferring with his people they should accept Christianity, we would come to instruct them and arrange for them a mode of living to prepare them for baptism. He replied that he would propose it to his people, but during the whole afternoon he did not return to give a report on which to base a well-founded hope of their acceptance of the proposal. The Father, being rejoiced by the expression of the Lagunas, asked what this last one was called (we had already named the guide Silvestre), and learning that they called him Oso Colorado [Red Bear] he instructed all of them, explaining the difference between men and beasts, the purpose for which each was created, and the evil they did by naming themselves after wild beasts, making themselves thereby equal and even inferior to them. Then he told the Laguna that hereafter he should be called Francisco. The others, hearing this, began to repeat this name, although with difficulty, the Laguna being pleased that they should call him by this name. It happened also that when the Father gave the name of Captain to the one who was ruling the ranchería, this person replied that he was not the chief, and that the real chief was a youth, a good looking fellow who was present. And when the Father asked if the chief was already married, he replied in the affirmative, saying he had two wives. This mortified the youth (to whom the other paid the compliment indicated because he was the brother of a very much venerated chief among the Sabuaganas whom they call Yamputzi) and he tried to convince them that he had only one wife, from which it is inferred that these barbarians have information or knowledge of the repugnance we feel for a multiplicity of wives at one time. Thereupon the Father took occasion to instruct them on this point, and to exhort them not to have more than one. After all this, he bought from them a little dried buffalo meat, giving them glass beads for it, and when he asked them if they wished to trade some horses for some lame ones which we had, they answered that they would exchange them in the afternoon. This done, the Father returned to the camp.

A little before sunset the chief, some old men, and many of the others, came to where we were. They began to urge us to turn back from here, setting forth anew and with greater force the difficulties and dangers to which we would expose ourselves if we went forward. They declared that the Cumanches would not permit us to do so, and protested that they were not telling us this to prevent us from going where we desired, but because they esteemed us greatly. We reciprocated these good wishes and told them that the one God whom we adore would arrange everything and would defend us, not only against the Cumanches but also against all others who might wish to injure us, and that being certain that His Majesty was on our side, we had no fears on the score of what they told us. Seeing that their pretexts were of no avail, they said that since we did not pay any attention to the warnings they had given us, and insisted on going forward, we must write to the Great Captain of the Spaniards, (as they call the Señor Governor) telling him that we had passed through their territory, so that if we had any mishap, and did not return, the Spaniards would not think they had killed us. This was the idea of some of our companions who desired to go back or remain with them. We replied to them that we would write the letter and leave it with them, so that when any of them should go to New Mexico they might carry it. They replied that they could not take it, and that we must send it by some one of our men. We said that none of our men could go back nor remain with them. Finally, since they found no other way of keeping us from going forward without declaring themselves our enemies, they said that if we would not turn back from here they would not trade with us for our lame horses. To this we replied that even though they should not trade we must go forward, because under no circumstances could we turn back without knowing the whereabouts of our brother, the Father who had been among the Moquis and Cosninas and might be wandering about lost.* To this they replied, inspired by those of our men who understood their language and were secretly conspiring against us, that the Fathers could not

---

*He refers to Father Garcés.

get lost because they had painted on paper all the lands and roads. They again insisted, repeating all the foregoing arguments to get us to turn back from here. Seeing our unshakable determination, they repeated that they were urging us not to go forward because they loved us, but that if we persisted they would not prevent it, and that next morning they would exchange horses. After nightfall they took their leave, not without hope of overcoming our determination next day. According to what we noticed, they were given this hope by Felipe of Abiquiú, the interpreter Andrés, and his brother Lucrecio, they being the ones who, either through fear or because they did not wish to go on, had secretly connived with the Sabuaganas ever since they learned they were opposed to our plan.

By this we were caused much grief, and even more by the following: before we left the town of Santa Fé we had warned the companions that no one who wanted to come with us on this journey could carry any kind of merchandise, and that those who would not agree to this must stay at home. All promised not to carry anything whatever, nor to have any purpose other than the one we had, which was glory to God and the salvation of souls. For this reason they were given whatever they requested for their equipment and to leave for their families. But some of them failed to keep their promise, secretly carrying some goods which we did not discover until we were near the Sabuaganas. Here we charged and entreated everybody not to trade, in order that the heathen might understand that another and higher motive than this had brought us through these lands. We had just told the Sabuaganas that we did not need arms or soldiers, because we depended for our security and defense on the omnipotent arm of God, when Andrés Muñiz, our interpreter, and his brother Lucrecio, showed themselves to be so obedient, loyal and Christian that they traded what they had kept hidden, and with great eagerness solicited arms from the heathen, telling them they were very necessary to them because they were going to pass through the lands of the Cumanches. By this conduct, greatly to our sorrow, they manifested their little or entire lack of faith and their total unfitness for such enterprises.

September 2. Early in the morning the same Indians, even more of them than yesterday afternoon, assembled at the camp.

They again urged the arguments set forth above, adding another serious difficulty, for they dissuaded the Laguna completely from his intention of guiding us, and made him return to us what we had given him to persuade him to accompany us to his land. After having argued more than an hour and a half without inducing the guide to take back what we had given him and to keep his word, or the rest of them to stop opposing us, we told them, with the anger justified in such a situation, that the Laguna had consented voluntarily to accompany us as far as his land. Furthermore, since they had raised such objections, we knew perfectly well that they were taking away our guide and trying to prevent us from going forward. We told them, however, that we would not go back, do what they might, for even without a guide we would go on, but that if the Laguna refused to accompany us they would learn immediately that we no longer considered them our friends. Thereupon they yielded and the above-mentioned youth, brother of Chief Yamputzi, talked to the rest, saying that since they had consented to our going forward and the Laguna had promised to guide us, it was useless to impede us any longer, and therefore they should stop talking about the matter. Another, also said to be a chief, followed with the same exhortation. Then all of them told the Laguna that now he could not avoid accompanying us, but he, because of what they had previously told him, now did not wish to do so. But after much urging and coaxing he accepted his pay, although with some ill grace, and agreed to go with us. The ranchería now pulled up stakes and traveled toward the place where Chief Yamputzi had been when we left the disagreeable campsite of San Antonio Mártir. We did not know what direction we ought to take because the guide, regretting the arrangement, did not want to go on or to show us the way. He remained at the site of the ranchería with the horse we had given him pretending to look for a saddle, while we continued by the route taken by the Sabuaganas, although unwillingly because we wanted to get away from them. We told the interpreter to get the guide immediately and try to encourage him. He did so and all the Yutas having left, the guide now told the interpreter the road we must take and sent him to take us back to the ranchería where he was. Here we found him saying goodbye to his countrymen who were remaining with the Sabuaganas, who charged him to conduct us with care, telling him how he was to proportion the days' marches. Besides the guide Silvestre, we found here another Laguna, still a youth, who wished to accompany us. Since we had not previously known of his desire we had not provided him with a horse, and so to avoid any further delay Don Joaquín Laín took him behind him on his horse.

Very gladly we left the trail the villagers were taking, and with the two Lagunas, Silvestre and the boy, whom we named Joaquín, we continued our journey. Having gone back a league to the west from San Antonio, we took another trail and traveled less than a league and three quarters to the northwest, then more than a quarter of a league to the west-northwest. We camped in a small valley with good pasturage near a little stream of good water which we named San Atanasio.[32] We traveled today over good terrain and through groves of cottonwood and clumps of dwarf oak, traveling three leagues but advancing only two. Tonight it rained heavily.

September 3. It rained again early in the morning and we had to wait for it to stop. Then, about eleven o'clock, we set out from San Atanasio toward the north. Having traveled a quarter of a league we turned northwest and went two and a quarter leagues through a valley with many groves of cottonwood and royal pine and an abundance of water and pasturage. We turned north-northwest for a league then northwest somewhat more than a league and three quarters, over good terrain without stones but with some hills, passing groves of royal pine, cottonwood and clumps of somewhat troublesome dwarf oak. We swung north-northwest a quarter of a league through a low valley in which runs as much water as two good-sized furrows would hold, although it does not continue throughout the valley, for in places it completely disappears, yet in some places it runs and in others it can be seen in pools like stagnant rainwater. It appears to be permanent because throughout the valley there were huts or little houses which indicate that this is a residence of the Yutas. Following the bed of an arroyo where the water disappears and comes out again on the north bank, we traveled northwest a league and a half and camped in the bed of the arroyo almost at the foot of a hill which the Yutas call Nabuncari. We named the campsite San Silvestre.[33] — Today seven leagues.

[32]They apparently camped on one of the headwaters of Buzzard Creek.
[33]South of Battlement Mesa near the foot of North Mam Peak.

September 4. We set out from San Silvestre toward the northwest, following the same arroyo. After going a short distance we swung west-northwest, and having traveled two leagues we turned again to the northwest, climbed a low hill, leaving the bed of the arroyo toward the south, and through hills bearing various species of broom we traveled more than half a league. We descended to another small stream which enters the arroyo mentioned, crossed it, climbed another hill with some stones and a grove of piñon, and having traveled a quarter of a league almost west-southwest we again passed close to the arroyo. Here the beaver have made with logs such ponds that at first they looked like a fairly good-sized river. Then on the south side we traveled through a plain of chamise about three-fourths of a league west, and turned to cross the stream again in order to continue on the other side and leave it at the south. Having crossed it we turned west-northwest through a small grove of piñon trees and entered a chamise thicket in which there were three Yuta women and a child, drying the berries which they had gathered for food along the arroyos and creeks which are here. We went to talk with them and immediately they offered us their fruits, which were chokecherry, garambullo, limes and some of this year's piñon. The garambullo which grows in these parts is very bitter while on the bushes, but when dried in the sun as these Yutas had done, it is bitter-sweet and very savory. We continued on our way, and having traveled a league and a half to the west-northwest from the little river mentioned (crossing another near the Yutas on whose farther bank there is a standing rock about five palms high shaped like a washbowl in which some of the animals slipped), we entered a valley or little glen with good pasturage. Another road comes in here, which, from Santa Monica and Río de San Javier, runs straight across the Sierra del Venado Alazán, which we have just descended today, and it is only half as long as the one we have been following. We turned northwest through the valley for a little more than half a league, swung west-northwest, and having traveled another half league, climbing and descending a somewhat long hill, steep but not stony, we crossed a small stream of very cold water and camped on its bank.[34] We named it and the little valley of good pastures here,

---

[34] Apparently on Kimball Creek.

Santa Rosalia. Last night and tonight we felt the cold very much. — Today six leagues (Total 201).

September 5. We set out from Santa Rosalia toward the northwest, and ascended a hill without troublesome stones but extremely steep and dangerous to climb because there are turns where the trail is less than a third of a vara wide. The footing is of very loose soft earth, so it is very easy for an animal to slip, and if he should lose his footing he would not be able to stop until he reached the plain below. The ascent must be somewhat more than a quarter of a league counting the distance which we have already covered. We descended it by a long valley which in some places produces nothing but dwarf oak and chokecherry and in other places spruce and white cottonwoods. Having traveled a little more than four leagues to the northwest we entered a little grove of juniper, swung half a league to the north-northwest, and after crossing a small chamise patch we arrived at a river which our people call San Rafael and which the Yutas call Rio Colorado. We crossed it and halted on its north bank in a meadow with good pasturage and a fair-sized grove of cottonwoods.[35] On this side there is a chain of high mesas, whose upper half is of white earth and the lower half evenly streaked with yellow, white, and not very dark colored red earth. This river carries more water than the Rio del Norte. It rises, according to what they told us, in a great lake which is toward the northeast near the Sierra de la Grulla. Its course along here is to the west-southwest, and it enters the Rio de los Dolores. At the ford it is split into two channels. The water reached above the shoulder blades of the animals, and some of them which crossed above the ford swam in places. From what we could see the river has many large stones, consequently if it should be necessary for any group of men to cross, it would be very desirable to ford it on good horses. — Today five leagues.

Tonight we observed the latitude and found ourselves in 41° and 4′. Thinking we had not come so far above Santa Monica, and fearing some defect in the observation, we decided to take it by the sun next day, stopping at a suitable hour in order not to remain here where the Sabuaganas might bother us.

September 6. We set out toward the west from the river and

---

[35] On the Colorado River in the vicinity of Una.

meadow of San Rafael (which lacks the facilities necessary for a settlement). We traveled downstream half a league, another half through some valleys toward the west-northwest, leaving the river to the south; northwest a quarter of a league and through ravines without stones for a league and a quarter west by west-northwest. To the west-northwest we went about a mile and then having gone nearly two more leagues west over broken ground with some stones and a great deal of small cactus, we descended to a small valley through which a little river of good water runs. On the bank, near its only cottonwood, we halted at eleven o'clock in the forenoon, sending some companions forward with the pack animals and the loose herd. We made an observation by the meridian and found ourselves in 41° 6' and 53" of latitude, and found that in the observation of the previous night there had been no error. We overtook the others, who having traveled two leagues northwest had stopped. They were disgusted with the guide because, leaving a road which went west upstream and appeared according to reports more direct, he led us by another which, entering a canyon, goes directly north. He said that although that road went north by the canyon it soon turned back toward the west. The companions who knew the Yuta language tried to convince us that the guide Silvestre was leading us by that route either to delay us by winding around so that we could not go on, or to lead us into some ambush by the Sabuaganas who might be awaiting us. In order to make us more distrustful of the guide, they assured us that they had heard many Sabuaganas in the ranchería tell him that he must lead us by a road which did not go to the Lake, and that after he had delayed us for eight or ten days in useless wanderings, he must make us turn back. Although it was not entirely incredible that some of them might have said this, we did not believe that the guide could ever have agreed to it nor even that it had really happened, because up to now none of our companions had told us a thing about it; for at the ranchería they had not neglected to magnify greatly other difficulties, less fearsome and less likely, as well as the fact that in any catastrophe they would risk little less than we. We well knew that if we went to the north we would have to take a more circuitous route. But when Silvestre said he was leading us by that route because on the other there was a very bad hill, we wished to accept his opinion. But all the companions except Don Joaquín Laín insisted on taking the other road, some because they feared the Cumanches too greatly and without foundation, and some because that route did not conform with their own opinions, which were considerably opposed to ours. Soon a Yuta Sabuagana, one of the most northern, arrived and said the road to the north went up very high. Therefore we had to continue to the west, and having traveled two leagues and crossed another and smaller river we camped on its bank, naming the campsite La Contraguía.[36] — Today seven leagues.

Here were three ranchos of Sabuaganas from which six men came to the camp. Among them there was one who had just come from the land of the Cumanches Yamparicas, whither with four others he had gone to steal horses. He said the Cumanches had withdrawn, and that judging from their trail they were going to the Río Napeste or to the east. With this report our companions were somewhat encouraged. These Sabuaganas were the last ones we saw.

September 7. We set out from La Contraguía through a wide valley, and having traveled in it a league to the west we came to a meadow with abundant pasturage. We turned to the northwest in the same valley, and having traveled three leagues we halted for a time so the animals might drink, because we did not know whether we should find water tonight. Afterward we continued in the same direction, and having gone a little more than a quarter of a league we swung to the north-northeast, climbing a grade that was so difficult that we were afraid we could not reach the top, because in addition to being very rugged in places there was not even a trail, and since the soil was very loose the animals could not put their feet down anywhere with safety. The ascent must be about half a league, and at the top there are some benches of very brittle shale where two pack mules lost their footing and rolled down more than twenty varas at the least. But God willed that none of those who were coming behind should be trampled upon and that the mules should not be injured. We climbed the mountain on foot, suffered much fatigue, and had some very great scares, for which reason we called it Cuesta del Susto. On the way up the guide gave us irrefutable proof of his sincerity and his innocence. Having reached the top of the hill we traveled

---

[36]Camp was in the Roan Creek Valley to the west of Highmore.

to the north-northwest half a league, descending into a small valley, and camped by a very scanty spring of water,[37] where there was fair pasturage for the animals. We named the campsite La Natividad de Nuestra Señora. — Today a little more than five and a quarter leagues.

September 8. We set out from La Natividad de Nuestra Señora toward the north, traveled half a league, crossing a permanent arroyo of good water, then ascending a hill which was rugged but without ledges or stones, we struck a trail and better terrain than that of yesterday. Having traveled two and a half leagues northwest through gently sloping hills and some cottonwood groves, we arrived at a high ridge from which the guide Silvestre pointed out to us the sierra on whose northern slope the Cumanches Yamparicas dwell, who are therefore north of the Sabuaganas. And at the point of the same sierra, toward the west of the place from which he pointed it out to us, are his people. We descended from the summit by an extremely long slope, rugged in places but without stones, and with many groves of dwarf oak and chokecherry, which served to prevent the horses from slipping and rolling. We entered a wide canyon* with good terrain, and having traveled a league to the north-northwest, counting the descent from the summit, we descended by the same canyon to the north a league and a half, and halted in order that the animals might drink, because a goodly amount of water which flows down from here in the bed of the canyon either runs underground or dries up. In the afternoon we continued downstream through the canyon, and having traveled a league to the west-northwest we camped without water, because the arroyo has none, in a glade with good pasturage which we called Santa Delfina.[38] Today five leagues.

September 9. We set out from the campsite of Santa Delfina down the same canyon, went half a league northwest, then swung north-northwest. Having traveled in the canyon nine leagues in all in this direction, over a very well beaten trail with only one bad stretch which can be avoided by crossing the arroyo a little sooner, and traversing a grove of tall chamise and jara [rockrose] of the kind they call *latilla*, we emerged from the canyon. Half way

---
[37]On Roan Plateau, perhaps near the head of Spring Creek.
[38]In the upper [southern] end of Douglas Canyon.
*Douglas Canyon.

down this canyon toward the south there is a very high cliff on which we saw crudely painted three shields or *chimales* and the blade of a lance. Farther down on the north side we saw another painting which crudely represented two men fighting. For this reason we called this valley Cañon Pintado. It is the only way by which one can go from the summit mentioned* to the nearest river, because the rest of the intervening country is very broken and stony. On the same side of this canyon near the exit a vein of metal can be seen, but we did not know the kind or quality, although one companion took one of the stones which roll down from the vein, and when he showed it to us Don Bernardo Miera said it was one of those which the miners call *tepustete*, and that it was an indication of gold ore. On this matter we assert nothing, nor will we assert anything, because we are not experienced in mines, and because a more detailed examination than the one we were able to make on this occasion is always necessary. Having crossed the canyon we traveled half a league to the north-northwest, arrived at a river which we called San Clemente, crossed it and camped on its north bank[39] where there is a fair-sized meadow of good pasturage. This river is medium-sized, along here runs to the west, and the region adjacent to it does not have advantages for settlement. — Today ten leagues.

September 10. Because, according to the interpreter, the guide declared the next watering place was far distant, and that even if we started early we could not reach it today, we decided to split the journey.** And so, after noon we set out from Rio de San Clemente toward the northwest, over hills without stones and small plains without pasturage or trees and of very loose earth, and having traveled a league we swung west-northwest for two leagues, over terrain almost level but with many dry arroyos and ravines. Because night was now coming on, and in the darkness the terrain was impassable and dangerous, we camped in the bed of an arroyo which we called El Barranco.[40] In it there was neither water nor pasturage and so it was necessary to watch the animals and keep them corraled all night. From the river to this

---
[39]At the mouth of Douglas Creek where it joins the White River just east of Rangely.
[40]Northwest of Rangely and about half way to the Utah state line.
*Roan Mountain.
**Travel in the afternoon, camp for the night, and finish the journey the next morning.

place we traveled in a straight line and without a trail, because although there are several, they are trails of the buffalo which come down to winter in this region. — Today three leagues.

September 11. As soon as it was daylight we set out from El Barranco toward the west-northwest, and having traveled a league and a half through arroyos and ravines, some of them deeper than those of yesterday, we found in one of them a small spring of water from which the animals were unable to drink. We continued west-northwest for a league, climbing to a ridge by a good and not very high ascent, and from it traveled three leagues over good country with fair pasturage. In the distance we saw a cottonwood grove and asked Silvestre if the watering place to which he was leading us was there. He said "No," that this was an arroyo, not a river, but that it might have water now. Thereupon we went toward it and found plenty of running water for ourselves and for the animals, which were now very much fatigued from thirst and hunger, and a pack mule was so worn out that it was necessary to remove the pack which it carried. To reach the arroyo we swung half a league to the north. — Today six leagues.

A short distance from the ravine we saw a recent buffalo trail. In the plain we saw it again where it was fresher, and observed that it ran in the same direction in which we were going. By now we were short of supplies because we had found it necessary to travel so far and because of what we had distributed among the Sabuaganas and the other Yutas. And so, a little before reaching the arroyo two companions turned aside to follow this trail. A little after midday one of them returned, telling us that he had found the buffalo. We despatched others on the swiftest horses and having chased it more than three leagues they killed it, and at half past seven at night returned with a large supply of meat, much more than comes from a large bull of the common variety. In order to prevent the heat from spoiling it for us, and at the same time to refresh the animals, we did not travel on the 12th, but camped at this place, which we named Arroyo del Cibolo.[41] Tonight it rained for several hours.

September 13. About eleven o'clock in the morning we set out from Arroyo del Cibolo through the plain which lies at the foot

---

[41]On Cliff Creek just south of the white cliffs of Yampa Plateau.

SPLIT MOUNTAIN AND THE GREEN RIVER

"The river enters this meadow between two high cliffs which, after forming a sort of corral, come so close together that one can scarcely see the opening through which the river comes." Diary, September 13, 1776

Photo Hal Rumel

of a small sierra which the Yutas and Lagunas call Sabuagari.*
It extends from east to west and its white cliffs can be seen from
the high hills which are reached before Cañon Pintado. Having
traveled two leagues and three-quarters to the west, we arrived
at the watering place known to the guide. It is a small spring at
the foot of the sierra, almost at its western extremity. We continued in the same direction for a quarter of a league along a
well beaten trail near which, toward the south, rise two large
springs of fine water, a musket shot apart, which we named Las
Fuentes de Santa Clara and whose moisture produces much good
pasturage in the small plain to which they descend and in which
they disappear. From here we traveled a league northwest over
the same trail and crossed an arroyo which comes from the plain
of Las Fuentes, and in which there were large pools of water.
From here downstream there is much good pasturage in its bed,
which is wide and level. We again crossed the arroyo, ascended
some low hills which were stony in places, and after traveling
two leagues to the northwest we arrived at a large river which
we called San Buenaventura. — Today six leagues.

This Río de San Buenaventura is the largest river we have
crossed,** and is the same one which Fray Alonso de Posada, who
in the [past] century was custodian of this Custodia of New
Mexico, says in a report, divides the Yuta nation from the
Cumanche, according to the data which he gives and according
to the distance which he places it from Santa Fé. And in fact, on
the northeast and the north it is the boundary between these two
nations. Its course along here is west-southwest; farther up it
runs west to this place. It is joined by San Clemente River, but
we do not know whether this is true of the previous streams.
Here it has meadows abounding in pasturage and good land for
raising crops, with facilities for irrigation. It must be somewhat
more than a league wide and its length may reach five leagues.
The river enters this meadow between two high cliffs which,
after forming a sort of corral, come so close together that one
can scarcely see the opening through which the river comes. According to our guide, one can not cross from one side to the
other except by the only ford which there is in this vicinity. This

---
*Cf. Sabuagana.
**They had not yet crossed it.

is toward the west of the northern crest and very close to a chain of hills of loose earth, some of them lead colored and others yellow. The ford is stony and in it the water does not reach to the shoulder blades of the horses, whereas in every other place we saw they can not cross without swimming. We halted on its south bank about a mile from the ford, naming the camp La Vega de Santa Cruz.[42] We observed the latitude by the north star and found ourselves in 41° 19′ latitude.

September 14. We did not travel today, remaining here in order that the animals, which were now somewhat worn out might regain their strength. Before noon the quadrant was set up to repeat the observation by the sun, and we found ourselves no higher than 40° 59′ and 24″. We concluded that this discrepancy might come from the declination of the needle here, and to ascertain this we left the quadrant fixed until night for the north stands on the meridian of the needle. As soon as the north or polar star was discovered, the quadrant being in the meridian mentioned, we observed that the needle swung to the northeast. Then we again observed the latitude by the polar star and found ourselves in the same 41° 19′ as on the previous night. In this place there are six large black cottonwoods* which have grown in pairs attached to one another and they are the nearest to the river. Near them is another one standing alone, on whose trunk, on the side facing northwest, Don Joaquín Laín with an adz cleared a small space in the form of a rectangular window, and with a chisel carved on it the letters and numbers of this inscription—"The Year 1776"—and lower down in different letters—"LAIN"—with two crosses at the sides, the larger one above the inscription and the smaller one below it.

Here we succeeded in capturing another buffalo, smaller than the first, although we could use little of the meat because the animal had been overtaken late and very far from the camp. It happened also this morning that the Laguna, Joaquín, as a prank mounted a very fiery horse. While galloping across the meadow, the horse caught his forefeet in a hole and fell, throwing the rider a long distance. We were frightened, thinking that the Laguna

---

[42]They camped on Green River a short distance above the mouth of Brush Creek, some miles above the bridge of Jensen, and about a mile south of Dinosaur Quarry.
*The six cottonwoods are still there, and are now huge trees.

had been badly hurt by the fall because when he had recovered from his fright, he wept copious tears. But God was pleased that the only damage was that done to the horse which completely broke its neck, leaving it useless.

September 15. We did not travel today either for the reasons indicated above.

September 16. We set out from the Vega de Santa Cruz on Río de San Buenaventura, ascended about a mile toward the north, arrived at the ford, and crossed the river. Then we turned west, and having traveled a league along the north bank and meadow of the river, we crossed another small stream which comes down from the northwest and entered it by the same meadow. We swung south-southwest for a league and crossed another small stream, a little larger than the first, which descends from the same northwesterly direction and enters the [main] river. From both of them canals can be made with which to irrigate the land on this bank, which also is very good for crops, although it will not be possible to bring the waters of the Río Grande to them. We continued to the southwest leaving the river which swings to the south through some hills and ravines which were stony in places. We descended to a dry arroyo by a high and very stony ridge, whose slope on the other side is not so bad. As soon as we reached the top we found a trail, one or two days old, of about a dozen horses and some people on foot, and on examining the vicinity, indications were found that on the highest part of the hill they had been lying in ambush or spying for some time without turning their horses loose. We suspected they might be some Sabuaganas who had followed us to steal the horseherd in this place, where it would be likely that we would attribute the deed to the Cumanches rather than to the Yutas, since we were now in the land of the former not the latter. Besides this, it gave us strong grounds for suspecting the guide Silvestre, because the preceding night he casually and without being noticed went off from the camp a short distance to sleep. During the whole journey he had not worn the cloak that we gave him, but today he left the campsite with it, not taking it off during the whole day, and we suspected that he, having come to an understanding with the Sabuaganas, put it on so that he could be recognized in case they attacked us. Our suspicions were increased when he stopped for a time before reaching the peak where we found the tracks, as if thoughtful and confused, wishing first to go along the banks of the river and then to lead us through here. We gave him no indications of our suspicion, dissimulating it entirely, and in the course of our march he gave us emphatic proofs of his innocence. We continued here along the same trail, descended again to the Río de San Buenaventura and saw that the people who made the trail had stayed a long time in the leafy grove and meadow which is situated here. We continued on the trail through the meadow, crossed some low hills, and camped in another meadow[43] with good pasturage on the bank of the river, naming the campsite Las Llagas de Nuestro Padre San Francisco. We traveled through the hills, canyons, peaks, and meadows mentioned six leagues to the southwest, and in the whole day's march eight leagues. As soon as we halted two companions followed the trail southwest to explore the terrain hereabouts and concluded that the Indians had been Cumanches.

September 17. We set out from the meadow of Las Llagas de Nuestro Padre San Francisco toward the southwest, ascended some low hills, and having traveled a league, we left the trail we were following, along which the tracks of the people on foot and of the horses continued. Silvestre told us that they were Cumanches who were going in pursuit of the Yutas, whom they had perhaps learned about while hunting buffalo. We were convinced that this was the case, both because of the direction in which they were traveling and on account of other signs they left. We crossed a dry arroyo, ascended a hill, and having traveled a league and a half to the west over good terrain, dry and almost level, we came to a high ridge from which the guide pointed out to us the junction of the rivers San Clemente and San Buenaventura which, now joined, ran south from this place. We descended to the plain and a large meadow of another river, and having traveled another league and a half to the west we arrived at the junction of two medium-sized streams. These come down from the nearby sierra north of the Río de San Buenaventura and now being joined flow eastward across the plain until they unite with the Río de San Buenaventura. The more eastern of the two streams, before reaching the junction, runs southeast, and we called it Río de San Damián; the other runs to the east and we

---

[43] On Green River beyond Horseshoe Bend.

called it Río de San Cosme. We continued up the latter stream, and having traveled a league to the west we saw near its banks the ruins of a very old pueblo, where there were fragments of metates, jars, and jugs made of clay. The pueblo was circular in form, judging from the ruins, which are now almost completely leveled to the ground. We turned southwest through the plain which lies between the two rivers, ascended some hills of loose stone, very troublesome for the animals, which were now sorefooted. We descended to another meadow of Río de San Cosme, and having traveled southwest half a league and west a league and a half through this meadow, we camped in it, naming it Ribera de San Cosme.[44] — Today eight leagues.

A little after crossing we saw columns of smoke at the foot of the sierra, and asking the guide who he thought had sent them up, he said they might be Cumanches, or some Lagunas who were accustomed to range through here hunting.

September 18. We left Ribera de San Cosme and the guide, wishing to cross to the other side of the river and travel on it, led us into a grove or thicket of almost impenetrable rockrose and through marshy creeks which forced us to go back and cross the river three times, making many useless turns. Then through a plain near the meadows of the river, we traveled three leagues to the southwest, swung to the west-southwest for a league, crossed the river a fifth time and again turned west, in which direction, now through the meadow of the river, now along the adjacent plain, we traveled three leagues and a quarter. We ascended a not very high mesa which was level on top and very stony, traveled about three quarters of a league including the ascent and the descent, crossed another small river which near here enters the San Cosme, named it Santa Catarina de Sena, and camped on its bank.[45] — Today nine leagues.

From the ranchería of the Sabuaganas and the campsite of San Antonio Mártir to this place we counted eighty-eight leagues and from Santa Fé two hundred and eighty-seven.

Along these three rivers we have crossed today there is plenty of good land for crops to support three good settlements, with

---

[44] On Duchesne River about five miles east of the site of Myton.
[45] Near Duchesne River and three or four miles northeast of the town of Duchesne.

opportunities for irrigation, beautiful cottonwood groves, good pastures, with timber and firewood nearby.

From the country of the Cumanches a very long high sierra descends, running from northeast to southwest as far as the country of the Lagunas. This ridge we could see for more than seventy leagues. Toward the north of Río de San Buenaventura at this season its highest hills and peaks are covered with snow, for which reason we named it Sierra Blanca de los Lagunas, and we shall begin to ascend and cross it tomorrow where it is least elevated.

September 19. We set out from Río de Santa Catarina de Sena toward the southwest without a trail, ascended a short gentle but very stony slope, and having traveled a quarter of a league swung to the west. We descended to the bank of the Río de San Cosme and traveled along it two and a quarter leagues, making several turns, through almost impassable terrain, now through many stones, now along rocky precipices, one of which lamed one of our horses and forced us to go back about a mile and go down to another meadow by the river. We crossed it, breaking through a thicket of rockrose and tall reeds, and after going half a league to the west we swung to the northwest, taking as a road the bed of an arroyo. Now climbing the sierra and leaving the San Cosme River, we continued along the arroyo which led us imperceptibly into a closed canyon, high on both sides, with no passable terrain other than the bed of the arroyo. Half way up the canyon there is another arroyo which runs from north to south. We followed the one which led us northwest, which with its many windings ran generally west-northwest, and having traveled four leagues we left the canyon which we called Cañon de las Golondrinas because there are many nests of swallows in it, formed with such symmetry that they look like little pueblos. Then we continued on good terrain through a chamise thicket and having traveled half a league west-northwest we swung to the west, ascending a long hill with some timber, and having descended it we entered a plain which is crossed from north to south by a well beaten trail. Having crossed the plain we descended by way of a high, stony and rough ridge to the watering place, which we named San Eustaquio,[46] having traveled two leagues and a half to the

---

[46]Camp was somewhat east of Fruitland, probably on Red Creek.

west. This watering place is permanent and well-filled and around it there is abundant pasturage. We arrived very much fatigued, partly because of the difficulty of the day's journey and partly because a very cold wind blew unceasingly from the west. — Today ten leagues.

September 20. We set out from San Eustaquio, leaving for dead one of our strongest horses, the one which had broken his neck at Santa Cruz del Río de San Buenaventura. We climbed a long but gradual slope toward the southwest, then swung to the west a little less than three leagues and a quarter through a level but troublesome chamise growth with much small cactus. We entered a small valley, wide and gently sloping, and after going a quarter of a league to the south-southwest we again turned west, descended to a small river which runs east and is perhaps the one which we formerly called the San Cosme. We crossed the river to the west-southwest, ascended another hill, long but gentle and passable, and after going a mile we swung southwest for about two leagues through a very pleasant and pretty valley with very abundant pasturage. We camped at the end of the valley at a small marsh with plentiful pasturage in the middle of which there was a good spring of water which we called Ojo de Santa Lucía.[47] Tonight it was so cold that even the water which was near the fire all night was frozen in the morning. — Today five leagues.

September 21. We set out from Ojo de Santa Lucía to the southwest by the same valley which we had just ascended, through a grove of white cottonwoods, and having traveled a quarter of a league we swung west a league and three quarters, now through thickets of troublesome chamise, now through low valleys of very soft earth, the animals sinking and stumbling every instant in the many little holes which were hidden in the grass. Then we descended to a fair-sized river in which there is an abundance of good trout, two of which the Laguna, Joaquín, killed with an arrow and caught, and each one of which would weigh somewhat more than two pounds. This river runs to the southeast through a pretty valley with good pastures, many creeks and pretty groves of white cottonwoods, neither very tall nor large around.

In this valley, which we named Valle de la Purísima, there

---

[47] In Strawberry Valley, apparently at Soldier Springs, a short distance east of Strawberry Reservoir.

are all the advantages necessary for a good settlement. The guide Silvestre told us that part of the Lagunas, who used the fish of the river as their customary food, lived in this valley at one time, and that they withdrew for fear of the Cumanches who were beginning their raids into this part of the sierra. Having crossed the river and ascended a hill, we entered the floor of the valley and, having traveled a league to the south-southwest, we swung to the west through a ravine with much chamise and bad terrain, and, having gone three-fourths of a league, we crossed a small stream of very cold water. We continued west another quarter of a league and entered a dense grove of white cottonwoods, dwarf oak, chokecherry, and royal pine. Through the same grove we took the south slope of a wooded ravine and, having traveled a league west by south, we crossed to the other side. The guide, anxious to arrive as quickly as possible, went so fast that at every step he disappeared in the thicket and we were unable to follow him, for besides the great density of the wood, there was no trail, and in many places his track could not be seen, so he was ordered to go slowly and to remain always in our sight. We continued through the grove which became more dense the farther we went, and having traveled half a league west, we emerged from it, arriving at a high ridge from which the guide pointed out to us the direction to the Lake, and, to the southeast of it, another part of the sierra in which he said there lived a great many people of the same language and character as the Lagunas. By this ridge we traveled southwest a quarter of a league and descended it to the west, breaking through almost impenetrable thickets of chokecherry and dwarf oak, and then through another grove of cottonwood so dense that we thought the packs would not get through without being unloaded. In this grove the guide again annoyed us by his speed, so that we were forced to keep him back and not let him go ahead alone. In this dense growth Father Fray Atanasio got a hard blow on one of his knees by hitting it against a cottonwood. Finally with great difficulty and labor we descended to a deep and narrow valley where we found sufficient pasturage, which abounds in all the sierra, and water for ourselves and for the animals. We camped here[48] after having traveled in the descent a league to the west, naming the place San Mateo. —

---

[48]On the western slope of the divide, perhaps on Fifth Water Creek.

Today six and one-half leagues. Tonight it was much colder than on previous nights.

September 22. We set out from San Mateo to the southeast along the north slope of this valley in which there were many perilous defiles and slides with no other trail than the one which we were opening. The rough and uneven ground of the sierra here forced us at each step to change our direction and to make many turns. Suffice it to say that after going up and down hills and high elevations, some of them rough and stony, for about five leagues, we descended by a long passable slope with plentiful pasturage to a small plain between two creeks which join in it, after traveling along the slope a league to the southwest. When we arrived the animals were all worn out. There was plentiful pasturage and so we camped in this place, naming it San Lino.[49] —Today we traveled six leagues which, on account of the many windings, would take us with respect to San Mateo, three leagues west-southwest.

From the top of the last ridge we saw in front of us and not very far away many large columns of smoke arising in the same sierra. The guide Silvestre said they must have been made by his people who were out hunting. We replied to them with other smoke signals so that if they had already seen us they would not take us to be enemies and thus flee or welcome us with arrows. They replied with larger smoke signals in the pass through which we must travel to the Lake, and this caused us to believe they had already seen us, because this is the most prompt and common signal used in any extraordinary occurrence by all the people of this part of America. Consequently, we warned Silvestre that tonight he must be on the *qui-vive* lest some of his people who knew of our arrival should approach the camp to see what people had come here. And about two o'clock in the morning, the hour when according to his opinion there might be one or more Indians close at hand, he made a long speech in his language, giving them to understand that we were peaceable people, friendly and good, but we do not know whether or not anyone heard him.

September 23. Knowing that we were now arriving at the Lake, in order that the two Indians, Silvestre and Joaquin, might enter their land or settlement feeling happier and more friendly

---

[49]On Diamond Creek where Wanrhodes Canyon meets Diamond Canyon.

toward us, we again gave each one a vara of woolen cloth and another vara of red ribbon with which they at once set about adorning themselves. The guide Silvestre donned the cloak previously given him, wearing it like a mantle or cape, and the cloth which we now gave him he wore like a wide band around his head, leaving two long ends hanging loose down his back. And so he paraded about on horseback, the living image of the captives whom the father redemptors bring out in their processions on this feast day of Nuestra Señora de la Merced. This event seemed to be a happy omen of the friendly disposition of these captives, whose liberty we desired and besought of the Redeemer of the World, through the intercession of His Immaculate Mother, who, in order to encourage us in this, wished to give the name which the Church celebrates today.

We set out early from San Lino to the southwest, ascended a small hill on whose summit we found a large ant hill, composed of very fine alum rock, pure and crystalline. We descended to the little river of San Lino, and having traveled a league through its small meadows, which are very level, we swung to the west without leaving the river and continued downstream. Here the river is joined by a smaller one, and in both there are pretty meadows and everything else necessary for stock-raising. Having traveled west downstream three-fourths of a league, we saw and passed three large springs of hot water which we tasted and liked. It is of the same sulphurous character as the spring which is near the pueblo of San Diego de los Hemes in New Mexico. We continued west another three-quarters of a league, entered the narrowest part of the river canyon and swung a mile to the north. Here there are three other springs of water like the foregoing, all of which rise on this north bank at the foot of a very high hill close to the river into which they flow. For this reason we named the stream Río de Aguas Calientes. In these narrows of the canyon there are some places that are difficult but which can be made passable.

We continued northwest half a league, crossed to the other side of the river, climbed a small hill, and beheld the lake and the wide valley of Nuestra Señora de la Merced de los Timpanogotzis, as we shall call it henceforth. We also saw that all around us they were sending up smoke signals one after another,

Photo Biddulph

MT. TIMPANOGOS
As seen from the floor of Utah Valley

thus spreading the news of our coming. We went down to the plain, and entering the valley, crossed the river again. After traveling through the wide meadows on its north bank somewhat more than a league, we crossed to the other side, and camped in one of its southern meadows,[50] which we named Vega del Dulcísimo Nombre de Jesús. — Today five and one-half leagues.

We found that the pasture of the meadows through which we were traveling had been recently burnt, and that others nearby were still burning. From this we inferred that these Indians had thought us to be Cumanches or some other hostile people, and since they had perhaps seen that we had horses, they had attempted to burn the pastures along our way, so that the lack of grass might force us to leave the plain more quickly. But since the plain is so large and extensive they could not do this in such a short time even though they had started fires in many places. As soon as we camped, therefore, while the rest of our small company remained here, Father Fray Francisco Atanasio set out for the first ranchos with the guide Silvestre, his companion Joaquín and the interpreter, Andrés Muñiz. In order to get there this afternoon, they pushed the horses as hard as they could, to the point of tiring them out, for six and one-half leagues to the north-northwest, and arrived at the ranchos.[51]

Some men came out to meet them with weapons in their hands to defend their homes and their families, but as soon as Silvestre talked to them, the guise of war was changed into the finest and simplest expression of peace and affection. They took them very joyfully to their poor little houses, and after the father [Father Atanasio] had embraced each one separately and made known to them that we came in peace and that we loved them as our best friends, he gave them time to talk at length with our guide Silvestre. The latter gave them an account of what he had observed and seen ever since he had joined us and of our purpose in coming, and it was so much in our favor that we could not have wished for a better report. He told them at great length how well we had treated him and of our love for him. Among other things, he told them with great surprise that although the Lagunas had

---

[50]A short distance south and east of the present site of the town of Spanish Fork.
[51]The Indian villages which they visited were on Provo River to the east of Utah Lake and north of the city of Provo.

told us that the Cumanches would kill us or steal our horses, we had passed through the regions which they most frequent, and even found their very fresh tracks, but they had not attacked us nor had we even seen them, thus verifying what the fathers had said, namely, that God would deliver us from all our enemies and from these in particular, in such a way that although we might pass through their very territory, they would not detect us nor would we see them. He concluded by saying that only the fathers told the truth, that in their company one could travel through all the land without risk, and that only the Spaniards were good people. They were further confirmed in this belief on seeing that the boy Joaquín was on such good terms with us that he paid no attention to his own people. He even refused to leave the father except to care for the horses which they brought. He would scarcely talk to his people or even stay near them, but clung to the father, sleeping at his side during the brief space of time that was left in this night. Such an attitude found in an Indian boy so far from civilization that he had never before seen fathers or Spaniards was an occasion for surprise not only to his own people but to us as well. When they had talked a long time concerning this matter, and many persons had assembled from the nearby ranchos, the father gave all of them something to smoke, and explained to them through the interpreter and Silvestre, who already had some understanding, our reasons for coming. Of these the principal one was to seek the salvation of their souls and to make known to them the only means whereby they could obtain it, the primary, first and most necessary being to believe in the true and only God, to love Him and obey Him completely, doing what is provided in His holy and immaculate law. Furthermore, if they wished to be Christians he would teach them all this more clearly and at greater length and would sprinkle upon them the water of holy baptism, and that fathers would come to instruct them and Spaniards to live with them, in which case they would be taught likewise to plant crops and raise cattle, and then they would have food and clothing like the Spaniards. For this purpose, if they consented to live as God commands and as the fathers would teach them, everything necessary would be sent by our Captain, who is very grand and rich and whom we call King. For if he saw that they wished to become Christians, he would regard them as his children, and he would care for them just as if they already were his people. Afterwards he [the father] told them that, since we must continue on our way in order to get news of the other padre, our brother [Father Garcés], we needed another of their people to guide us to some other tribe known to them who might furnish us still another guide. In all this we were aided by the good offices of Silvestre. They listened gladly and replied that they were ready to do all this, thereby exhibiting from then on their great docility. Although two chiefs were present, the one who ruled these people as head-chief was absent, and so the father requested that they send for him. They replied that he was at his house, which was distant and that he would come the next day. Thereupon they withdrew to their homes, some remaining and conversing all night with our Silvestre.

September 24. We sent word by Joaquín and another Laguna to the other companions that they should come from El Dulcísimo Nombre de Jesús to the rancho where we were and where the Indians of this and other rancherías were gradually assembling, and they arrived here a little before noon. Early in the morning the head-chief came with the two other chiefs, several old men and many other persons. We explained to them at greater length the things already mentioned, and all of them unanimously replied that if the fathers should come, that they [the Indians] would live with the Tatas (as the Yutas call the friars), who would rule and teach them. They offered the Spaniards all their land so they might build their houses wherever they pleased, adding that they would scout through the country and be always on the watch for the inroads of the Cumanches, so that if they tried to enter the valley or the vicinity of the sierra, the Spaniards would be promptly warned and they all could go out together to punish them. Seeing such admirable docility, and having achieved our purpose, we told them that after finishing our journey we would return with more fathers and Spaniards to baptize them and live with them, but that from now forward they must be careful what they said so that later on they might not have to repent. They replied that they were sincere in what they were promising, adding with earnest supplication that we must not delay our return for long. We told them that although our people would believe what we might say about them, they must give us a token showing that they wished to be Christians, et cetera, so we could show it to our Great Captain, and to the rest of the Spaniards, so that by means of it they would be more convinced of their good intentions and be encouraged to come more quickly. We did this the better to sound out their intentions, and they replied that they would very gladly give us the token the next morning.

We then presented the chief, who was a man of good presence, with a hunting knife and strings of beads, and Don Bernardo Miera gave him a hatchet. We gave some white glass beads to the others for which they were happy and grateful, though we could give only a few to each one because the Indians were numerous. Afterward we reminded them of their promise regarding a guide, and we told them that if they were agreed we would take Joaquín who wanted to go on with us. They replied that they had already discussed the matter and had decided that not only Joaquín, but also a new guide should go with us, perhaps as far as our land, and that they should return with us when we came back. They added that none of them knew much about the country in the direction which they knew we had to take, but that with the two, Joaquín and the guide, we should make inquiries of the tribes along our route. This most sincere expression of their sentiments, so clear and satisfactory, filled us with an inexpressible joy and assured us completely that without the least duplicity and with spontaneous and free will, moved by the Divine Grace, they accepted and desired Christianity. We put in front of them the same present which we had given to Silvestre, so that on seeing it the one who was to go with us as guide might make himself known. Immediately one of those present accepted it and became, thereupon, our guide and companion, who from that time we called José María. This being arranged, we decided to continue our journey to the establishments and port of Monterey next day.

They informed us that there was a sick child, in order that we might go to see him and baptize him. We went and, finding that he was rather large and that he was now almost recovered from a long illness, and in no immediate danger, we did not think it desirable to sprinkle upon him the water of baptism. Afterward his mother brought him to where we were, begging us to baptize him, and we consoled her by saying that we should soon return, when everyone, large and small, would be baptized.

Finally, we told them that we now had only a few provisions and would be grateful if they would sell us a little dried fish. They brought it and we purchased a considerable quantity of it. All day and a part of the night they kept coming and conversing with us, and we found them all very simple, docile, peaceful, and affectionate. Our Silvestre was now looked upon with respect, and acquired authority among them for having brought us and being so much noticed by us.

September 25. In the morning they again assembled and brought us the requested token, explaining what it contained. As soon as we had asked for it the day before, we warned the interpreter that neither he nor the rest should say anything to the Indians about the matter, in order to see what they of their own accord would produce. When the token was brought, a companion, who did not know of the order that had been given, saw the pictures on it and showing them the cross of the rosary, he explained to them that they should paint it on one of the figures, and immediately they took it back and painted a little cross above each one. They left the rest of it as it was and gave it to us, saying that the figure which on both sides had the most red ochre or, as they called it, the most blood, represented the head-chief, because in the battles with the Cumanches he had received the most wounds. The two other figures which were not so bloody, represented the two chiefs subordinate to the first, and the one which had no blood represented one who was not a war chief but a man of authority among them. These four figures of men were rudely painted with earth and red ochre on a small piece of buckskin. We accepted it, saying that the Great Captain of the Spaniards would be very much pleased to see it, and that when we returned we would bring it with us so that they might see how much we esteemed their things and in order that the token itself might be a guarantee of their promises and of everything we had discussed. We told them that if, while awaiting us, they should have any difficulty in the way of sickness or enemies they must call upon God, saying, "Oh true God, aid us! Favor us!" But seeing that they were unable to pronounce these words clearly, we told them that they should say only "Jesús María! Jesús

María!" They began to repeat this with ease, our Silvestre very fervently leading them, and all the time we were preparing to leave they kept on repeating these holy names. The time for our departure arrived and all of them bade us goodbye with great tenderness. Silvestre especially embraced us vigorously, almost weeping. They again charged us to come back soon, saying they would expect us within a year.

DESCRIPTION OF THE VALLEY AND LAKE OF NUESTRA SEÑORA DE LA MERCED DE LOS TIMPANOGOTZIS OR TIMPANOCUTZIS OR COME PESCADOS, ALL OF WHICH NAMES ARE GIVEN TO THEM.

To the north of the Río de San Buenaventura, as we have said above, there is a sierra which in the parts we saw runs from northeast to southwest more than seventy leagues, and its width or breadth must be at most forty leagues, and where we crossed it, thirty. In the western part of this sierra in latitude 40° 49′ and about northwest by north of the town of Santa Fé, is the valley of Nuestra Señora de la Merced de los Timpanocutzis, surrounded by the peaks of the sierra, from which flow four fair-sized rivers which water it, running through the valley to the middle of it where they enter the lake. The plain of the valley must be from southeast to northwest, sixteen Spanish leagues long (which are the leagues we use in this diary), and from northeast to southwest, ten or twelve leagues. It is all clear and, with the exception of the marshes on the shores of the lake, the land is of good quality, and suitable for all kinds of crops.

Of the four rivers which water the valley, the first on the south is that of Aguas Calientes, in whose wide meadows there is sufficient irrigable land for two good settlements. The second, which follows three leagues to the north of the first and has more water, could sustain one large settlement or two medium-sized ones with an abundance of good land, all of which can be irrigated. This river, which we named Río de San Nicolás, before entering the lake divides into two branches, and on its banks besides the cottonwoods there are large sycamores. Three and one-half leagues northwest of this river is the third, the country between them being of level meadows with good land for crops. It carries more water than the two foregoing streams, and has a larger cottonwood grove and meadows of good land, with opportunities for irrigation sufficient for two or even three good settlements. We were close to it on the twenty-fourth and twenty-fifth, and we named it Río de San Antonio de Padua. We did not reach the fourth river although we could see its grove of trees. It is northwest of the Río de San Antonio and has in this direction a great deal of level land which is good, judging from what has been seen. They told us that it has as much water as the others, and so some ranchos or pueblos could be established on it. We named it Río de Santa Ana. Besides these rivers, there are many pools of good water in the plain and several springs running down from the sierra.

What we have said regarding settlements is to be understood as giving to each one more lands than are absolutely necessary, for if each pueblo should take only one league of agricultural land, the valley would provide for as many pueblos of Indians as there are in New Mexico. Because, although in the directions indicated above we give the size mentioned, it is an understatement, and on the south and in other directions there are very spacious areas of good land. In all of it there are good and very abundant pastures, and in some places it produces flax and hemp in such quantities that it looks as though they had planted it on purpose. The climate here is good, for after having suffered greatly from the cold since we left the Río de San Buenaventura, in all this valley we felt great heat both night and day.

Besides these most splendid advantages, in the nearby sierras which surround the valley there are plentiful firewood and timber, sheltered places, water and pasturage for raising cattle and horses. This applies to the north, northeast, east and southeast. Toward the south and southwest close by there are two other extensive valleys, also having abundant pasturage and sufficient water. The lake, which must be six leagues wide and fifteen leagues long, extends as far as one of these valleys. It runs northwest through a narrow passage, and according to what they told us, it communicates with others much larger.

This lake of Timpanogotzis abounds in several kinds of good fish, geese, beaver, and other amphibious animals which we did not have an opportunity to see. Round about it are these Indians, who live on the abundant fish of the lake, for which reason the Yutas Sabuaganas call them Come Pescados [Fish-Eaters]. Besides this, they gather in the plain grass seeds from which they make atole, which they supplement by hunting hares, rabbits and fowl of which there is great abundance here. There are also buffalo not very far to the north-northwest, but fear of the Cumanches prevents them [the Come Pescados] from hunting them. Their habitations are chozas or little huts of willow, of which they also make nice baskets and other necessary utensils. In the matter of dress they are very poor. The most decent clothing they wear is a buckskin jacket and long leggings made of the same material. For cold weather they have blankets made of the skins of hares and rabbits. They speak the Yuta language but with notable differences in the accent and in some of the words. They have good features and most of them have heavy beards. In all parts of this sierra to the southeast, southwest and west live a large number of people of the same tribe, language, and docility as these Lagunas, with whom a very populous and extensive province could be formed.

The personal names of the chiefs contained in the token described above, in their own language are as follows: of the head chief, Turuñianchi; of the second, Cuitzapununchi; of the third, who is our Silvestre, Panchucumquibiran (which means "Talker"); of the fourth, who is not a chief but is brother of the head chief, Picuchi.

The other lake with which this one communicates, according to what they told us, covers many leagues, and its waters are noxious and extremely salty, for the Timpanois assure us that a person who moistens any part of his body with the water of the lake immediately feels much itching in the part that is wet. Round about it, they told us, live a numerous and peaceful nation called Puaguampe, which in our ordinary speech means "Witch Doctors" and who speak the Cumanche language. Their food consists of herbs. They drink from several fountains or springs of good water which are around the lake, and they have houses of grass and earth (the earth being used for the roofs). They are not enemies of the Lagunas, according to what they intimated, but since a certain occasion when [the Puaguampes] approached and killed one of their men they do not consider them as neutral as formerly. On this occasion they entered by the last pass of the Sierra Blanca de los Timpanosis (which is the same one in which they live), to the north by northwest, and they say that right here the Cumanches make their entries, which did not appear to be very frequent.

The Timpanogotzis were so-called from the lake on which they live, which they call Timpanogó, and this is the special name of this lake, for the name or word with which they designate any lake in general is "pagariri." This one must be six leagues wide and fifteen leagues long to the narrows and the junction with the large one.

September 25. About one o'clock in the afternoon we set out from these first ranchos and the river of San Antonio where we had been, and having traveled a little more than three and one-half leagues, we camped for the night on the bank of Río de San Nicolás.[52]

September 26. With the two Lagunas, José María and Joaquín, we set forth from the Río de San Nicolás, arrived at the Río de Aguas Calientes, crossed it, and having traveled beyond it two leagues to the south, we halted, still in the plain, near a creek of good water which we called Arroyo de San Andrés.[53] It appears to flow continuously and therefore is rather a small river or creek than an arroyo. On its banks there is a species of medium-sized trees on whose foliage live a vast number of little insects as strange to us as are the trees. — Today two leagues.

September 27. We set out toward the south from the Arroyo de San Andrés and having traveled a league still in the plain, we crossed another small stream with as much water as is contained in a fair-sized irrigation ditch. It runs along the surface of the land through which it passes, which is very good for crops. We continued south through the same plain for a league and a half, left it through the southern pass, which we named Puerto de San Pedro, and entered another large valley. Because the salt flats from which the Timpanois get their salt are very close to this valley toward the east, we called it the Valle de las Salinas, which is one of the nearby valleys mentioned above. It must be

---
[52] On Hobble Creek northwest of present-day Springville.
[53] Near the site of Payson.

about fourteen leagues long from north to south and five wide from east to west. It is all of level land with abundant water and pasturage, although only one small river flows through it. In it there are large numbers of fowl of the kind which we have already mentioned in this diary. We traveled four more leagues south along the plain of the valley and camped at a large spring of good water which we called Ojo de San Pablo.[54]

As soon as we halted, José María and Joaquín brought five Indians from the nearby ranchos. We gave them something to eat and to smoke, and told them the same things that we had told the others at the lake in-so-far as was appropriate to the circumstances. We found them as docile and affable as the others. Manifesting great joy on hearing that more fathers and Spaniards were coming to live with them, they remained with us until nearly midnight. — Today six and one-half leagues to the south.

September 28. We set out from the Ojo de San Pablo toward the south, and having traveled four leagues we arrived at a small river which comes down from the same eastern part of the sierra in which the salt flats are, according to what they told us. We stopped here a short time in the shade of the cottonwoods on the bank to get some relief from the great heat, and we had scarcely sat down when, from among some thick clumps of willows, eight Indians very fearfully approached us, most of them naked except for a piece of buckskin around their loins. We spoke to them and they spoke to us, but without either of us understanding the other, because the two Lagunas and the interpreter had gone ahead. By signs we gave them to understand that we were peaceful and friendly people. We continued toward the south, and having traveled three leagues we swung southeast half a league and another half to the south and camped,[55] while still in the valley, near a spring which we named San Bernardino. —Today eight leagues almost all to the south.

September 29. We left San Bernardino, going south-southwest, and immediately met six Indians. We talked with them a long while and preached to them through the interpreter and the Lagunas, and they listened with great docility. Having traveled two and one-half leagues, we swung to the southwest, now leav-

---
[54]In the vicinity of the town of Starr, just east of Mona Reservoir.
[55]Near the town of Levan.

ing [Valle de] Las Salinas which continues on to the south. Here we met an old Indian of venerable appearance. He was alone in a little hut, and his beard was so thick and long that he looked like one of the hermits of Europe. He told us about a river nearby and about some of the country which we still had to traverse. We traveled southwest half a league, swung westnorthwest through some little valleys and dry hills, and having traveled a league and a half we arrived at the river not discovering it until we were on its very bank. We camped in a meadow with good pasturage,[56] which we named Santa Ysabel. Here we observed the latitude by the north star and found ourselves in 39° 4' of latitude. — Today four leagues.

A short time after we halted, four Indians arrived at the other bank. We had them cross over to where we were, treated them with courtesy, and they remained with us all the afternoon, telling us about the country which they knew and of the wateringplace to which we must go the next day.

This river, according to the name which these Indians give it, appears to be the San Buenaventura, but we doubt whether this is the case, because here it carries much less water than where we crossed it in 41° 19', although after it unites with the San Clemente it is joined by the San Cosme, the San Damián, and several other small streams. Moreover, it seems likely that when we crossed it in that latitude Silvestre would have told us that this river ran near his country, as he told us other things about the sierra and of other rivers and lakes, which we found to correspond with his account, and in which I include this river which passes through Santa Monica.

September 30. Very early twenty Indians arrived at the camp together with those who were here yesterday afternoon, wrapped in blankets made of the skins of rabbits and hares. They remained conversing with us, very happily, until nine in the morning, as docile and affable as the preceding ones. These people here have much heavier beards than the Lagunas. They have holes through the cartilage of their noses and they wear as an ornament a little polished bone of deer, fowl or some other animal thrust through the hole. In features they look more like Spaniards than like the other Indians hitherto known in America, from

---

[56]On Sevier River near the site of Mills.

whom they are different in the foregoing respects. They speak the same language as the Timpanogotzis. At this river and place of Santa Ysabel this tribe of bearded Indians begins. It is they, perhaps, who gave rise to the report of the Spaniards that they live on the other side of the Río del Tizón which according to several coinciding reports is the Río Grande, formed from the Río de los Dolores and others and which joins the Navajó.

At nine o'clock we set out from Santa Ysabel, crossed the river, and traveled three and one-half leagues to the south through a plain covered with chamise, troublesome for the animals. We entered a little canyon of good land, and a little farther on came to a plain with abundant pasturage but without water. Having traveled through it a league and a half to the south, we found behind some small hills a spring of water which we named Ojo de Cisneros,[57] by which there are two small trees which mark the place. — Today five leagues to the south.

October 1. We set out from Ojo de Cisneros, going back nearly half a league to the north, then again swung south, traveled a quarter of a league through a ravine that was stony in places, and through it we went a mile up the sierra (which from the valley of Las Salinas continued southward). Swinging southwest now for a quarter of a league, we came upon a vast plain surrounded by sierras in which they told us the Río de Santa Ysabel entered another lake and then emerging from that lake it continued west. Descending the valley or pass, we swung westnorthwest over low and very stony hills, and having traveled two long leagues we entered a chamise thicket. Then along the bank of a dry arroyo and without a trail we went three leagues west, then left the arroyo, and having traveled two leagues west by north, we descended to the plain. It appeared to us that nearby there was water in a marsh or lake. We quickened our pace and found that what we had thought to be water was in places salt, in others saltpeter, and in others *tequesquite*. We continued west by south along the plain and the salt flats, and having traveled more than six leagues we camped[58] without having found any water fit to drink or pasturage for the animals, for which reason they were unable to travel any farther. There was some

---
[57]In the vicinity of the town of Scipio.
[58]They camped on Salt Lake, which lies northeast of Clearlake and south of Deseret.

PAHVANT BUTTE

Prominent landmark on the Sevier Desert. Escalante passed to the west of this butte. Miera marked it on his "Bearded Indian" map.

Photo Frank Beckwith

pasturage where we stopped, but it was bad and there was little of it. Hitherto in the whole plain, there had been no pasture, good or bad. — Today fourteen leagues.

Two companions had gone ahead seeking water and they reported that a league beyond this place they had seen some. On hearing this we decided that as soon as the moon came up they should take the animals a few at a time so they might drink, and they should also bring water for the men. They were not certain about the water they had seen and so, leaving two men with the horses, the other three went to look for it in the direction in which they had told us the Río de Santa Ysabel was.

October 2. Morning dawned without our hearing from the five men who had gone with the horses in search of water. One of the two who had remained with the herd came at six o'clock but was unable to tell us anything about the herd, his companion or any of the rest because these two had fallen asleep. Meanwhile the horse herd, driven by thirst, strayed away, and the men waking at various times, each took a different route to hunt for the animals. Immediately Don Juan Pedro Cisneros set out on the trail riding bareback and overtook the herd seven leagues back, that is, midway in the preceding day's march, returning with it only a little before noon. Shortly afterward the men who had gone seeking water arrived, accompanied by some Indians whose ranchos they accidentally reached on the bank of the Río de Santa Ysabel. These were some of the people with long beards and pierced noses who, in their language, are called Tirangapui. The five who first came with their chief had such long beards that they looked like Capuchin or Bethlemite fathers. The chief was an attractive man of mature years but not aged.

They remained very happily talking with us and in a short time they became very fond of us. The chief learned that one of our companions was still missing, and immediately he ordered his four Indians to go as quickly as possible to look for him in the plain and bring him to where we were, each one going in a different direction. This was an action worthy of the greatest gratitude and admiration in people so wild that they had never before seen persons like us. While the chief was giving these orders, he saw that the absentee was already coming and very gladly he told us the news. We preached the Gospel to them as well as the interpreter could explain it, telling them of the Unity of God, the punishment which He has in store for the bad and the reward ready for the good, the necessity of holy baptism, and of the knowledge and observance of the divine law. While this was going on, three of their men were seen coming toward us, and then the chief told us that these also were his people, and that we must suspend the conversation until they arrived in order that they also might hear everything that we were saying for their benefit. When they arrived he told them that we were padres and that we were instructing them in what they ought to do in order to go to Heaven and so they must pay attention. He said this so forcefully that although we understood only a word of Yuta now and then, we gathered what he was telling them before the interpreter had translated it for us, solely by the gestures with which he was expressing himself. We told them that if they wished to obtain the proposed benefit we would return with more fathers so that all might be instructed, like the Lagunas, who already were awaiting religious teachers, but that then they must live together in a pueblo and not scattered as they do now.

They all replied very joyfully that we must return with other fathers, that they would do whatever we might teach and command them, the chief adding that if then we wished and thought it better, they would go to live with the Lagunas (which we had already proposed to him). We said goodbye to them and all, especially the chief, took our hands with great fondness and affection. But the time when they most emphatically expressed themselves was when we were leaving this place. They scarcely saw us depart when all of them, imitating their chief, who set the example, broke out weeping copious tears, so that even after we were a long distance away we still heard the tender laments of these miserable little lambs of Christ who had strayed only for lack of The Light. They so moved us that some of our companions could not restrain their tears. In this place, which we named Llano Salado, where, because of some delicate white shells which we found, it appears there has been a lake much larger than the present one, we observed the latitude and found it in 39° 34' 36". This observation was made by the sun almost in the middle of the plain, which from north to south must be little less than thirty leagues, and from east to west fourteen leagues. In most places it is very short of pasturage and although two rivers enter it, the Santa Ysabel from the north, and a medium-sized one whose waters are very salty, from the east, we saw no place whatever suitable for settlement.

In the afternoon we continued on our way toward the south-southeast because the marshes and lakes would not permit us to go south, which was the direct route to the pass through which we were to leave the plain. Having traveled three leagues we camped near a small hill which is in the plain, giving the name of El Cerrillo to the campsite,[59] where there were marshes with much pasturage but salty water. — Today three leagues south-southeast.

October 3. Leaving El Cerrillo we made many turns, because we were surrounded by marshes, so we decided to cut through from the east, crossing the river which abounds in fish and apparently disappears in the marshes and in the other lakes of the plain. The ford was miry, and in it the horse which the interpreter Andrés was riding fell and threw him into the water, giving him a hard blow on the cheek. Having crossed with some difficulty and traveled six leagues south by west over good level land, we arrived at an arroyo which appeared to have much water, but we found only some pools in which it was difficult for the animals to drink. Nevertheless, because there was good pasturage, we camped here.[60] All along the arroyo there was a sort of white, dry and narrow bank which from a distance looked like stretched canvas, for which reason we named it Arroyo del Tejedor. — Today six leagues south by west.

October 4. We set out from El Tejedor upstream and toward the south, and after traveling one fourth of a league, we swung a little to the south-southwest, then having traveled less than five leagues, we arrived at the south pass. After we had left the salty plain we found in this arroyo more and better water than that of yesterday, and beautiful meadows, very abundantly supplied with good pasturage for the animals, which were now badly fatigued because the salty water had done them much harm, and so we camped here, naming the campsite Las Vegas del Puerto.[61] — Today five leagues.

---
[59]Southeast of the town of Clearlake, probably just south of Pahvant Butte.
[60]Apparently in the vicinity of Borden on the Union Pacific Railroad.
[61]On Beaver River in the pass east of Cricket Mountains, some ten miles northeast of Black Rock.

October 5. We left Las Vegas del Puerto, traveled south on the banks of the same arroyo, and having gone two leagues we swung southwest three leagues and camped in another meadow of the arroyo, naming it San Atenógenes.[62] — Today five leagues.

This morning before we set out from Las Vegas del Puerto, the Laguna, José María, left us and went back without saying goodbye. We saw him leave the camp but we did not wish to say anything to him nor to have anyone follow him and bring him back, preferring to leave him in complete liberty. We did not know what moved him to make this decision but, according to what the interpreter told us afterward, he was now somewhat disconsolate on seeing that we were going so far from his country. But doubtless the decision was hastened by an unexpected event of the preceding night. This was that when Don Juan Pedro Cisneros sent for his servant, Simón Lucero, in order that with him and the rest they might say the rosary of the Virgin, Lucero objected to coming. Don Juan reprimanded him for his laziness and lack of devotion, whereupon the servant attacked him, and they struggled with each other. From where we were saying the matins of the following day we heard the hullabaloo, and we went over at once, but not in time to prevent José María's getting a great scare. We tried to convince him that these persons were not angry, saying that although a father might chide his son, as just now had been done, he never would wish to kill him, as he thought, and that therefore he must not be afraid. Nevertheless, he turned back from here, leaving us without anybody who knew the country ahead even from hearsay. We felt very sorry about this incident because we desired to hasten his salvation which now he would not be able to obtain so quickly.

As soon as we halted two men went to see if the western part of the sierra and a valley which was in it were passable, and if they gave any hope of finding in them water and pasturage for the animals. After nightfall they returned saying they had found no pass whatever by which to cross the sierra, that it was very rough and high in this direction, and that in front of it there was a wide plain without any pasturage or water whatsoever. Therefore we were unable to take this direction, which was the

---

[62]Apparently in the Beaver River valley southwest of the town of Black Rock.

best for reaching Monterey, which was our objective, and we decided to continue south until we emerged from this sierra through a very wide valley beginning at this campsite of San Atenógenes, which we named Valle de Nuestra Señora de la Luz. Through it continues the Arroyo del Tejedor, with sufficient wells and pools of good water, and very spacious meadows abundant with pasturage, both of which in the valley are very scarce.

On the preceding days a very cold wind from the south had blown fiercely and without ceasing, followed by a snowfall so heavy that not only the peaks of the sierra but likewise all the plains were covered with snow tonight.

October 6. In the morning it was snowing and it continued all day without ceasing, so we were unable to travel. Night came and, seeing that it still did not stop, we implored the intercession of Our Mother and Patroness, saying in chorus the three parts of her Rosary and of all the saints, and singing the litanies, and God willed that at nine o'clock at night it should cease to snow, hail, and rain.

October 7. Although we were greatly inconvenienced by the lack of firewood and the excessive cold, we were unable to leave San Atenógenes today either, because, with so much snow and water, the land, which here is very soft, was impassable.

October 8. We set out from San Atenógenes through the plain toward the south but traveled only three and one-half leagues with great difficulty because it was so soft and miry everywhere that many pack animals and saddle horses, and even the loose ones, either fell down or mired in the mud. We camped about a mile west of the arroyo, naming the campsite Santa Brígida,[63] where, having observed by the north star, we found ourselves in 38° 3′ 30″of latitude. — Today three and one-half leagues to the south.

Today we suffered greatly from cold because all day a very sharp north wind never stopped blowing. Hitherto we had intended to go to the presidio and new establishments of Monterey, but thinking them still distant because, although we had to descend only 1° 23½′ to this place of Santa Brígida, we had not advanced toward the west, according to the daily directions, more than 136½ leagues. According to the opinion which we had

---

[63]They camped farther up the Beaver River valley.

formed, partly on account of not having heard among all these last people any report of the Spaniards and fathers of Monterey, partly because of the great difference in longitude between this port and the town of Santa Fé as shown on the maps, there were still many more leagues to the west. Winter had already begun with great severity, for all the sierras which we were able to see in all directions were covered with snow. The weather was very unsettled and we feared that long before we arrived the passes would be closed and we would be delayed for two or three months in some sierra, where there might be no people nor any means of obtaining necessary sustenance, for our provisions were already very low, and so we would expose ourselves to death from hunger if not from cold. Moreover, we reflected that even granting that we might arrive at Monterey this winter, we would not be able to reach the Villa de Santa Fé before the month of June next year. This delay, together with that which would arise in the regular and necessary pursuit of such an interesting undertaking as the one now in hand, might be very harmful to the souls who, according to what has been said before, desired their eternal salvation through holy baptism. Seeing such delay in what we had promised them, they would consider their hopes frustrated or would conclude that we had intentionally deceived them, whereby their conversion and the extension of the dominions of His Majesty in this direction would be made much more difficult in the future. To this it might be added that the Laguna, Joaquín, terrified and weary of so many hardships and needs, might stray away from us and return to his country, or to other people of whom he might have heard, as was done by the other [Laguna]. Added to these considerations was the possibility that by continuing south from Santa Brígida we might discover a shorter and better road than the one by way of the Sabuaganas by which to go from Santa Fé to the Laguna de Timpanois and to these other Indians, the Long Beards, and perhaps to some other nation hitherto unknown who may always have lived on the north bank of the Río Grande. Therefore, we decided to continue to the south, if the terrain would permit it, as far as the Río Colorado, and from there proceed toward Cosnina, Moqui, and Zuñi.

NEW ITINERARY AND THE BEGINNING OF OUR RETURN FROM 38° 3 MINUTES AND 30 SECONDS OF LATITUDE

October 9. We left Santa Brígida, going south, and having traveled six leagues with less difficulty than yesterday, because the ground now was not so soft nor so wet, we camped near a bend[64] formed by the valley and the great plain of Nuestra Señora de la Luz, where it becomes wider, and from which place it continues for many leagues to the southwest. We named the campsite San Rústico, where we found everything convenient, it being unnecessary for us to go to the arroyo for water or to its meadows for pasturage. The water was rainwater and not permanent. — Today six leagues south.

October 10. We set out from San Rústico toward the south, traveled a league, and then went three more south-southwest, to a small and very low hill in the middle of the plain to ascertain by the view the extent of this valley and plain of La Luz. Ascending the hill we saw that from here it extended southwest more than thirty-five or forty leagues, for we could scarcely see the sierras where it ends in this direction, although they are very high as we afterward discovered.

We saw also three springs of hot sulphurous water which are on top of and on the eastern slope of these hills, near and below which there are small patches of ground covered with saltpeter. We continued across the plain, and having traveled two leagues south we camped,[65] fearing that farther on we might not find water for the night. Here there was a great deal collected from the melted snow in a kind of lake, and there was also good pasturage. We named the campsite San Eleuterio. — Today six leagues.

The Long Bearded Yutas (Yutas Barbones) extend this far south, and here apparently their territory ends.

October 11. We set out from San Eleuterio south by east, letting the companions go ahead so that we two might discuss between ourselves the means we ought to adopt to relieve the companions, especially Don Bernardo Miera, Don Joaquín Laín,

---
[64]Below the town of Milford, at the southern end of the valley where it divides and swings off toward the southwest.
[65]Apparently some twelve miles southwest of the site of Minersville.

and the interpreter Andrés Muñiz, of the great dissatisfaction with which they were leaving the route to Monterey and taking this one. The latter we thought was now desirable and according to the most holy Will of God, in accord with which alone we desired to travel, and to obey which we were disposed to suffer and if necessary to die. We had already told them at Santa Brígida the reasons for our new decision, but instead of listening to the force of our arguments, they opposed our views and so from then on they were very insubordinate. Everything was now very onerous to them and everything insufferably difficult. They talked of nothing but how useless so long a journey would now be. For to them it was of no value to have already discovered so great an extent of country, and people so willing to attach themselves readily to the Vineyard of the Lord and the dominions of His Majesty (God spare him); nor to have become acquainted with such extensive provinces hitherto unknown; nor finally, to bring one soul, now almost assured to the fold of the Church, an achievement more than great, and worth an even longer journey of greater difficulties and fatigues. Moreover, we had already made much progress toward reaching Monterey later. But to all this they paid no attention, for the first of the persons here mentioned [Don Bernardo Miera], without any cause whatsoever, at least on our part, had conceived great hopes of honor and profit by merely reaching Monterey, and had communicated these hopes to the others, building great castles in the air. And now he assured them that we were robbing them of these blessings which they imagined would be so great, with the result that even the servants greatly tried our patience. Shortly before this decision was made, Don Bernardo had said that we had advanced but little toward the west, and that it was still a long distance to Monterey, but now even the servants frequently maintained that we would have arrived within a week. Many times, before leaving the Villa de Santa Fé, we had told each and every one of our companions that in this journey we had no other destination than the one which God might give us, and that we were not inspired by any temporal aim whatsoever; and that any one of them who might attempt to trade with the heathen, or to follow out his personal desires instead of devoting himself to the one purpose of this enterprise, which had been and is the greater honor of God and the spread of the Faith, had better not go with us.

On the way we repeatedly admonished them to purify any intentions they might have, because otherwise we would suffer trouble and misfortunes, and would fail to achieve all our aims, a thing which in part they now saw happen under circumstances which, unless they close their eyes to the Light, they will never be able to attribute to accident. With all this we were more mortified each day, and we were disconsolate to see that instead of the interests of Heaven, those of Earth were first and principally sought. And so, in order that the cause of God might be better served, and to make them see more clearly that not through fear nor by our own will had we changed our plan, we decided to abandon entirely the heavy responsibility of the foregoing reflections. Having implored the divine clemency and the intercession of our patron saints we decided to inquire anew the will of God by means of casting lots, putting in one the word "Monterey" and in the other "Cosnina," and following the route which might come out.

We now overtook the companions, and had them dismount. When all were assembled, Father Fray Francisco Atanasio set forth to them the inconveniences and difficulties which now prevented our continuing to Monterey; what we would be able to achieve by returning by way of Cosnina; and finally, the mistakes and set-backs which we would have suffered hitherto if God had not interfered with some of their projects. He pointed out to them all the evil which might result from continuing now to Monterey, especially from the straying or the return of the Laguna, Joaquín. He warned them that if the lot fell to Monterey, there would be no other director than Don Bernardo Miera, for he thought it so near at hand, and all this dissatisfaction was a result of his ideas. Then Father Atanasio gave them a brief exhortation to the end that, putting aside every sort of passion, they should subject themselves entirely to God, and beg Him, with firm hope and lively faith, to make known His Will. They all submitted in a Christian spirit and with fervent devotion they said the third part of the Rosary and other petitions, while we said the penitential Psalms, and the litanies and other prayers which follow them. This concluded, we cast the lot, and it was decided in favor of Cosnina. Now, thank God, we all agreeably and gladly accepted this result.

We now continued on our way, quickening our pace as much as possible and having traveled ten leagues from San Eleuterio, two south by east, three south-southeast (now leaving the plain of Nuestra Señora de la Luz), a fourth of a league southeast, one and a quarter south-southeast, three and one-half southeast over good terrain, and going through a wood of piñon and juniper, crossing a long valley with much pasturage, and afterwards some grass-covered hills, we descended to a beautiful valley and camped after nightfall near a small river in one of its meadows, which have a very great abundance of pasturage. We named them the Valley of Señor San José.[66] — Today ten leagues.

We observed by the polar star and found ourselves in 37° and 33′ of latitude.

THE ITINERARY AND DIARY CONTINUES FROM 37° 33 MINUTES OF LATITUDE, AND FROM THE SMALL RIVER OF SEÑOR SAN JOSÉ, IT IS DIRECTED TOWARD THE RÍO COLORADO AND COSNINA.

October 12. We set out from the small river of Señor San José, where there were some miry places, crossed a large marsh with much water and pasturage and through the middle of which runs another stream of water like an irrigation ditch. We crossed this stream by going northwest, then turned straight south on the west side of the meadows of the plain. Having traveled over good terrain four and one-half leagues, we saw that the companions who were some distance ahead of us left the road hurriedly. We quickened our pace to learn the cause, and when we overtook them they were already talking with some Indian women whom they had forcibly* detained because they had begun to run away with other Indian women, of whom there were about twenty in number gathering grass seeds in the plain, as soon as they saw them [the companions]. We were sorry to see them so frightened for they could not even speak, and through the interpreter and the Laguna, Joaquín, we tried to relieve them of their fear and timidity. When they had somewhat recovered their composure,

---
[66]On Coal Creek some ten miles north of Cedar City.
*Evidently should read "a fuerza" for "afuera."

they told us that in this vicinity there were many of their people; that they had heard it said that toward the south there were people who wore blue clothes and that the Río Grande was not very far from here. We were not able to learn from them with certainty from what nation they obtained these blue garments or rags, nor to form concerning this matter any opinion from what they said. But we knew that the Payuchis traded only for red clothes, and immediately it occurred to us that the Cosninas buy their blue woolen cloth in Moqui, so we concluded that it was of these they were talking, from which we inferred that this place was near the Río Colorado and the Río Cosnina. These Indian women were so poorly dressed that they wore only some pieces of buckskin hanging from their waists, which hardly covered what can not be looked at without peril. We bade them goodbye, telling them they must notify their people that we were coming in peace, that we harmed nobody and loved everybody, and therefore the men who were able to do so should come without fear to the place where we were going to camp. We continued along the plain and valley of Señor San José, and having traveled three more leagues to the south, we saw other Indians who were running away. We despatched the interpreter with the Laguna, Joaquín, and another companion, to try to bring an Indian to the campsite, which was now nearby, in order to inquire whether the Río Grande was as near as the Indian women had said, and to see if one of them would accompany us as a guide as far as Cosnina. They ran so fast that our men were barely able to stop one of them. Don Joaquín Laín brought that one behind him on his horse to the place where, having traveled another half-league to the south, we had already camped near a small stream which we called Río de Nuestra Señora del Pilar de Zaragoza,[67] where, as in all the valley, there was much good pasturage. — Today eight leagues south.

This Indian whom the companions brought to the camp, as we have just said, was very excited and so terror-stricken that he seemed to be insane. He looked in every direction, watched everybody, and was excessively frightened by every action or movement on our part and to escape what his extreme cowardliness led him to fear, he gave such close attention when

---

[67]In the vicinity of Kanarraville on one of the tributaries of Ash Creek.

we talked to him and responded so quickly that he appeared rather to guess at our questions than to understand them. He quieted down a little, and we gave him something to eat and a ribbon, putting it on him ourselves. He carried a large net very well made of hemp, which he said he used to catch hares and rabbits. When we asked him where he got these nets, he replied that it was from other Indians who live down the Río Grande, from whence, we also learned later, they obtained colored shells, and according to the distance and the direction in which he placed them, they appear to be the Cocomaricopas. With respect to the distance to the Río Grande and the blue clothing, he said the same as the Indian women, adding that some colored woolen threads which he possessed he had purchased this summer from two of those who wear the blue clothing and who had crossed the river. We questioned him in different ways about the Cosninas, but he gave us no information about them, either because these people knew them by another name, or perhaps because he feared that if he admitted he knew them, we would take him by force so that he might conduct us to them, or, finally, because he did not know them. We asked him if he had heard it said that toward the west or west-northwest (pointing in these directions) there were fathers and Spaniards, and he answered, "No," for although many people lived there, they were of the same language and tribe as himself. They showed him a kernel of maize, and he said that he had seen how it was grown, adding that at a rancho to which we would come next day there was a little of this grain, which they had brought from the place where it is raised. We made great efforts to get him to tell us the name of these people who were now planting maize, and to clarify other things of which he was giving a confused account, but we were able to learn only that they lived on this side of the Río Grande on another small river. He remained with us voluntarily all night and promised to lead us to the rancho mentioned.

October 13. We set out southward from the small river and campsite of Nuestra Señora del Pilar, accompanied by this Indian, to whom we had promised a hunting knife if he would guide us to where we might find other Indians. We traveled two and a half leagues south and arrived at the rancho mentioned, which belonged to him. In it there were an old Indian, a young man, several children and three women, all of them very good looking.

They had very good piñon nuts, dates, and some little sacks of maize. We remained in conversation with the old man for a long time, but he told us only what the others had. We gave the promised hunting knife to the one who had conducted us to this place, and told them that if any of the three would accompany us to those who they said planted maize, we would pay him well. From the response we saw that they were still very suspicious and much afraid of us, but at the suggestion of the companions we put before them a hunting knife and some glass beads. The old man seized them, and impelled by his great fear, he offered to guide us, in order to get us away from there, as later became evident to us, and to give his family time to reach a place of safety by withdrawing to the nearby sierra.

We continued on our way accompanied by this old man and the Indian who had passed the preceding night with us. We traveled a league and a half to the south, descended to the little Río del Pilar, which here has a leafy cottonwood grove, crossed it, now leaving the valley of Señor San José, and entered a stony cut in the form of a pass between two high sierras. In the roughest part of this cut the two guides disappeared and we never saw them again. We admired their cleverness in having brought us through a place well suited to the sure and free execution of their plan, which we had already suspected not only because of their cowardliness, but also from the manner in which they had consented to guide us. We continued without a guide, and having traveled with great difficulty over the many stones for a league to the south, we descended a second time to the Río del Pilar and halted on its bank in a pretty cottonwood grove, naming the place San Daniel.[68] — Today five leagues south.

The Valley of Señor San José through which we have just passed, in its most northern part is in 37° 33' of latitude. From north to south it is about twelve leagues long, and from east to west in some places it is more than three, in others two, and in still others, less. It has very abundant pasturage, large meadows, fair-sized marshes, and plenty of very good land for a settlement with seasonal crops, although there is not [enough] water

---

[68]On Ash Creek just across the ridge from the valley and some five miles north of the town of Pintura.

in the two small rivers of Señor San José and Pilar to irrigate more than a few small areas. However, the great moisture of the land may supply this lack so that the irrigation will not be missed, because the moisture in all the valley is so great that not only the meadows and the flats, but even the high places at this season had green and fresh pasturage, like the most fertile meadows of rivers in the months of June and July. Round about the valley and very near at hand there is plentiful timber, firewood of spruce and piñon, and good sites for raising large and small stock. The Indians who live in the valley and in its vicinity to the west, north, and east are called in their language Hauscari. They dress very poorly, and eat grass seeds, hares, piñon nuts in season, and dates. They do not plant maize, and judging from what we saw, they obtain very little of it. They are extremely cowardly and different from the Lagunas and Barbones. On the northwest and north they border on the latter and speak the same language, although with some differences. The Sierra de los Lagunas ends in this place of San Daniel, having run directly south from the Valley of Las Salinas to here. From here to the Río Grande all the land is poor, although it appears rich in minerals.

October 14. We set out from San Daniel going south by west along the west side of the river, swung a short distance away from it, and having traveled two leagues over hills of very brilliant white sand, very stony in places, we passed two large springs of good water which flow into the river. We swung south now over stony malpaís (which is like slag although heavier and less porous) but not very difficult, now among small sandy stretches, now over sand banks, and having traveled two more leagues we descended a third time to the river and halted on its banks where there was a very good pasture. We named the campsite San Hugolino.[69] Here the climate is very mild for although we felt great heat yesterday, last night and today the cottonwoods of the river were so green and leafy, the roses and flowers which grow here so flaming and undamaged that they showed that through here they had not yet been frozen nor frosted. We also saw mesquite trees, which do not grow in very cold lands. — Today four leagues south.

---

[69] On Ash Creek about midway between the towns of Toquerville and Pintura.

October 15. We set out from San Hugolino on the west bank of the river and along the slopes of some nearby hills, and having traveled two and one-half leagues to the south-southeast, we returned to the bank and to the grove* along the river. Here we found a well made mat with a large supply of ears and husks of green corn which had been placed on it. Near it, in the small plain and on the bank of the river, there were three small corn patches with their very well made irrigation ditches. The stalks of maize which they had already harvested this year were still untouched. For this reason we felt especially pleased, partly because it gave us hope that we should be able to provide ourselves farther on with assured supplies, and principally, because it was evidence of the application of these people to the cultivation of the soil, and because of finding this preparation for reducing them to civilized life and to the Faith when the Most High may so will, for it is already known what it costs to get other Indians to do this, and how much their conversion is impeded by their aversion to this labor which is so necessary for living a civilized life especially in pueblos. From here downstream and on the mesas on either side for a long distance, according to what we learned, live Indians who sustain themselves by planting maize and calabashes, and who in their language are called the Parussi.

We continued downstream toward the south, and having traveled half a league, we swung southwest, leaving the river, but a high cliff without any way to get down forced us to go back more than a quarter of a league and return to the river which here runs southwest. Two other small rivers join it here, one which comes from the north-northeast, and the other from the east. The latter consists in great part of hot and sulphurous water, and for this reason we named it Río Sulfúreo. Here there is a beautiful grove of large black cottonwoods, some willows, and wild grape vines. In the stretch where we retraced our steps there are ash heaps, veins and other signs of minerals, and many stones of reddish mica. We crossed the Río del Pilar and the Sulfúreo near the place where they join, then going south we ascended a low mesa between crags of shiny black rock. Having reached the top, we came to good open country, crossed a small plain which toward the east has a chain of very high mesas and to the west, hills

---

*Seville edition reads "alameda" which is evidently the correct wording.

of chamiso (the plant which in Spain is called *brezo*) and red sand. In the plain we might have gone to the edge of the mesas and finished our day's march over good level country, but the men who went ahead changed the direction in order to follow some fresh tracks of Indians and led us over these hills and sand flats where our animals now became very much fatigued.

After having traveled by the mesa and plain two leagues to the south we went three leagues southwest through the above-mentioned hills. We now turned south a little more than two leagues and descried a small valley surrounded by mesas, from one of which we found ourselves unable to descend to the valley. On it there was neither water nor pasturage for the animals, which now were unable to go forward, so we were forced to descend from a high, rugged and very stony ridge. Having traveled three-fourths of a league to the south, we stopped after sunset at an arroyo where we found large pools of good water with sufficient pasturage for the animals. We named the place San Dónulo,[70] or Arroyo del Taray, because here there were some tamarisk trees or *palo taray*. — Today ten leagues, which in a direct line would be seven leagues south by west. We observed by the north star and found ourselves 36° 52′ 30″ of latitude.

In this plain or little valley besides the tamarisk there is much *hediondilla*, which is a bush with very medicinal qualities, according to what has been learned in New Mexico. Tonight our supplies were completely exhausted, leaving us only two little cakes of chocolate for tomorrow.

October 16. We set out from San Dónulo with the intention of continuing south as far as the Río Colorado, but after traveling a short distance we heard some people shouting behind us; turning around to see where the noise came from, we saw eight Indians on the hills near the campsite which we had just left, and which are in the middle of the plain, extend almost entirely across it, and abound in transparent gypsum and mica. We returned to them, giving orders that the interpreter, who had gone ahead, should come also. We arrived at the foot of the little hill and told the Indians to descend without fear because we had come in peace and were friends. Thereupon they took courage and

---

[70]Camp was apparently near the site of Old Fort Pierce, southwest of the town of Hurricane on Fort Pierce Creek, just north of the Arizona state line.

descended, showing us for barter some sartas or strings of *chalchihuite* [stones of an emerald color], each string having a colored shell. This gave us something to think about, for from below, the strings of *chalchihuite* looked to us like rosaries and the shells like medals of saints. We remained here with them a short time, but they spoke the Yuta tongue so differently from all the rest that neither the interpreter nor Joaquín, the Laguna, could make them understand clearly nor understand much of what they said. Nevertheless, partly by signs, partly because about some matters they spoke the Yuta tongue more like the Lagunas, we understood them to say that all were Parusis (except one who spoke more of an Arabic tongue than Yuta, and which we thought was Jamajab) and that they are the ones who plant the crops on the banks of the Río del Pilar and live downstream for a long distance. We took them to be Cosninas but afterward we learned that this was not the case. They offered their chalchihuites for trade, and when we told them we did not have a thing there, but if they would come with us until we overtook the rest of the companions, we would give them what they asked for and would talk with them at length, all came very cheerfully though with great fear and suspicion on the part of those who appeared the most intelligent. We stopped and talked with them more than two and a half or three hours. They told us that in two days we would reach the Río Grande, but would not be able to go the way we wanted to, because there was no watering place, nor would we be able to cross the river in this region because it ran through a great canyon and was very deep and had on both sides extremely high cliffs and rocks, and finally, that from here to the river the terrain was very bad. We gave them a present of two hunting knives and to each one a string of glass beads, and then told them that if one of them would guide us to the river we would pay him. They replied that they would go and put us on the trail through a canyon which was in the mesa east of the plain, and that from there we could go alone, because they were barefoot and could not travel very well. In spite of this explanation we did not wish to give up going south as far as the river, for we suspected that the Moquinos might have become unfriendly toward the Cosninas because they had escorted Father Garcés and that, fearful that they might lead other fathers and Spaniards to Moqui, they had tried to keep them back with threats; and that these people having heard the news, now intended to lead us astray in order that we might not reach the Cosninas or their neighbors, the Jamajabas. But at the urging of the companions, to whom it was not desirable at present to make known our suspicions, we consented to go by the canyon. We offered these Indians soles of satchel leather for sandals if they would guide us. They said that two of them would go with us until they had put us on a good straight road. With them we entered the canyon mentioned, traveled through it a league and a half with extreme difficulty, the animals being hindered by the many pebbles and flint stones and the frequent difficult and dangerous stretches in it. We arrived at a narrow pass so bad that in more than half an hour we were able to make only three saddle animals enter it. This was followed by a rocky cliff so rough that even on foot it would have been difficult to ascend it. The Indians, seeing that we would not be able to follow them, fled, impelled doubtless by their excessive cowardice. Thereupon it was necessary for us to go back and turn once more to the south. Before doing so we stopped a short time in order that the animals might eat a little and drink some of the water which was here, but it was so bad that many of the animals would not touch it. In the afternoon we retraced the full length of the canyon, and having traveled half a league along the plain toward the south, we camped near the southern entrance of the valley,[71] without water for ourselves or for the animals. This night we were in great need, having no kind of food, so we decided to take the life of a horse in order not to lose our own, but because there was no water we deferred the execution until we should have some. Today, in so difficult a journey, we advanced only a league and one-half south.

October 17. We continued on our way toward the south, threaded the aforesaid pass from the little valley along the bed of an arroyo in which we found a pool of good water where all the animals drank. We traveled south two leagues and swinging southeast two more, we found in another arroyo a large supply of good water, not only in one place but in many, and although it is rain-water which accumulates during the floods, it appears not to dry up in the course of the whole year. Here we found

---

[71]Camp may have been at the southern end of Black Rock Canyon.

some of the herbs which they call *quelites*. We thought it possible by means of them to supply our most urgent need, but were able to gather only a few and these were very small. We continued southeast, and having traveled four and a half leagues over good level country, although it was somewhat spongy, we stopped partly to see if there was water in the washes from the mesa and partly to give Don Bernardo Miera some of these ripe herbs as food, for since yesterday morning we had not had a thing to eat and he was now so weak that he was scarcely able to talk. We ordered the bags and other containers in which we had brought the supplies ransacked, to see if there were any left-overs, but found only some pieces of calabash which the servants had obtained yesterday from the Parusis Indians, and which they had hidden to avoid having to share them with the rest. With this and a little sugar, which we also found, we made a stew for everybody and took a little nourishment. We did not find water so we could spend the night here and therefore decided to continue the journey toward the south. The companions, without telling us, went to examine the eastern mesa and the country beyond. Those who went to make the reconnaissance returned saying that the ascent of the mesa was very good and that afterward the land was level, with many arroyos in which there could not fail to be water, and that it appeared to them that the river was at the end of the plain which lay beyond the mesa. Thereupon everybody favored changing our direction, but we knew very well how they had been deceived on other occasions and that in so short a time they could not have seen so much; and we were of the opposite opinion because toward the south we had much good level land in sight, and had found so much water today, contrary to the story told by the Indians, and had traveled all day over good land. All of these facts increased our suspicion. But since now we were without food, and water might be far away, and so that the adoption of our plan should not make the thirst and hunger which (for our sake) they might endure on either route more intolerable for them, we told them to take the one they thought best calculated to take us southeast toward the mesa. We ascended it by a rough and very stony wash or arroyo in which there is very good gypsum rock of the kind which is used for white-washing. We had just finished climbing the mesa by a very rough black stone slope when night fell, and we camped there on the mesa in a small plain of good pasturage but without water, naming it San Ángel.[72] — Today nine leagues.

We were very sorry to have changed our route because, according to the latitude in which we now found ourselves, by continuing to the south we would very soon have arrived at the river. As soon as we halted, those who had previously been on the mesa told us that at a short distance from here they thought they had seen water. Two of them went to bring some for the men, but they did not return all night, and the next day dawned without our having heard from them. Since we concluded that they had continued seeking Indian ranchos where they could relieve their hunger as soon as possible, for this reason, and since there was no water here, we decided to go forward without waiting for them.

October 18. We set out from San Ángel to the east-southeast and having traveled half a league, we swung to the east by south for two leagues over hills and extensive valleys with plentiful but very stony pasturage. Then, not finding water, we swung east by north for two more leagues, ascending and descending stony hills which were very troublesome for the animals. There were five Indians spying upon us from a small but high mesa, and as we two passed the foot of it, for we were following behind our companions, these Indians spoke to us. When we turned toward where they were, four of them hid, only one remaining in sight. We saw how terrified he was, but we could not persuade him to come down, and the two of us ascended on foot with very great difficulty. At each step we took toward him he wanted to run away. We gave him to understand that he must not be afraid, that we loved him like a son, and wished to talk with him. Thereupon he waited for us, making a thousand gestures which showed that he was greatly afraid of us. As soon as we had ascended to where he was we embraced him and, seating ourselves beside him, we had the interpreter and the Laguna come up. Having now recovered his composure, he told us that the other four were hiding near by and that if we desired it, he would call them in order that we might see them. When we answered in the affirmative, he laid his bow and arrows on the ground, took the interpreter

---

[72]On the top of Hurricane Cliff, a short distance northeast of Diamond Butte.

by the hand, and went with him to bring them. They came and we remained about an hour in conversation, and they told us that we now had water near at hand. We begged them to go and show it to us, promising them a piece of woolen cloth and after much urging three of them consented to go with us. We continued with them a league to the southeast, much fatigued by thirst and hunger, and having traveled another league to the south over a bad and very stony road, we arrived at a little grove of cedar and at an arroyo where deep holes held two large pools of good water. We took enough for ourselves and brought the horses which, since they were now very thirsty, drained both pools. Here we decided to spend the night, naming the campsite San Samuel.[73] — Today six leagues.

The three Indians mentioned came with us so fearfully that they did not wish to go ahead nor to have us come near them until they questioned Joaquín, the Laguna, but with what he told them about us they quieted down. Greatly surprised at his valor, they asked him, among other things, how he had dared to come with us? He, wanting to rid them of their fears in order to relieve the privation which, greatly to our sorrow, he was suffering, answered them as best he could; and thus he greatly lessened the fear and suspicion they had felt. Doubtless it was because of this that they did not leave us before arriving at the watering place. As soon as we camped we gave them the promised woolen cloth with which they were greatly pleased. Learning that we came without provisions, they told us to send one of our men with one of theirs to their huts which were somewhat distant, and they would bring some food, the rest meanwhile remaining with us. We sent one of the genízaros with Joaquín, the Laguna, giving them the wherewithal to purchase provisions and pack animals on which to bring them. They left with the other Indian, and after midnight they returned, bringing a small supply of wild sheep, dried tuna* made into cakes, and grass seeds. They also brought news of one of the two men who the preceding night had gone for water, saying he had been at this rancho. The other had arrived at camp about ten o'clock tonight.

October 19. Twenty of these Indians came to camp with some cakes or loaves of tuna and several bags of the seeds of various

---
[73]Apparently at Cooper's Pockets, some twenty miles north of Mt. Trumbull.
*Prickly pear.

herbs to sell to us. We paid them for what they brought and told them that if they had meat, piñon nuts or more tunas, they should bring them and we would buy them all, especially the meat. They said they would do so but that we must wait for them until mid-day. We agreed and they went away. One of them promised to accompany us as far as the river if we would wait until afternoon, and we agreed to this also. After mid-day many more Indians came to camp than those who previously had been with us, among them being one who was said to be a Mescalero Apache, and to have come with two others from his country to this one, crossing the river a few days previously. His features were not very pleasing, and he was distinguished from the rest of the Indians by the disgust which he showed at seeing us here and by the greater display of animosity which we noticed he was purposely making. They told us that these Apaches were their friends. They did not bring meat but many bags of the seeds mentioned and some fresh tunas, partly exposed to the sun, and dried ones made into cakes. We purchased from them about a fanega of seeds and all of the tunas. We talked a long while concerning the distance to the river, the road to it, their numbers and mode of living, the neighboring peoples, and the guide for whom we were asking. They showed us the direction we must take to the river, giving confused reports of the ford, and saying that in two or three days we would arrive there. They told us they were called Yubuincariris and that they did not plant maize; that their foods were seeds, tunas, piñon nuts, of which they gathered very few, judging from the small quantity they gave us, and what hares, rabbits and wild sheep they hunted, adding that on this side of the river only the Parusis planted maize and calabashes; that on the other side just across the river were the Ancamuchis (who, we understood, were the Cosninas) and that they planted much maize. Besides these, they gave us the names of other people, their neighbors to the south-southwest, on this west bank of the river, saying these were the Payatammumis. They also told us of the Huascaris, whom we had already seen in the Valley of Señor San José. Concerning the Spaniards of Monterey they did not give us even the least indication that they had ever heard them mentioned. One of the Indians who had spent the preceding night with us gave us to understand that he had already heard of the journey of the Reverend Father Garcés, which, together with the denial by all these that they knew the Cosninas (unless they know them by the above name of Ancamuchi), seems to verify what we have already said we suspected. Having finished the conversation, they began to leave, and we were unable to get any of them to consent to accompany us as far as the river. Today Don Bernardo Miera was sick at his stomach, so we were unable to leave here this afternoon. A little farther away we found other pools of water for tonight.

October 20. We set out from San Samuel toward the north-northeast, directing our way toward the ford of the Río Colorado, avoiding a low wooded sierra with many stones on this side of it. Having traveled a little more than two leagues, we swung northeast, entering a level country without rocks, and traveled four leagues, when we found in an arroyo several pools of good water. Then traveling a league to the east-northeast, we camped on the bank of the arroyo between two little hills in the plain nearby,[74] where there was a large supply of water and good pasturage. We named this place Santa Gertrudis, whose latitude we observed by the north star, finding it is in 36° 30′. — Today seven leagues.

October 21. We set out from Santa Gertrudis toward the east, and after traveling half a league we swung to the northeast. Several times we crossed the Arroyo de Santa Gertrudis, which in most places had large pools of water, and wound our way along the twists and turns over very poor terrain for five and a half leagues to the northeast. Then we went a little more than four leagues to the east-northeast through some not very troublesome chamise thickets and good land, and camped after nightfall near a little valley[75] with good pasturage but without water even for the men. Lorenzo Olivares, driven by his thirst because he had eaten too many of the seeds, piñon nuts, and tuna which we had bought, went looking for water in the nearby arroyos as soon as we camped and did not appear all night, causing us much worry. We named the campsite Santa Bárbara. — Today ten leagues.

October 22. We set out from Santa Bárbara toward the north-northeast looking for Olivares, and after going about two leagues we found him near a pool with a small amount of water,

---

[74]In Antelope Valley on one of the western headwaters of Kanab Creek.
[75]In Kimball Valley near Johnson Creek and some eight miles southeast of Fredonia.

there being only enough for the men to drink and to fill a little barrel which we carried in case we should not find water tonight. We continued through the plain, and having traveled four leagues northeast, we saw a trail which ran to the south, and when the interpreter said the Yubuincariris had told him this was the one we ought to take to go to the river, we took it. But having traveled along it a league to the south we found that the interpreter was uncertain about the signs because, after going a little distance, the trail turned back. And so, going east, we ascended the low sierra which we were intending to avoid. It runs from north to south the whole length of the eastern side of this plain. We crossed it with great labor and fatigue for the animals because, besides having many canyons, it is very stony and full of pebbles. Night overtook us as we were going down the other side of a very high ridge from which we saw below us several fires on the far side of a small plain. We thought the interpreter, Andrés, and the Laguna, Joaquín, who had gone ahead seeking water for the night, had made them in order that we might know where they were. But having finished the descent, and having traveled five leagues to the east-northeast from the place where we left the trail mentioned, making several turns in the mountain valleys, we arrived at the fires where there were three little Indian huts and where we found our interpreter and Joaquín. We decided to spend the night here because nearby on both the east and the west there were water and pasturage for the animals which were now almost completely worn out. We named the campsite San Juan Capistrano.[76] — Today twelve leagues.

Since it was night when we arrived at these huts, and the Indians were unable to distinguish the number of men who were coming, they were so afraid that in spite of the coaxing by the interpreter and the Laguna, Joaquín, most of them fled on our arrival, there remaining only three men and two women, who, greatly disturbed, said to our Laguna, "Little brother, you are of the same race as ourselves. Do not permit these people with whom you come to kill us." We embraced them and tried by every possible means which occurred to us to remove the suspicion and fear which they felt toward us. They quieted down somewhat,

---

[76] Near the state line in Utah, on one of the western branches of Paria River approximately in longitude 112°.

and trying to please us, they gave us two roasted hares and some piñon nuts. Besides this two of them went, although with great fear, to show the servants the watering place in order that the animals might drink. This campsite is east of the northern point of the small sierra mentioned, near a number of small hills of red earth, to the south of which, very close by, on some rocky hills having some piñon and juniper trees, are two good pools of rain water. Nearer to them in a small arroyo there are also some pools of water, but these are small and not very good. To the west-southwest of the same little hills, at the foot of the sierra, there is also a small permanent spring.

After we had retired, some of the companions, among them Don Bernardo Miera, went to one of the huts to chat with the Indians. They told him that Don Bernardo was ill, and an old Indian, one of those present, either because our men ordered it or because he wanted to, set about doctoring him with songs and ceremonies which, if not openly idolatrous (for such they might be) were at least entirely superstitious. All of our people permitted them willingly, and among them the sick man, and they applauded them as harmless compliments, when they ought to have stopped them as contrary to the evangelical and divine law which they profess, or at least they ought to have withdrawn. We listened to the songs of the Indian but did not know what their purpose was. Early in the morning they told us what had taken place. We were deeply grieved by such harmful carelessness, and we reprimanded them, telling them that at another time they must not sanction such errors by their voluntary presence nor in any other way. This is one of the reasons why the heathen who deal most with the Spaniards and Christians of these regions, more stubbornly resist the evangelical truth, making their conversion more difficult each day. When we were preaching to the first Sabuaganas we saw regarding the necessity of holy baptism, the interpreter either in order not to displease them nor to lose the ancient friendship which they maintain with them through the vile commerce in skins (even in violation of just prohibitions by the governors of this kingdom, by whom it has been ordered re-repeatedly that no Indian, genízaro, or citizen shall enter the lands of the heathen without having obtained a license for it from the governor of his province), translated for them in these very words:

"The Father says that the Apaches, Navajós and Cumanches who do not become baptized cannot enter Heaven, but go to Hell, where God punishes them, and where they will burn forever like wood in the fire." The Sabuaganas were greatly pleased at hearing themselves thus exempted from and their enemies included in the inescapable necessity either of being baptized or of being lost and suffering eternally. The interpreter was reprimanded, and seeing that his foolish infidelity had been discovered, he reformed. We might give other examples from the lips of these same persons who have been among the Yutas and who perhaps had applauded and even cooperated in many idolatrous actions, but the two referred to above, of which we are obviously certain, will suffice. For if, in our company, after having many times heard these idolatries and superstitions refuted and condemned, they witness them, encourage them, and applaud them, what will they not do when they wander two, three or four months among the heathen Yutas and Navajós with nobody to correct and restrain them? Besides this, some of them have given us sufficient cause in this journey to suspect that while some go to the Yutas and remain so long among them because of their greed for peltry, others go and remain with them for that of the flesh, obtaining there its brutal satisfaction. And so in every way they blaspheme the name of Christ and prevent, or rather oppose, the extension of His faith. Oh, with what severity ought such evils be met! May God in His infinite goodness inspire the best and most suitable means!

October 23. We did not travel today, in order to give time for the people here to quiet down and to enable those of the vicinity to assemble. The grass seeds and other things which we had purchased and eaten made us very sick, weakening instead of nourishing us. We were not able to induce these people to sell us any ordinary meat, so we had a horse killed and the flesh prepared so that it could be carried. Today Father Fray Francisco Atanasio was very ill from a pain in the rectum so severe that he was not able even to move.

All day the Indians kept coming from the nearby ranchos, all of whom we embraced and entertained to the best of our ability. These people now gave us a clearer account of the Cosninas and Moquinos, calling them by these very names. They also told us where we had to go to reach the river, (which is twelve leagues from here at most) giving us a description of the ford. We bought from them about a fanega of piñon nuts and gave them as a present more than half a fanega of grass seeds.

Very early the next day twenty-six Indians assembled, among them being some who were with us yesterday afternoon, and others whom we had not seen. We told them of the Gospel, reprimanding and explaining to them the wickedness and idleness of their sins, especially in the superstitious doctoring of their sick. We admonished them to rely in their troubles upon the true and only God, because only He has at His command health and sickness, life and death, and is able to help everybody. And although our interpreter could not explain this to them clearly, one of them, who doubtless had dealt extensively with the Yutas Payuchis, understood it well and explained to the others what he had heard. Since we saw that they listened with pleasure, we told them that if they wished to be Christians, fathers and Spaniards would come to instruct and live with them. They replied that they would like this, and when we asked them where we would find them when we should come they said they would be in this little sierra and on the nearby mesas. Then to increase their affection for us, we distributed thirteen varas of red ribbon, giving to each one half a vara, with which they were very much pleased and grateful. One man had already agreed to go with us as far as the river to direct us to the ford, but after all the others had said goodbye, and he had traveled with us half a league, he became so frightened that we could not persuade him to continue. The companions, inconsiderately, wanted to use force to make him keep his word, but knowing his reluctance, we let him go freely.

October 24. About nine o'clock in the morning, or a little later, we set out from San Juan Capistrano toward the south-southeast, through a valley and having traveled four leagues we turned to the southeast in the same valley. Here at the foot of the eastern mesa in the valley there are three pools of good water, but there was not enough for the animals. From the campsite to here we traveled over good country. Having advanced two more leagues to the southeast, we swung to the east-southeast for about three leagues over sandy and difficult country, and although we did not find water for the animals, we did find pasturage, so we camped because the horses were very tired and it was already nightfall. We named the campsite San Bartolomé.[77] Here there is an extensive valley but the land is poor, for the part which is not sandy is a kind of earth which on the surface has about four fingers [about three inches] of gravel and beneath it loose soil of different colors. There are many deposits of transparent gypsum, some of mica and apparently there are also some of metals. — Today nine leagues.

Through this region the Río Colorado flows from north-northeast to south-southwest and runs through a deep canyon so that although the land might be good, the river banks are of no use for planting. This afternoon we thought we saw the canyons and cliffs of the river bed which, seen from the west side, look like a long row of houses, but we concluded that it was the canyon of one of the many arroyos which are in the plain.

October 25. We set out from San Bartolomé to the east-southeast and traveled less than a league and a half to the east. We did not try to reach the canyon which [we afterward learned] was really the channel of the Río Grande, because we had crossed several arroyos which had canyons as large as that one. So we concluded that the river did not run there but in some other arroyo. Therefore, we turned toward the north-northeastern portion of the valley for it appeared to us that it was possible to avoid the mesas which surround it. Seeking water for the animals which were now tired out from thirst, we followed the bed of an arroyo, and having traveled along it two leagues to the northeast we were unable to get out so we went on westward climbing a very difficult slope. We turned again to the north-northeast and having traveled two leagues we saw some cottonwoods at the foot of the mesa. We went toward them and found there a good spring of water. Around its edges there was a substance something like saltpeter and we thought the water would be salty, but when we tried it we found it had a good taste. We camped here, naming the place San Fructo.[78] — Today five leagues.

In the afternoon Don Juan Pedro Cisneros went to explore

---

[77]They camped on the southwestern edge of the Paria Plateau near House Rock.
[78]Camp was at the foot of a mesa on the southern edge of Paria Plateau probably at Jacob's Pools.

the northern corner of the valley to see if there was a pass and if he could find or get a glimpse of the river and its ford. He returned after midnight with the desired report that he had reached the river, but said that he did not know whether or not we would be able to cross some mesas and high crests which were on the other bank. Nevertheless, because he said the river appeared to him to be all right and to have a ford here we decided to go to it.

October 26. We set out from San Fructo toward the north, traveled three and a half leagues, and reached the place where previously we thought the northern exit from the valley was. It is a bend completely surrounded by very high cliffs and crests of red earth of various formations; and since the intervening plain below is of the same color, it has an agreeably confused appearance. We continued in the same direction with excessive difficulty because the animals, breaking through the surface gravel, sank to their knees in the ground, and having traveled a league and a half we arrived at the Río Grande de los Cosninas. Here it is joined by another small river which we named Santa Teresa. We crossed this latter stream and camped on the banks of the Río Grande near a high gray rock, naming the campsite San Benito Salsipuedes.[79] All the terrain from San Fructo to here is very difficult and in places where a little moisture has been left from snow or rain it is entirely impassable. — Today five leagues north.

We decided to reconnoiter this afternoon to learn whether, having crossed the river, we might continue from here to the southeast or east. On all sides we were surrounded by mesas and inaccessible heights. Therefore, two men who knew how to swim well entered the river naked, carrying their clothing on their heads. It was so deep and wide that the swimmers, in spite of their prowess, were scarcely able to reach the opposite shore, and they lost their clothing in the middle of the river, never seeing it again. Since they arrived very tired, naked, and barefoot they were unable to walk the distance necessary for the reconnaissance and returned after having eaten something.

October 27. Don Juan Pedro Cisneros went up the bed of the Río de Santa Teresa to see whether by way of it he could

---

[79]On Colorado River close to the place where the Paria River joins it at Lees Ferry.

find a pass by which to cross the eastern mesa and return to the Río Grande in more open country where, being wider, the river might be fordable or at least where it would be possible for the horses to cross without the danger, encountered here, of being drowned in its waters. He traveled all day and part of the night without finding a way out. He saw an acclivity very near here by which it would be possible to cross the mesa but it appeared to him to be very difficult. Others went to reconnoiter in different directions but found only insuperable obstacles in the way of reaching the ford without going back a long distance.

October 28. We returned to the same undertaking, but all in vain. In a short time a raft of logs was constructed and with it Father Fray Silvestre, accompanied by the servants, attempted to cross the river. But since the poles which served for propelling the raft, although they were five varas long, failed to touch the bottom a short distance from the shore, the waves caused by the contrary wind drove it back. So it returned three times to the shore it had left, but was unable to reach even the middle of the river. Aside from being so deep and so wide, the river here has on both banks such deep, miry places that in them we might lose all or the greater part of the animals. We had been assured by the Yubuincariri and Pagampachi Indians that the river everywhere else was very deep, but not at the ford, for when they crossed it the water reached only a little above their waists. For this reason and on account of other landmarks which they gave us, we conjectured that the ford must be higher up, so we dispatched Andrés Muñiz and his brother Lucrecio with orders to travel until they found a place where we might cross the mesa mentioned above, and that, when they arrived at the river, they should seek a good ford, or at least some place where we could cross on the raft and the animals could swim without danger.

October 29. Not knowing when we might leave this place, and having consumed all the flesh of the first horse, and the piñon nuts and other things we had purchased, we ordered another horse killed.

October 30 and 31. We remained here awaiting the men who went to look for a pass and a ford.

November 1. They returned at one o'clock in the afternoon, saying that they had found a pass, although a difficult one, and a ford in the river. The pass over the mesa was the acclivity which Cisneros had seen, and since it was very high and rugged, we decided to approach it this afternoon. We set out from the bank of the Rio Grande and the unfortunate campsite of San Benito de Salsipuedes, followed the Río de Santa Teresa, and having traveled a league northwest we camped on its bank at the foot of this acclivity.[80] — Today one league.

This night, from sunset until seven o'clock in the morning, we suffered greatly from the cold.

November 2. We set out from Río de Santa Teresa and climbed the acclivity, which we called Cuesta de las Ánimas and which must be half a league long. We spent more than three hours in climbing it because at the beginning it is very rugged and sandy and afterward has very difficult stretches and extremely perilous ledges of rock, and finally it becomes impassable. Having finished the ascent toward the east, we descended the other side through rocky gorges with extreme difficulty. Swinging north, and having gone a league, we turned northeast for half a league through a stretch of red sand which was very troublesome for the animals. We ascended a little elevation, and having traveled two and a half leagues also to the northeast, we descended to an arroyo which in places had running water which although saline was fit to drink. There was pasturage also, so we camped here, naming the place San Diego.[81] — Today four and a half leagues.

Today we camped about three leagues in a direct line northeast from San Benito Salsipuedes near a multitude of narrow valleys, little mesas and peaks of red earth which at first sight look like the ruins of a fortress.

November 3. We set out from San Diego to the east-southeast, and having traveled two leagues we came a second time to the river, that is to say, at the edge of the canyon which here serves it as a bed, whose descent to the river is very long, high, rough and rocky, and has such bad ledges of rock that two pack animals which went down to the first one were unable to climb up it in return, even without the pack saddles. The men who had

---

[80]On Paria River about three miles upstream from its junction with the Colorado River.

[81]Apparently on Wahweap Creek some distance above the point where it enters the Colorado River.

come here previously had not told us of this precipice, and we now learned that they had neither found the ford, nor in so many days even made the necessary reconnaissance of such a short stretch of country, because they spent the time seeking some of the Indians who live hereabouts, and accomplished nothing. The river was very deep here, although not so deep as at Salsipuedes, but for a long distance it was necessary for the animals to swim. The good thing about it was that they did not mire, either going in or getting out. The companions insisted that we should go down to the river, but on the other side there was no way to go forward after having crossed the river, except by a deep and narrow canyon of another little river which here joins it. And not having learned whether or not this could be traveled, we feared that (if we descended and crossed the river) we should find ourselves forced to go back, which on this cliff would be extremely difficult. In order not to expose ourselves to this predicament, we stopped above and sent the genízaro, Juan Domingo, to cross the river to see if that canyon had an outlet. But if this afternoon he should not find one, he was to return in order that we might continue upstream on this bank until we should find the ford and trail of the Indians. We sent Juan Domingo on foot. Thereupon Lucrecio Muñiz said that with our permission he would go also, on a horse, bareback, carrying equipment for making a fire, and if he found an exit he would send up smoke signals for us, in order that upon this advice we might try to descend so that the delay would be less. We told him to go, but informed him that whether or not he found the exit we would wait for him this afternoon. They did not return, so we spent the night here, not being able to water the animals although the river was so close by. We named the campsite El Vado de los Cosninas, or San Carlos.[82] — Today two leagues east-southeast.

November 4. Day broke without our getting news of the two we sent yesterday to make the reconnaissance. We had used up the flesh of the second horse, and today we had not taken any nourishment whatsoever, so we broke our fast with toasted leaves of small cactus plants and a sauce made of a berry they brought from the banks of the river. This berry is by itself very pleasant to taste, but crushed and boiled in water as we ate it today it is

---

[82] On the cliffs of Glen Canyon.

very insipid. Since it was already late, and the two emissaries had not appeared, we ordered that an attempt should be made to get the animals down to the river, and that on its banks another horse should be killed. With great difficulty they got the animals down, some of them being injured because, losing their footing on the rocks, they rolled down long distances. Shortly before nightfall the genízaro, Juan Domingo, returned, declaring that he had not found an exit, and that the other emissary, leaving his horse in the middle of the canyon, had followed some fresh Indian tracks. Thereupon we decided to continue upstream until we should find a good ford and passable terrain on both banks.[83]

November 5. We set out from San Carlos although Lucrecio had not returned. His brother Andrés remained with orders to await him only until afternoon, and to attempt to overtake us before morning. We traveled on this west bank over many ridges and gullies for a league and a half to the north, then descended to a dry arroyo and a very deep canyon, in which there was a great deal of copperas. In it we found a little-used trail, followed it, and by it left the canyon, passing a small bench of white rock, difficult but capable of being made passable. We continued on our way and having traveled a league and a quarter to the north-northeast, we found sufficient pasturage and some water, although not much, and since it was almost night we camped near a high mesa, naming the campsite Santa Francisca Romana.[84] — Today three short leagues.

Tonight it rained heavily here and in some places it snowed. At day break it was raining and continued to do so for several hours. About six o'clock in the morning Andrés Muñiz arrived, saying his brother had not appeared. This report caused us great anxiety, because by now he had traveled three days without provisions and with no more shelter than a shirt for he had not even worn trousers. Although he crossed the river on horseback the horse swam for a long stretch and where it faltered the water reached almost to its shoulders. And so the genízaro decided to go to look for him, following the trail from the place where he had last seen him, and we sent him off, giving him meat from our sup-

---

[83] They spent this night on the river bank in Glen Canyon, below the campsite of the previous night.
[84] At the foot of a high mesa near Warm Creek Canyon, across the Utah state line.

ply and instructing him that if the horse could not get out of the canyon he should leave it and follow on foot; that if he found Lucrecio on the other bank, from that side they should look for signs of us and follow us, and if on this side, they should try to overtake us as quickly as possible.

November 6. The rain having ceased we set out from Santa Francisca toward the northeast, and having traveled three leagues we were stopped for a long time by a heavy storm and a torrent of rain and large hail, with horrible thunder and lightning. We chanted the Litany of the Virgin in order that She might ask some relief for us and God was pleased that the storm should cease. We continued half a league toward the east and camped near the river[85] because it continued to rain and our way was blocked by some boulders. We named the campsite San Vicente Ferrer. — Today three and a half leagues.

Don Juan Pedro Cisneros went to see if the ford was in this vicinity, and returned with the report that he had seen that here the river was very wide, and judging from the current it did not appear to him to be deep, but that we would be able to reach it only through a nearby canyon. We sent two other persons to examine the canyon and ford the river, and they returned saying that it was very difficult. But we did not give much credence to their report and decided to examine everything ourselves next day in company with Don Juan Pedro Cisneros. Before nightfall the genízaro arrived with Lucrecio.

November 7. We went very early to inspect the canyon and the ford, taking along the two genízaros Felipe and Juan Domingo, so that they might ford the river on foot since they were good swimmers. In order to lead the animals down the side of the canyon mentioned it was necessary to cut steps in a rock with axes for the distance of three varas or a little less. The rest of the way the animals were able to get down, although without pack or rider. We went down to the canyon and having traveled a mile we descended to the river and went along it downstream about two musket shots sometimes in the water, sometimes on the bank, until we reached the widest part of its current where the ford appeared to be. One of the men waded in and found it good,

---

[85]On the cliffs above the Colorado River at the spot now known as the Crossing of the Fathers.

not having to swim at any place. We followed him on horseback a little lower down, and when half way across, two horses which went ahead lost their footing and swam a short distance. We waited, although in some peril, until the first wader returned from the other side to guide us and then we crossed with ease, the horses on which we crossed not having to swim at all. We notified the rest of our companions, who had remained at San Vicente, that with lassoes and ropes they should let the pack saddles and other effects, down a not very high cliff to the bend of the ford, and that they should bring the animals by the route over which we had come. They did so and about five o'clock in the afternoon they finished crossing the river, praising God our Lord and firing off a few muskets as a sign of the great joy which we all felt at having overcome so great a difficulty and which had cost us so much labor and delay, although the principal cause of our having suffered so much since we reached the Parusis was our lack of someone to guide us through such bad terrain. For through lack of an experienced guide we went by a very roundabout route, spent many days in such a small area, and suffered hunger and thirst. And now, after having suffered all this, we learned the best and most direct route where there were water holes adjusted to an ordinary day's travel. Most of this we heard of as we traveled, especially after we left our southerly direction on the day we set out from San Dónulo or Arroyo del Taray. Because from that place we might have gone to the large water hole which we found in the next plain. From here we might conveniently have reached another water hole which is about three leagues to the northeast of San Ángel. From this latter place we might have reached Santa Gertrudis. From here we might have gone on three leagues and stopped in the same arroyo with good water and sufficient pasturage, going on in the afternoon as far as possible to the northeast, following the same direction, avoiding the sierra entirely, and arriving next day at the Río de Santa Teresa three or four leagues north of San Juan Capistrano. From this river we could have gone east-southeast to San Diego and from there to the ford without any special inconvenience and avoiding many windings, acclivities and bad stretches. But doubtless God disposed that we should not obtain a guide, perhaps as a benign punishment for our sins, or perhaps in order that we might acquire some knowledge of the people who live in these parts. May His holy will be done in all things and His holy name glorified.

The ford of the river is very good and here it must be a mile wide, or a little more. Before reaching this place the Navajó and Dolores rivers have united, together with all those which we have mentioned in this diary as entering one or the other. And in no place which we have seen along here is it possible to establish on the banks any settlement whatsoever, or even to travel on either bank a good day's journey either downstream or upstream with the hope that its water might serve for men and animals, because, aside from the bad terrain, the river runs in a very deep gorge. All the region nearest to the ford has very high cliffs and peaks. Eight or ten leagues to the northeast of the ford there is a high, rounded peak which the Payuchis, whose country begins here, call Tucané, which means Black Peak, and it is the only one hereabouts which can be seen close at hand from the river crossing.

On this eastern bank, at the very ford which we called La Purísima Concepción de la Virgen Santísima, there is a fair-sized valley of good pasturage. In it we spent the night[86] and observed its latitude by the north star, and it is 36° and 55'.

BRIEF ACCOUNT OF THE PEOPLE WHOM WE SAW, DEALT WITH, AND LEARNED OF BY REPORT, FROM THE VALLEY OF SEÑOR SAN JOSÉ TO THE FORD OF THE RÍO GRANDE DE COSNINA, INCLUSIVE.

In this land, which, although we traveled in it one hundred long leagues counting the turns we made, must be sixty Spanish leagues from north to south, and forty from east to west, there live a large number of people, all of pleasing appearance, very friendly, and extremely timid. For this last reason, and because all whom we saw spoke the Yuta language in the same way as the western-most Payuchis, we call all these of whom we are speaking Yutas Cobardes. The particular names correspond to the country which they inhabit, and distinguish them as belonging

---

[86] After fording the Colorado River they camped a little farther downstream on the opposite bank.

to various provinces or territories, not as different nations, since all the Yutas known hitherto compose a single nation, or they might be called a kingdom divided into five provinces, known by the common name of Yutas: the Yutas Muhuachis, the Yutas Payuchis, the Tabehuachis, the Sabuaganas, and the Yutas Cobardes. These last are divided into the Huascaris, who live in the Valley of Señor San José and its vicinity; the Parusis, who follow them on the south and southwest, inhabit the banks and vicinity of the little river of Nuestra Señora del Pilar, and are the only ones among all these we saw who apply themselves to the planting of maize; the Yubuincariris, who live almost south of the Parusis and through here are the nearest to the Río Grande; the Yutas Ytimpabichis, who live on the mesas and peaks which are near to and north of the campsite of Santa Bárbara; the Pagampachis, who likewise live in the bad country of mesas and barren gorges, because although they have a spacious valley through which the Río Grande runs, as we have already said, they are not able to utilize the waters of this river for irrigation. According to the account given by the Yubuincariris, to the south-southwest of them downstream there live other people whom they call Payatammunis. To the west and west-northwest of the Huascaris, we learned also, there live other people of the same language as themselves. All the rest (and they are many) who live on this western or northern side, upstream, in all the sierra which runs down from the Lagunas, and the land which lies between it and the last northern rivers which we crossed before they joined, are, according to the reports which we obtained, of this same sort of Indians, and belong partly to the Yutas Barbones, partly to the Huascaris, and partly to the Lagunas, depending upon their proximity to each one of these groups, judging by the greater similarity with which those nearest speak the general language.

November 8. We set out from the ford and camp of La Concepción, and ascended from the bed of the river by a long ridge which was not very difficult, then turned south-southeast following a well-beaten trail, and traveled five leagues over sandy land with some rugged places. Swinging now to the east for a league, we halted near the last cliff of the range which runs from the river to this place, naming the campsite San Miguel,[87] in

---
[87] On the mesa to the north of Navajo Creek.

which there was good pasturage and plentiful rain water. — Today six leagues.

Today we found many tracks of Indians but saw none. Through here wild sheep live in such abundance that their tracks are like those of great flocks of domestic sheep. They are larger than the domestic breed, of the same form, but much swifter. Today we finished the horse meat we had brought, so we ordered another horse killed. Tonight we felt much colder than on the other bank.

November 9. We lost the trail and were unable to find a way by which to descend to a canyon which lay immediately to the southeast of us, or to cross more than a half league of rocks and ridges which prevented us from continuing along our route. For this reason we turned east-northeast, and having traveled two leagues over bad terrain, the same difficulty obliged us to halt on a mesa without being able to take a step forward.[88] Near this mesa we found some ranchos of Yutas Payuchis, neighbors and friends of the Cosninas. We made great efforts through the Laguna and other companions to induce them to come near to where we were, but either because they suspected that we were friends of the Moquinos, toward whom they are very hostile, or because they had never seen Spaniards and greatly feared us, we were unable to induce them to come.

November 10. Very early we two went with the interpreter and the Laguna to their ranchos, but we were unable even on foot to get to the place where they were. We sent the two persons mentioned away, we ourselves remaining on an elevation from which we saw them and were seen by them, in order that seeing us alone they might approach with greater willingness and less fear. After the interpreter had urged them for more than two hours, five of them came, but when they were about to reach us they turned and fled, and we were unable to stop them. The interpreter went back to see if they would sell us some provisions but they replied that they had none. They told him that the Cosninas lived very near here, but at present were wandering not far away in the woods, gathering piñon nuts, and that a short distance from here we would find two roads, one leading to the Cosninas and

---

[88] Near an Indian village some five miles east of the previous campsite and still on the rim of the canyon of Navajo Creek.

Photo *Hal Rumel*

MONUMENT VALLEY
Which borders Escalante's route on the east

the other to the Pueblo of Oraybi, in Moqui. They also gave him signs of the trail which we had lost, saying that we would have to go back as far as San Miguel and from there descend to the canyon mentioned. In this way we spent most of the day, and during the remainder we returned to the campsite of San Miguel, going half a league closer to the arroyo or canyon to which formerly we had been unable to descend. We camped at the beginning of the descent.[89] —Today half a league southeast.

November 11. Very early the descent was examined and the lost trail was found, and we continued on our way. We descended to the canyon with great difficulty because it has some dangerous places and is made up entirely of cliffs. The Indians have repaired it with loose rocks and logs and in the last bad place they have a stairway of the same materials, more than three varas long and two wide. Here two small streams come together, entering the Río Grande near the site of San Carlos. We ascended to the opposite side along a ridge of rocks and crags which is between the two small streams, making many turns and passing some perilous benches of rock which could be made passable only by the use of crowbars. We finished the ascent at nearly midday, having traveled in the descent and the ascent two leagues to the east-southeast. Here, to the northeast of the trail, there are two small peaks. From the smaller we swung southeast, and having traveled three leagues over good terrain, we camped,[90] although without water, because there was good pasturage for the animals and plentiful firewood to withstand the severity of the cold which we suffered, naming the campsite San Proto. — Today five leagues.

November 12. We set out from San Proto to the south-southeast. We traveled now over an open road and good terrain for three leagues, and right on the road we found a small spring of good water from which, after we had broken the ice, all the men and all the animals drank. Judging from the vestiges, it is a campsite of the Cosninas when they go to the Payuchis. We continued south along the same road, experiencing excessive cold, and having traveled four leagues over very good terrain we left the direct road for Moqui, according to the instructions of the Payuchis,

---

[89]Having retraced their steps they again camped on the rim of Navajo Canyon near the campsite of November 8.
[90]On the eastern bank of Kaibito Creek.

and followed the more used one of the Cosninas toward the south-southwest. Having traveled a league, we found several uninhabited little houses or ranchos, and indications that many cattle and horses had pastured here for some time. We continued over the same road, and after we had traveled a league and a half to the southwest, night fell and we camped without water, naming the campsite San Jacinto.[91] — Today nine and one-half leagues.

Because of the great cold part of us stopped for a while, the rest of the companions going forward, to make a fire and massage Don Bernardo Miera, who was now about to freeze on our hands, for we feared he could not withstand such extreme cold. For this reason the rest of the companions arrived at the above-mentioned spring ahead of us, and before we overtook them they went on without putting water in the vessels which they carried for this purpose, for which inadvertence we suffered great thirst tonight.

November 13. We set out from San Jacinto toward the south-southwest along the same road, over good land with timber and abundant pasturage, and having gone two leagues we swung to the south one and one-half leagues, and found in some rocks plenty of water for the men and almost enough for all the animals. We continued across a sandy plain two leagues to the south, and half a league to the southeast, and camped[92] about a league beyond another pool which contained bad water which we found on the same road. We named the campsite El Espino because we caught a porcupine here, and we tried its flesh, which is very appetizing. We were all greatly in need of food for since the night before we had not tasted anything except a piece of toasted hide, so the porcupine distributed among so many persons served only to stimulate the appetite. For this reason we ordered another horse killed, which we had not done sooner because we expected to find some food in some of the ranchos of the Cosninas, but we have not seen even recent vestiges of them. — Today six leagues.

November 14. We set out from El Espino toward the south-southeast, and having traveled a little less than a league we found on the road a large pool of good water, from which all the animals drank to their satisfaction. We continued southeast, and having

---

[91]On Kaibito Plateau, just north and west of Preston Mesa.
[92]Midway between Whitmore Pools and Tuba City.

gone three-fourths of a league, we entered a canyon in which four springs of good water rise. We traveled along it half a league to the southeast and arrived at a small farm and some ranchos of the Cosninas, which were very beautiful and well arranged. This farm is irrigated by the four springs mentioned and two other large ones which rise near it. This year the Cosninas planted maize, beans, calabashes, water melons and cantaloupes on it. When we arrived they had already gathered their harvest, and judging from the refuse or remains which we saw of everything, it was abundant, especially the beans, for if we had stopped here we could have gathered half a fanega of them. The farm was surrounded by peach trees, and, besides several huts made of branches, there was a little house very well made of stone and mud. In it were the baskets,* jars, and other utensils of these Indians. Judging from the tracks, they had been absent for several days, perhaps to seek piñon nuts in the high sierra close by toward the south-southwest. From the rancho, roads led out in different directions, and we did not know which we ought to take to go to Moqui, because now we could not go farther afield to seek the Cosninas, both because of the lack of provisions as well as on account of our severe suffering from the winter weather.

We took a road which runs to the southeast and traveled two leagues over very level terrain, passing some springs of good water, and crossed a small river which flows from northeast to southwest and carries as much water as a fair-sized ditch. It has its small grove and medium-sized meadows but very bad pasturage where we crossed it. After leaving the river we climbed a mesa on which there was a small lake, and several pools of rain water which serve as drinking places and watering holes for the cattle of Moqui, which we now began to see in large herds. We traveled along the mesa two and one-half leagues to the east-southeast, ascended a high hill, and because night was coming on and there was good pasturage for the animals, we stopped, naming the campsite Cuesta de los Llanos,[93] because from this place wide plains and fields begin without mesas, trees, or sierras, but with very good pasturage, that extend to the southeast beyond Moqui. — Today six and one quarter leagues.

---

[93]On Moenkopi Plateau some eight miles south of Moenkopi.
*Evidently cuevanos.

November 15. We left the Cuesta de los Llanos, going east-southeast, traveling along the plains nine leagues without finding water in the whole day's march, because we did not wish to turn aside to look for it. We found some in a valley in which there was chamise of the kind they call *chizo*, and we camped in the valley, naming it La Cañada de los Chizos.[94] — Today nine leagues to the east-southeast.

We [the fathers] had nothing for supper tonight because the horse meat which we had did not suffice for all. Here there were large herds of cattle, and all the companions wished to kill a cow or a calf, impatiently urging us to permit them in this way to relieve the hunger we all were suffering. Considering that we were now near the pueblo of Oraybi and that this might stir up some trouble for us with the Moquinos and defeat our purpose, which was to use again the means of the evangelical light and meekness to combat their willful blindness and inveterate obstinacy, we ordered another horse killed, and that no one should go near the cattle even though they might be strays or common stock, as the companions assured us they were.

November 16. We set out east-southeast from La Cañada de los Chizos, traveled three leagues, and near a high mesa swung east-northeast for a quarter of a league. Here we found a very much used road. Concluding that it would go to one of the pueblos of Moqui we followed it, and having traveled over good and entirely level country for three leagues to the northeast and a little less than two to the north, we arrived at the mesa of the Pueblo of Oraybi. Ordering the companions to halt at the foot of the mesa, and that no one except those who were accompanying us in the ascent should go to the pueblo until we should instruct them to do so, we ascended without incident and on entering the pueblo we were surrounded by a great number of Indians, large and small. In a language which they did not understand we asked them for the cacique and the chiefs, and when we wished to go to the house of the cacique, they restrained us, one of them saying in the Navajó tongue that we must not enter the pueblo. Don Juan Pedro Cisneros, in the same tongue spiritedly asked if they were not our friends. Thereupon they

---

[94]Near Dennebito Springs on Dennebito Wash a little north and west of Padilla Mesa.

quieted down, and an old man led us to his house and made us welcome in it, assigning us a room in order that we might pass the night there,[95] and giving us the viands which they eat. — Today seven leagues.

Tonight the cacique and two old men came to visit us, and after having given us to understand that they were our friends, they offered to sell us the provisions we might need, as we had intimated that we would be grateful for them.

November 17. Very early in the morning they brought for us to the lodging some baskets or small trays of flour, beef tallow, guavas, and other kinds of food. We purchased promptly all we could because of the most necessary things they brought us the least. For lack of an interpreter we were unable to take up the matter of their conversion, as was desirable and as we wished to do, but we explained some things to them, especially to the cacique and to our host and benefactor. They listened attentively but said nothing except that they wanted to maintain friendship with the Spaniards. The cacique told us he had already sent word to the other pueblos in order that they might offer us hospitality and sell us the provisions we might need until we reached Zuñi. We gave them to understand that we were very grateful for this favor and the others we had received at their hands. In the afternoon we set out from Oraybi for the pueblo of Xongopabi, and having traveled about two and a quarter leagues to the southeast we arrived after sunset, and they welcomed us courteously, promptly giving us lodging.[96] — Today two and a quarter leagues to the southeast.

November 18. After the principal Indians of this pueblo and of the others nearby, Xipaolabi and Mossonganabi, had assembled, and we had told them of our gratitude for the favors and the warm welcome they had given us, we preached to them, partly by signs and partly in the Navajó tongue. They replied that they were unable to answer us because they did not understand the Castilian tongue or we the Moquino, and that we should go to Gualpi where there were persons versed in Castilian and where, talking as much as we might desire with the caciques and chiefs, we would learn what everybody wished to know. But when we

---

[95] They spent the night at the Indian pueblo of Oraibi.
[96] They stayed at the Hopi pueblo of Xongopabi, at the southern end of Second Mesa.

urged them that if they had understood us they themselves should reply, they added that the cacique and chief of Oraybi had sent to tell them they must lodge us, listen to us, and sell us provisions, cultivating our friendship without treating of or admitting any other subject, since they wished to be our friends but not Christians.

This over, we gave to the Indian who had lodged us and extended to us many courtesies a woolen cloak for his wife, thinking that in this way they would better understand our gratitude and become more attached to us. But it did not turn out the way we expected, for although the Indian woman gladly accepted the cloak, a brother of hers took it away and threw it toward us with a deep frown. We concluded that his hostility toward this innocent recompense arose from a suspicion of some evil purpose, contrary to our honor and profession, so we tried, with the seriousness and circumspection which the case demanded, to explain to them our true motive. Then the Indian, wishing to make amends for the affront he had shown us, although his guilt was not as grave as it appeared, put us in another predicament even worse than the first, many of us finding ourselves unable to understand a thing. After causing us to think seriously and when the crowd had dispersed he pointed out Father Fray Silvestre and Don Pedro Cisneros and said in Navajó that he had heard what took place in Oraybi when the fathers Fray Silvestre and Don Juan Pedro had been there in the summer of the previous year, and he had been present in Gualpi when the Cosnina talked to Father Fray Silvestre and told him about the road from Moqui to the Cosninas, and that now we had come by this same road; that he would not permit his brothers-in-law and brothers to accept the cloak, because if they did so their relatives and neighbors would be angry with them. He said this to satisfy us, but we were unable to understand clearly the other thing regarding which he wished to tell us, although it is not very difficult to infer it from the foregoing events.

This afternoon we left for Gualpi, and having traveled nine* leagues, more than four of them to the east, we arrived at night. Some of our small following remaining at the foot of the mesa, we ascended with the rest of them. We were welcomed very

---

*Evidently should read two and one-fourth leagues.

joyfully by the Tanos and Gualpis and they lodged us in the house of the cacique of the Tanos, where we spent the night.[97] — Today two and one fourth leagues to the east.

After we had rested for a short time, we were told by an apostate Indian named Pedro, from the pueblo of Galisteo in New Mexico, who was now old and had great authority in this pueblo of the Tanos at Moqui, that they were now at fierce war with the Navajó Apaches, who had killed and captured many of their people. For this reason, he added, they were hoping that some fathers or Spaniards would come to these pueblos in order through them to beg from the Señor Governor some aid or defense against these enemies. So they had been especially delighted when they learned that we were coming to visit them because they hoped we would aid and console them. This appeared to us to be one of the finest opportunities to induce them to submit to the Faith and to enter the dominions of His Majesty, God spare him. So we replied, giving them great hopes and telling them they must summon the chiefs of the three other pueblos to come to Gualpi, so that next day all might assemble in this pueblo of Tanos to discuss this matter at length and seriously. Then Pedro said that if we wished to take him with us he would like to go to the Villa of Santa Fé to arrange with the Señor Governor, in the name of the Moquinos and the Tanos, the alliance which they desired, and to request the aid they needed. We replied to him that we would take him gladly, and would use our good offices with the Señor Governor, in favor of all the Moquinos, but that for this it was necessary that each one of the six pueblos should send some person of authority into the presence of his lordship. They promised that next day they would assemble in the way suggested and that they would send for us when they were assembled in a kiva, to talk over and discuss everything and decide what was best.

November 19. The chiefs of Mossonganabi came, and when they were assembled with the caciques and chiefs of these pueblos of the mesa of Gualpi in a kiva of the Tanos, the apostate Pedro led us to it, giving us as an interpreter another apostate, an Indian of the pueblo of Santa Clara named Antonio el Cuati, because he speaks and understands the Castilian language well.

---

[97]They spent the night at the pueblo of Gualpi, south of First Mesa.

He translated our words into the Tegua language, and Pedro into the Moquino, so that all of us in the assembly might understand. They related everything they had discussed before we arrived at the kiva, and said they had agreed that the apostate Pedro should go with us to the Villa of Santa Fé in order that in the name of all he might ask the Señor Governor for aid against the Navajó Apaches, and establish friendship with the Spaniards, and they begged us to do everything possible in their behalf. We replied to them that we would take their part in every way, because we loved them like children, and were very sorry for their troubles, but that since only God is allpowerful and rules all, so long as they remained in their infidelity and until they ceased to offend Him, they would not be able to free themselves from suffering these troubles. Then we explained to them the severity of the eternal punishments which, if they did not accept the Christian religion, they must inevitably suffer in Hell, taking advantage for greater clarity and force, of the afflictions of which they had just told us. We told them also that if they would submit, they would have constant and sure help from the Spanish arms against all the heathen who might attempt to attack them, as did the Christian pueblos of New Mexico. This caused them to see at the same time the uselessness and inconstancy of the friendships and alliances which they had celebrated many times before with the Yutas and Navajós. And after having told them everything we thought suitable and efficacious, we told them that they must make known their decisions, with the understanding that whether or not it accorded with our desires, we were firm in our promise to take their ambassadors to Santa Fé and aid them in every way possible. Three times we urged them, exhorting them to enter the fold of the Holy Church, impugning and proving false and insubstantial their arguments for not accepting the Faith. Regarding the first, they replied that they knew the governors were sending the fathers to persuade them to submit to their authority but that they had not and still did not wish to. Regarding the second, they gave us to understand that, since there were many more heathen nations than Christian, they wanted to follow the more numerous party, and that besides this, they lived in country which was very inconvenient for the service which, once converted, they would have to render the Spaniards.

When we had overcome the apparent force of each one of these arguments, finding now nothing to contradict, the men of the assembly talked a long time, each in turn, beginning with those of the greatest authority and continuing in the order of their importance. And although each one spoke individually, he expressed himself in the form of a dialogue, and concluded his discourse by asking various questions of the others, who replied by assenting or denying respectively according to the nature of the questions. In these discourses they related the traditions of their ancestors and exhorted that they be observed, concluding that it was better for them to suffer their present troubles and calamities than to violate these traditions. So they replied that they wished only our friendship but by no means to become Christians, because the old men had told them and counseled them never to subject themselves to the Spaniards. We tried to make them see the foolish impiety of such traditions and counsels but without any success whatsoever. Finally they decided that Pedro should not go to the Villa of Santa Fé, the reason for which decision he himself told us, saying, "Now they do not wish that I should go to see the Governor because, since I am a Christian, they say that he will not let me return to Moqui." He feared this much more than the others, and so we were unable to get him to carry out his first intention. The assembly having ended, we withdrew very sadly to our lodging, realizing that the obstinacy of these unhappy Indians was invincible. And so we decided to continue next day to Zuñi before the passes and roads should be closed, because it was now snowing constantly, for which reason we were unable to observe the latitude of these pueblos of Moqui.

November 20. In the afternoon we set out from the pueblos of Gualpi, and having traveled four leagues east by southeast, we camped for the night at the watering place called El Ojo del Cañutillo or Ojito de Moqui.[98] — Today four leagues.

November 21. We set out from El Ojo del Cañutillo to the northeast, and having traveled three leagues we swung to the east-southeast two, then going a little more than two additional leagues to the east, we camped more than half a league before

---

[98]Camp may have been south of Keams Canyon at Jadito Springs on North Jadito Wash.

reaching a small watering place named the Estiladero or Ojito del Peñasco.⁹⁹ — Today seven leagues.

November 22. We left the companions with the rest of the animals, which were now worn out, in order that they might follow slowly to Zuñi, and we with three of the companions set forth in light order, and having traveled nine leagues east by southeast, we arrived at the place called Cumáa. Here we rested a while, and then continued two more leagues to the east. The animals were now exhausted and we had to halt.¹⁰⁰ — Today eleven leagues.

November 23. We continued our journey although it snowed all day with troublesome flurries, and having traveled on the gallop for twelve leagues, we camped at the place called Kianatuna or Ojo de San José.¹⁰¹ Tonight we suffered greatly from the cold. — Today twelve leagues almost all toward the east.

November 24. As soon as it was daylight we left the Ojo de Señor San José, going southeast, and having traveled two leagues we halted for a time to make a fire with which to warm ourselves, because it was so cold that we feared we should freeze in this valley. We continued southeast more than three leagues, traveled two more east-northeast, and halted to change horses at a watering place which the Zuñis called Okiappá. We continued on our way, and having traveled five leagues to the southeast, we arrived after nightfall and greatly fatigued at the pueblo and mission of Nuestra Señora de Guadalupe de Zuñi.¹⁰² — Today twelve leagues.

Not having sufficient strength to continue immediately to the Villa de Santa Fé, we reported to the Señor Governor our happy arrival at this mission, together with a brief account of the contents of this diary.

November 26. In the afternoon the rest of the companions arrived.

On account of various incidents we remained at this mission until the thirteenth of December, when we set out for the Villa de Santa Fé, and having traveled thirty leagues, we arrived at

---

⁹⁹Apparently at a spring on the upper branches of Pueblo Colorado Wash, possibly Senatoa Spring south of Salahkai Mesa.
¹⁰⁰Camp was probably a few miles south of the site of Cornfields.
¹⁰¹They may have camped on Black Creek in the vicinity of Allantown.
¹⁰²The next three weeks were spent at the pueblo of Zuñi.

the mission of San Estéban de Ácoma[103] on the sixteenth of December. Immediately there fell a heavy snow which prevented us from continuing as soon as we desired.

December 20. We set out from Ácoma for the mission of Señor San José de la Laguna, where we arrived after traveling four leagues.[104] —Today four leagues.

December 22. We set out from La Laguna, and having traveled six leagues east-northeast, we halted at the place called El Alamo.[105] — Today six leagues.

December 23. We set out from here, and having traveled five leagues east by east-southeast, we arrived at the mission of San Angustín de la Isleta.[106] — Today nine leagues.

December 28. We set out from the pueblo of La Isleta, and having traveled four leagues we arrived at the mission of San Francisco Javier de Alburquerque.[107] — Today four leagues.

December 30. We set out from here, and having traveled four more leagues, we arrived at the mission of Nuestra Señora de los Dolores de Sandía.[108] — Today four leagues.

December 31. We continued on our way, and having traveled seven leagues, arrived at the mission of Nuestro Padre Santo Domingo.[109] — Today seven leagues.

On **January 2** of this year of '77 having set out from the mission just mentioned we arrived at the Villa de Santa Fé.

January 3. We presented this diary, the token of the Lagunas of which mention is made, and the Laguna Indian. And because everything stated in this diary is true and faithful to what happened and was observed in our journey, we signed it in this mission on the third of January of the year 1777.

      Fray Francisco Atanasio Domínguez
      Fray Silvestre Vélez de Escalante

---

[103] They spent four days at the Sky City of Ácoma.
[104] Near the present town of Laguna.
[105] They camped about half way between the San José and Puerco rivers, due west of Albuquerque.
[106] They spent the next five nights at the old Indian pueblo of Isleta, twelve miles south of Albuquerque.
[107] Present day Old Albuquerque.
[108] They stayed at the Sandía Mission, about twelve miles northeast of Albuquerque.
[109] Northeast of Bernalillo on the Rio Grande.

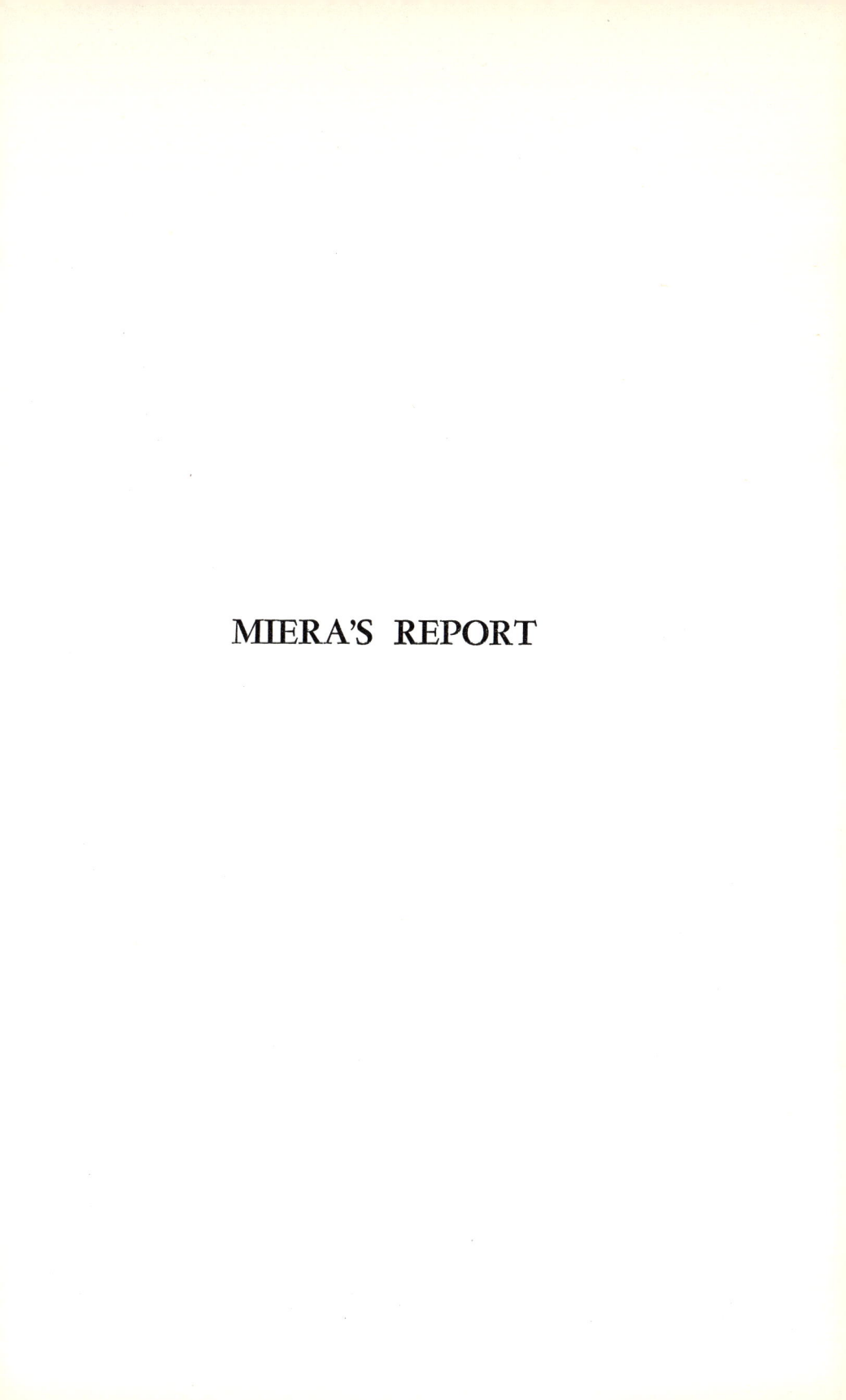

MIERA'S REPORT

MIERA'S REPORT TO THE KING OF SPAIN
October 26, 1777

Sacred Royal Catholic Majesty
My Lord:

    Because within me there burns a desire to spread our Holy Faith and to serve Your Majesty, the force of my loyal and sincere affection moves me to give you herewith a brief report, guiding myself by the experiences of many years, and by the services which I have rendered Your Majesty and which are on record in the archives of the viceroys of New Spain, during the time of the rule of the Conde de Revilla Gigedo and the Marqués de las Amarillas; and finally, by the one I have just finished rendering Your Majesty, with such risk of my life, in company with the Franciscan Fathers, Fray Atanasio Domínguez, visitor and custodian, and Fray Silvestre Vélez de Escalante. Indeed we were twelve persons in all [obviously an error for they add up to only ten], traveling over vast areas and through various tribes which are named in the Diary and Itinerary written by those Fathers, and shown on the map drawn by me and enclosed with the diary that we are sending to Your Majesty by order of Don Pedro Fermín de Mendinueta, Governor of New Mexico.

    From that province we set out to the northwest and went inland as far as the forty-second degree of latitude, intending to reach the Port of Monterrey on our return by the circle we were making, but, to the great sorrow of my heart, we failed to reach it for the reasons that are set forth in the Diary.

    It is certain, My Lord, that many tribes desire the water of baptism, especially the Timpanogos and the Barbones [Long Beards] of Valle Salado and Laguna de Miera, for those people, with tears in their eyes, manifested their ardent desire to become Christians. But in order to succeed in bringing about the salvation of these souls, some difficulties will have to be overcome, namely the great distance, and the obstacle imposed by the Apache nation, the one which at present ravages these provinces. But, by the will of God, the power of Your Majesty, and the righteous desires and deeds of your loyal ministers, all these difficulties will be overcome.

The basic and principal means of achieving the desired result is the strengthening of the port of Monterrey by two or three additional settlements in this vicinity, bringing the colonists by sea from the coast of Nueva Galicia, together with all the things necessary for a good pueblo. And, assuming that it is the intention of Your Majesty to facilitate the transit and communication between the two provinces of Sonora and New Mexico and the ports which are now established and in the future may be established on the coast of California, it will be necessary to provide those towns with large and small stock [cattle, sheep, and goats], and with horses to serve as mounts for the soldiers of the presidios. The animals will have to be brought by land as quickly as possible, and it can be done by way of the Pimería Alta or of New Mexico.

Ever since the time of the first discoverer and colonizer of New Spain, Don Fernando Cortés, and of the subsequent viceroys who have governed it, efforts have been made to explore that coast of California, both by land and sea, but they have never been successful until the time of Your Majesty. What is worth much costs much. Expenses will be incurred that must be paid from the royal treasury, but your Catholic Majesty will not be deterred by them, for always your royal aim and intention is the conversion of souls.

With three presidios, together with three settlements of Spaniards, the door will be open to a New Empire which may be explored and colonized. The chief one, and the one that should be the first objective, should be on the shores of the lake of the Timpanogos, on one of the rivers that flow into it, for this is the most pleasing, beautiful, and fertile site in all New Spain. It alone is capable of maintaining a settlement with as many people as Mexico City, and of affording its inhabitants many conveniences, for it has everything necessary for the support of human life. This lake and the rivers that flow into it abound in many varieties of savory fish, very large white geese, many kinds of ducks, and other exquisite birds never seen elsewhere, besides beavers, otters, seals, and some strange animals which are or appear to be ermines, judging by the softness and whiteness of their furs. The meadows of these rivers produce abundant hemp and flax without cultivation. The sierra or mountains toward the east are likewise very fertile, having many rivers and springs, good pastures for raising all kinds of cattle and horses, timber, including royal and other pines, and lands for the planting of all kinds of grain in their valleys. The veins that are seen in the sierra appear at a distance to have minerals, and to the south of this sierra there are some hills of very fine mineral salt.

The river which the inhabitants say flows from the lake, and whose current runs toward the west, they say is very large and navigable. And if it is as they say, I conjecture that it is the Río del Tizón discovered long ago by Don Juan de Oñate, first colonizer of New Mexico. And it is said that from this river he turned back because he was not able to cross it on account of its great width and depth, after having traveled three hundred leagues northwest from the Villa de San Gabriel de Yunqui, which was the first settlement founded by him (and is the one now called Chama). They told him that on the other side of the river there were large settlements in which lived civilized Indians.

The presidio could be placed in this Valle de Timpanogos (which is more than thirty leagues long from north to south and twelve leagues wide), for the protection of the missions of Indians whom they may convert, together with a settlement of a hundred families of Spaniards. And if among those who may go, there should be persons of all trades, and two skilled mechanics who know how to build barks and launches for sailing on this lake, and to transport whatever might present itself, they would serve also for fishing and for exploring its full extent, for visiting the tribes who live around it, and for learning whether or not the river mentioned is navigable and what tribes live on the other side of it. Thus, in a short time a very beautiful province would be formed, and it would serve to promote and supply the nearest ports of the coast of California.

The second presidio and the settlement of families attached to it also are very desirable, and should be founded at the junction of the river of Nabajóo with that of Las Ánimas, along the beautiful and extensive meadows which its margins provide for raising crops, together with the convenience of the timber, firewood, and pastures which they offer. There still remain in those meadows vestiges of irrigation ditches, ruins of many large and ancient settlements of Indians, and furnaces where apparently they smelted metals.

The region below these sites, from the place where the river is joined by the Río de los Zaguaganas, now called Río Colorado, is made uninhabitable because the river runs through a tremendous canyon between very high and steep red cliffs. Indeed not even the heathen live on this river for a distance of more than five leagues on either side, because of its extreme sterility, the terrain being rough and broken, and the canyon extending downstream through all the country of the Cosninas as far as the Jamajabas, Galchidunes, and Yumas. This presidio would serve as a way station for communication between New Mexico and the new establishments on the coast of Monterrey, and likewise for giving aid to the missions of the Cosninas, who for many years have clamored to receive our Holy Faith, and as a site to which to transplant the pueblos of Moqui, who rebelled and martyred their missionaries in the general uprising of the year [16]80.

These Moquis, for many reasons (which I shall not set forth, in order not to make this narrative too long), should be brought down by force from their cliffs. I will say only that even though they do not make war, they are obnoxious to New Mexico, for they serve as an asylum for many apostates from the Christian pueblos of that province. On the other hand, they are Indians who are very highly civilized, much given to labor, and not addicted to idleness. For this reason, although they live in that sterile region, they lack nothing in the way of food and clothing, and their houses are built of stone and mortar and are two or three storeys high. They raise cattle, sheep, goats, and horses, and weave good fabrics of wool and cotton. They live on the tops of three high and steep mesas in six separate pueblos. But they would come down from them without the shedding of blood, with only the threat of a siege of the principal cliffs of Oraibe and Gualpi by a company of soldiers stationed at the waterholes which they have at the foot of the cliffs, and in less than a week they would surrender and be ready to do whatever might be required of them. If these six pueblos were established in the immediate vicinity of the mentioned settlement and presidio [on the Navajó River] within a few years there would be in that place a rich and strong province, adjoining New Mexico and expanding toward these new establishments [on Lake Timpanogos].

The third presidio is likewise very desirable, and it is most necessary that it also be built strong enough, and provided with both soldiers and settlers. And if it were placed at the junction of the Jila River with the Colorado, or in that vicinity, which offers conveniences for its firm establishment, it would be useful in many ways. It would serve as a way station on the road from Sonora; for communication with the above-mentioned establishments; to protect and aid the converted tribes in its vicinity; and to check the ravages of the hostile Jila Apaches who live toward the east. It would serve also to give assistance to the above-named presidio northeast of it and between it and New Mexico, thus facilitating communication with all parts.

If the establishment of these three presidios with their adjacent settlements is carried out, much benefit may result through the spread of our Holy Faith and the extension of the dominions of Your Majesty. The Divine Majesty would reward you in every way, disclosing superabundant riches to compensate for the costs to your royal treasury, and increasing the stability of your Empire. These three presidios would be three firm columns to strengthen by land the coast of California, which is the object that should be kept in mind, for the three provinces that might be founded would expand with all vigor and reach as far as that coast.

For the more complete success of these objectives it is necessary to make every effort to remove the very great obstacle of the hostile Jila Apaches, who intervene between the three provinces of New Mexico, Sonora, and Nueva Vizcaya; to establish settlements and reap the profits from the mines which are in their mountains, ridding them of the Jila Apaches, and driving the latter toward the east and to the Buffalo Plains, where are found the two most obnoxious tribes, the Cumanches and Apaches, who by their fighting would soon destroy each other.

For this purpose, and for the achievement of the greatest success, it is my idea, My Lord, to apply the remedy where the danger arises. The fact is that from the province of Jila which, as I have said, is a pocket intervening between these three provinces, these Apaches sally forth to ravage them, with damage to life and property that becomes worse and worse every day. For so fierce are these attacks and so great the consternation they cause, that the majority of the haciendas, Spanish settlements, and the pueblos of Christian Indians on those frontiers have been ruined and abandoned and all mining stopped, thus reducing the royal income and multiplying the cost for troops, without providing any remedy.

The presidios being placed in a line, the Indians go in and out between them to perpetrate their thieveries, making it necessary to conduct a campaign every year, from which the Indians suffer very little damage. They hide their stolen goods and their families in the mountains, and the soldiers, since most of them are cavalrymen, are not able to operate nor to succeed in punishing them, but can only cross their plains and valleys, returning without achieving their purpose, while behind them the enemies follow proudly and haughtily, and succeed in whatever ravages they undertake.

From this province of Jila, I repeat, comes the greatest damage, and the greatest obstacle to success in the conversion and the colonization desired. So I say, My Lord, that here the remedy should be applied, for from here comes the injury. So, for the purpose in view, and for success in everything, the remedy is to place in the center of the province [of Jila] three strong settlements with a sufficient force of mounted and leather-jacket soldiers, who by continuous war may succeed in dislodging the enemy from that province, the troops and leather-jackets from the presidios serving to protect and transport the supplies.

Of the places most suitable in which to establish them, and from which to make the war a continuous campaign, the first is on the Jila River in a valley at the exit of the canyon called San Pedro de Alcántara, from which the river flows; the second is on the Río de Mimbres near the Sierra de Cobre Vírgen, and the third is on the Río del Norte opposite the place called San Pasqual. For this purpose the expense which would be added to the royal treasury would be in the establishment of families to settle in those places; in equipping three companies of militia of one hundred men each from the eight which are listed in New Mexico and its jurisdiction of El Paso; and in instructing them in the service of mounted infantry, with no other arms or impedimenta than a musket and a bayonet, two horses and one pack mule, and their salary of six and one-half reales daily as long as the war might last. Such would be the added cost of relieving the province of these enemies. And assuming that there should be four flying companies of leather-jackets and two pickets of dragoons, in addition to the presidios of the line, one of these companies with the pickets of dragoons might be trained by the same method as the mounted infantry so that they could continually aid in this service. From the Presidio of El Carrizal as far as El Altar, which make nine counting that of Buena Vista, twenty men might be detached from each one, and they could be alternated continually in the front ranks, to carry on the war in order to protect the settlements and to convoy supplies and other necessities.

After this province of Jila has been cleared of enemies the half line of presidios, which are the ones mentioned from El Carrizal to Tubac or El Altar, would cost the royal treasury less, and some troops could be moved up as needed and others could remain where it was most convenient. The other flying companies might reinforce the other half of the line from the Presido of Elceareo as far as that of San Juan Bautista, to ward off the incursions of the Apaches of the plains, who are the Carlanes, Natajees, and Lipanes. Since care would be taken to scout the land, these Indians would have no opportunity to enter the area between those presidios nor to take refuge in the Bolsón, called by them the Mapimí, which is the place through which they penetrate to the interior as far as Parras near Durango and the hills of Nueva Vizcaya. It appears to be desirable to be on the defensive along this half line because it faces on the vast area of the Buffalo Plains. These offer no spiritual or temporal advantages, and there is little hope of converting the wandering tribes which live in them. They are the Cumanches and the Apaches, who are very hostile to each other and for this reason they will become less numerous.

I again repeat, Sir, that the only safeguard for this North America depends on the settlement described, and, in order to extend our Holy Faith and the dominions of Your Majesty, it is necessary to remove the aforementioned obstacle, which is and has been the said province of Jila. What thousands of souls may be left without conversion in those peaceful tribes which live to the north and northwest of this treacherous nation! What damage has been caused under the pretended and deceitful peace agreements on these frontiers!

Your Majesty is our King and universal father. Have mercy on these poor people, your frontier vassals, who are suffering many calamities and miseries. Do not mind the costs which may arise from increasing the troops. Plant one with the hope that God will return one hundred. Do not delay the execution of this plan, because the enemies are achieving many advantages, the many captive apostates being the worst, and the longer the delay the more difficult the remedy. This, My Lord, is my opinion (saving a better one), born of the great love and loyal affection which I have for Your Majesty, and being moved to it by the experience of many years and many services rendered at my own expense with great willingness, to which I refer in the accompanying memoir which I place at your feet.

The Divine Majesty, who is all powerful, many times uses vile instruments to manifest His power and grandeur. And since I regard myself as one of these, the fire of love which I have for Your Majesty and for the extension of our Holy Faith and for your royal dominions has caused me to strive, breathing my fervent desires for the greatest success. The one who writes this missive to Your Majesty likewise promises, as I do promise (God giving me life and health) that in the term of three years counting from the first day that I arrive at the site of Las Mimbres with the troops which I have mentioned, to give quiet and peace to that province and to have the three settlements established, and at least one mine of gold, silver, and copper discovered and in operation. With my fervent desires and my firm hopes, as far as is possible, my promises will be fulfilled.

It is my desire, Sir, that on the arrival at this Villa, of the commandant general-in-chief, Don Teodoro de la Crois, whom Your Majesty has sent to govern us in his royal name, I may present to him a copy of this plan for his use. I hope it may be entirely successful through the favor of the All Powerful, to whom, humble and prostrate, I beg and pray that He may preserve the most important life of Your Majesty with very robust health for many years, for the achievement of such happiness as we, your children and vassals, have need.

San Phelipe El Real del Chiguagua, October 26, 1777. Sir, the feet of Your Catholic Majesty are kissed by your loyal servant and vassal.

Bernardo Miera y Pacheco
[Rubric]

BIBLIOGRAPHY

BIBLIOGRAPHY

There is extensive documentary material for the Escalante expedition, much of which was published by Otto Maas, O. F. M., in a volume entitled *Viajes de Misioneros Franciscanos a la Conquista del Nuevo México con un mapa y dos estadisticas de las Misiones Franciscanas en los años de 1786 y 1788.* Sevilla, 1915. Most of these were translated by Miss Jessie Hazel Power in her M. A. thesis written in my seminar at the University of California in 1920. Miss Power gives a full bibliography of both primary and secondary materials, which was a basis for the one that I insert here. She also includes the translations of many documents. Aside from the materials cited by Miss Power, the chief contribution to the Escalante story has been made by Herbert S. Auerbach in his excellent monograph entitled "Father Escalante's Journal, 1776-77," *Utah Historical Quarterly,* XI (1943). My own chief contribution has been my retracing of Escalante's route through many years, my map of the trail, the narrative herein contained, and the publication of the colored maps.

ABBREVIATIONS

A.G.I.—Archivo General de Indias, Seville, Spain
A.G.M.—Archivo General y Público de la Nación, Mexico City

MANUSCRIPT MATERIALS

Bucarely to Gálvez. Remite copia de carta de dos Misioneros de Nuevo Mexico. Mexico, February 24, 1777. A.G.I., 104-6-18.
Costansó, Miguel. Dictamen del Ingeniero D. Miguel Costansó. March 18, 1776. A.G.M., *Provincias Internas,* 169.
——Opinion of Costansó relative to expedition of Domínguez and Escalante. Mexico, March 18, 1776. A.G.M., *Historia,* 52.
Crespo, Francisco Antonio. Informe que hizo al Virrey. Altar, December 15, 1774. A.G.M., *Historia,* 25. Transcript in Documentos para la historia de Nuevo México, II, in Bancroft Library.
——To Hugo Oconór concerning the frontier and establishment of presidios. Tubac, November 25, 1774. A.G.M., *Historia,* 25. Transcript in Documentos . . . de Nuevo Mexico, II, Bancroft Library.

Croix, Teodoro to Gálvez. Remite copias de Diario y Mapa que hicieron dos religiosos del Nuevo México en demanda del camino por tierra al Puerto de Monterrey. Mexico, July 26, 1777. A.G.I., 104-6-18.

Domínguez, Francisco Atanasio to Fray Ysidro Murillo. Santa Fé, July 28, 1776. A.G.I., 154-7-16.

———To Murillo. Santa Fé, July 29, 1776. A.G.I., 154-7-16.

———To Murillo describing the journey to Zuñi. Zuñi, November 25 ,1776. A.G.M., *Historia,* 52.

———Viaje que comenzó el veinte y nueve de julio de mil setecientos setenta y seis. A.G.M., *Historia,* 25. Transcript in Documentos... , Bancroft Library.

Domínguez, Francisco Atanasio and Vélez de Escalante, Silvestre. Diario y derrotero de los R.R. P.P. Fray Francisco Atanasio Domínguez y Fray Silvestre Vélez de Escalante, para descubrir el camino desde el Presidio de Santa Fé del Nuevo-México, al de Monterey, en la California Septentrional. A.G.M., *Historia,* 26 and 62; A.G.I., 104-6-18. Copies in Bancroft Library, British Museum, and Library of Congress. Earliest printed copy in *Documentos para la Historia de México, Sér.* II, Tomo I, Mexico, 1854.

———To Mendinueta describing their journey to Zuñi. Zuñi, November 25, 1776. A.G.M., *Historia,* 52; A.G.I., 104-6-18.

Fermín de Mendinueta, Pedro. Informe del gobernador . . . sobre comunicación con Sonora. Santa Fé, November 9, 1775. A.G.M., *Historia,* 52; copy in *Provincias Internas,* 169.

———Report concerning route from New Mexico to Monterey and expedition of Domínguez and Escalante. Santa Fé, June 26, 1776. A.G.M., *Historia,* 52.

———Reports concerning discovery of route from Santa Fé to Monterey and plans of Garcés and Escalante. Santa Fé, August 5, 1776; December 25, 1776. Enclosure: letter by Father Garcés to the minister of Zuñi. July 3, 1776. A.G.M., *Californias,* 36.

Gálvez, José to the viceroy acknowledging report of the expedition of Domínguez and Escalante. Aranjuéz, June 3, 1777. A.G.I., 104-6-18.

Garcés, Francisco to the minister of Zuñi. Oraibe, July 3, 1776. A.G.M., *Historia,* 52; copies in *Historia,* 25, A.G.I., 104-6-18, and 154-7-16, Documentos... II, Bancroft Library.

———Diario y derrotero que siguió . . . al Río Colorado para reconocer las naciones que habitan sus márgenes, y á los pueblos del Moqui del Nuevo—México. A.G.M., *Historia,* 52; A.G.I., 104-6-18 and 154-7-16.

Miera y Pacheco, Bernardo to the King of Spain. Chihuahua, October 26, 1777. From the original in the Edward E. Ayer Collection, Newberry Library, Chicago.

Morfi, Juan, to Croix, giving views about results of Domínguez-Escalante expedition. 1777. A.G.I., 103-6-8.
Oconór, Hugo to viceroy proposing an expedition to Moqui. January 15, 1776. A.G.M., *Historia,* 52.
Rodríguez de la Torre, Mariano to Domínguez concerning 1755 expedition to Moqui. Santo Domingo, July 11, 1770. A.G.M., *Historia,* 25; copy in Documentos . . . Bancroft Library.
Rosete y Peralta, Mariano to Domínguez. Zuñi, July 6, 1776. A.G.I., 154-7-16.
Vélez de Escalante, Silvestre to Goméz. Zuñi, August 18, 1775. A.G.M., *Historia,* 52.
——Informe y diario de la entrada que en Junio de 1775 hizo á la Provincia de Moqui. To Mendinueta. Zuñi, October 28, 1775. A.G.M., *Historia,* 25; copy in Documentos . . . Bancroft Library.
——Diary of the journey to Moqui in June, 1775. Addressed to Murillo. Zuñi, April 30, 1776. A.G.I., 154-7-16.
——Letter to Murillo explaining reasons for suggesting force to subdue Moquis. Zuñi, May 6, 1776. A.G.I., 154-7-16.
——To Murillo. Santa Fé, July 29, 1776. A.G.I., 154-7-16.
——Carta escrita en 2 abril de 1778 años. A.G.M., *Historia,* 2.
——Expedition of Fray Francisco Vélez de Escalante from Santa Fé to Zuñi, 1776. Written in 1780. A.G.M., *Historia,* 25.

PRINTED DOCUMENTS

Documentos para la Historia de México, Segunda Série. Mexico, 1854.
Maas, P. Otto, O.F.M. *Viajes de Misioneros Franciscanos á la Conquista del Nuevo México, con un mapa y dos estadisticas de la Misiones Franciscanas en los años 1786 y 1788.* Sevilla, 1915.

SECONDARY MATERIALS

Arricivita, Juan Domingo. *Cronica Seráfica y Apostólica del Colegio de Propaganda Fide de la Santa Cruz de Queretaro en la Nueva España,* Dedicada al Santísimo Patriarca el Señor San Joseph. Segunda Parte. Mexico, 1792.
Auerbach, Herbert S. "Father Escalante's Journal, 1776-77," *Utah Historical Quarterly,* XI (1943).
Bancroft, Hubert Howe. *Arizona and New Mexico.* San Francisco, 1889.
Bolton, Herbert E. *Guide to the Materials for the History of the United States in the Archives of Mexico.* Washington, 1913.
——"Escalante in Dixie and the Arizona Strip," *New Mexico Historical Review,* III (January, 1928).

Chapman, Charles Edward. *Catalogue of Materials in the Archivo General de Indias.* Berkeley, 1919.
——*The Founding of Spanish California.* New York, 1916.
Coues, Elliott. *On the Trail of a Spanish Pioneer.* 2 vols. New York, 1900.
Hackett, Charles Wilson. *Historical Documents Relating to New Mexico.* 3 vols. Washington, 1923, 1926, 1937.
——*Pichardo's Treatise on the Limits of Louisiana.* 4 vols. Austin, Texas, 1931.
——*Revolt of the Pueblo Indians of New Mexico and Otermin's Attempted Reconquest 1680-1682.* 2 vols. Albuquerque, 1942.
Hafen, LeRoy R. *Colorado, The Story of a Western Commonwealth.* Denver, 1933.
Harris, W. R. *The Catholic Church in Utah.* Salt Lake City, 1909.
Harry, Philip. "The Journeyings of Father Escalante, 1776," in J. H. Simpson, *Explorations Across the Great Basin of Utah in 1859.* Washington, 1876.
Hill, Joseph J. "Spanish and Mexican Exploration and Trade Northwest from New Mexico into the Great Basin," *Utah Historical Quarterly,* III (January, 1930).
Hodge, Frederick W. *Handbook of American Indians North of Mexico.* 2 vols. Washington, 1907-1910.
——*Spanish Explorers in the Southern United States.* New York, 1907.
Roberts, H. H. *Early Pueblo Ruins in the Piedra District, Southwestern Colorado.* (Bureau of American Ethnology, Bulletin 96.)
Twitchell, Ralph E. *The Leading Facts of New Mexican History.* 2 vols. Cedar Rapids, 1911-12.
——*The Spanish Archives of New Mexico.* 2 vols. Cedar Rapids, 1914.

INDEX

A

Abiquiú, 17
Abiquiú Valley, 18
Agua Escondida, see Hidden Water
Agua Tapada, see Covered Pool
Aguas Calientes, 184
Aguilar, Juan de, 11, 133
Albuquerque, 239
Allantown, 124, 238
Allison, 25
American Fork River (Río de Santa Ana), 71, 185
Ancamuchis, see Havasupais
Ancapagari, see Uncompahgre
Antelope Valley, 213
Anza, 9
Apache Indians, 12, 17, 126, 212, 247, 249
Apache Nation, 243
Árboles, 23, 138
Arkansas River (Napeste River), 53
Arroyo del Belduque, see Hunting Knife Creek
Arroyo del Canjilón, see Arroyo Seco
Arroyo del Cíbolo, see Buffalo Creek
Arroyo del Taray, see San Dónulo
Arroyo del Tejedor, see Arroyo of the Weaver
Arroyo de San Andrés, 74, 187
Arroyo de Santa Gertrudis, 104, 213
Arroyo Seco (Arroyo del Canjilón), 133, 134
Arroyo of the Weaver (Arroyo del Tejedor), 81, 83, 193, 195
Ash Creek (Señor San José), 91, 93, 200, 201, 203
Ashley Creek, 59
Astronomical Observations, 130
Atanasio, Father Fray Francisco, 108, 140, 149, 153, 154, 156, 179, 199, 216
Aubrey Cliffs, 4
Austin (Santa Monica), 41, 155, 162
Aztec, 25

B

Barbones, see Bearded Indians
Basin Creek (Fuente de San Bernabé), 35, 146
Battlement Mesa, 52, 161
Bear River Valley, 83, 194, 195
Bearded Indians (Barbones, Long Bearded Yutas, Tirangapui, Yutas Barbones), 78, 79, 86, 87, 128, 186, 189, 190-192, 196, 197, 243
Beaver River, 82, 193
Bernalillo, 239
Black Creek (Tucané), 226, 238
Black Peak, 119
Black Rock, 82, 193
Black Rock Canyon, 99, 208
Black Rock (town), 194
Bloom, 81
Bolsón, see Mapimí
Book Cliffs, 52
Boulder Lake, 19
Borden, 81, 193
Bowie, 44, 155
Brush Creek, 59, 170
Buffalo Creek (Arroyo del Cíbolo, Cliff Creek), 56, 168
Burford Lake, 19
Buzzard Creek, 51, 161

C

Cachupín, Governor Don Tomás Vélez, 6, 12, 26, 140
Cahone (Cajón), 29, 142
Cajón del Yeso, see Gypsum Creek
Canjilón, 18
Cañon de las Golondrinas, 174
Cañon del Engaño, see Deceitful Canyon
Cañon Pintado, see Painted Canyon
Canyon of Deceit (Cañón del Engaño), 137
Canyon of the Swallows (Las Golondrinas), 61
Carlanes (Indians), 249
Carracas, 21, 137
Cebolla, 135
Cedar City, 89, 91, 200
Cedar Valley, 91
Cerro del Pedernal, 136
Chaco Canyon, 23
Chama (Villa de San Gabriel de Yumqui), 245
Chama River, 16, 17, 133
Chamita, 16
Chimney Rock Mesa, 24

INDEX

Cisneros, Don Juan Pedro, 11, 32, 79, 82, 111, 117, 123, 133, 144, 191, 194, 218, 219, 224, 234
Cisneros, Ojo de, 79
Clear Lake, 78, 81
Clearlake, 190, 193
Cliff of Acoma, 125
Cliff Creek (Buffalo Creek, Arroyo de Cíbolo), 56, 168
Coal Creek, 89, 200
Cobardes (Indians), 119
Cocomaricopas (Indians), 92, 202
Collbran, 51
Colorado, 14
Colorado River (Río del Tizón, Rio Grande de Cosnina, Río Grande, Río Colorado, San Rafael), 2-4, 31, 73, 85, 91, 92, 105, 108, 111-116, 127, 151, 152, 163, 196, 200, 207, 217, 219, 247
Comanche (Indians) (Cumanches), 12, 17, 126, 154, 165, 172, 176, 187, 247, 249
Comanches Yamparicas, 42, 53, 166
Come Pescados, see Timpanogos
Conchos River, 12
Cooper's Pockets, 102, 211
Copper (El Cobre), 151
Cordillera de las Grullas, see Rocky Mountains
Cornfields, 124
Coronado trail, 12
Cortés, Don Fernando, 244
Cosninas, see Havasupais
Coues, 5
Covered Pool (Agua Tapada), 30, 143
Coyote, 142
Cricket Mountains, 81, 82, 193
Crois, Don Teodoro de la, 250
Crossing of the Fathers (Crossing of the Colorado), 112, 118, 224
Cuesta de las Ánimas, 113
Cuesta de los Llanos, 231
Cuesta del Susto, 165
Cumaá, 124, 238
Cumanches, see Comanches
Currant Creek, 62

D

The Deaf One (El Surdo), 39, 152
Debeque, Colorado, 52
Deceitful Canyon (Cañon del Engaño), 20
Dennebito Spring, 123
Dennebito Wash, 232
Deseret, 190
Diamond Butte, 210

Diamond Canyon, 177
Diamond Creek, 63, 64, 177
Diaz, Father, 126
Dinosaur Quarry, 57, 59, 170
Disappointment Creek (Río de las Paralíticas), 32, 144
The Dividing Line, 14
Dolores River (Río de Nuestra Señora de los Dolores), 7, 14, 27, 28, 31, 119, 141, 144, 146, 147
Dolores (town), 27
Domingo, Juan, 115, 117, 142, 222
Domínguez, Fray Francisco Atanasio, 1, 5, 6, 9-11, 13, 16, 26, 27, 29, 46, 47, 53, 63, 65, 66, 90, 98, 106, 117, 121, 123, 127, 133 243
Douglas Canyon, 54, 55, 166
Douglas Creek (San Clemente River), 54, 169, 172
Dove Creek Town, 30
Duchesne River, 60, 173
Duchesne, Utah, 61, 173
Dulce, 136
Durango, 25, 249

E

El Alamo, 125, 239
El Barranco, 56
El Cerrilo, 81, 193
El Cobre, see Copper
El Espino, 122
El Ojito del Cañutillo, see Ojito de Moqui
El Paso, 6, 12, 248
El Purgatorio, 152
El Surdo, see The Deaf One
El Vado, 19
El Vado de los Cosninas, see Glen Canyon
Egnar, Colorado, 30, 143
Escalante, Fray Francisco Silvestre Vélez de, 1, 2, 5, 6, 9-13, 16, 21, 27, 31, 36, 39, 41, 47, 52, 53, 57-59, 63, 64, 66, 68, 71, 72, 76, 79, 82, 85, 86, 90-93, 95, 98, 99, 106, 117, 118, 121, 123, 127, 133, 243
Española, 16
Estiladero, see Ojito del Peñasco

F

Fages, Captain Pedro, 127
Farmington, 25
Felipe, 117, 142
Fewkes, Walter, 28
Fifth Water Creek, 176
Fillmore, 81

INDEX

Fish Eaters (Indians), *see* Timpanogos
Fora, Nicolás de la, 12
Fort Pierce Creek, 96, 206
Fountains of Saint Clara (Las Fuentes de Santa Clara), 57, 169
Francisco, *see* Oso Colorado
Fredonia, 104, 213
Friars, 181
Fruitland, 174
Fuente de San Bernabé, *see* Basin Creek

G

Galchidunes, 246
Galisteo, 12, 235
Garcés, Fray Francisco, 1, 3, 5, 37, 48, 104, 126, 127, 149, 158, 181, 207, 212
Genízaro, 17, 142
Gigedo, Conde de Revilla, 243
Gila River, 5, 6, 127
Glen Canyon (El Vado de los Cosninas, San Carlos), 115, 116, 121, 222
Grand Canyon, 5, 99
Grand Mesa National Forest, 155
Grand Valley, 52
Great Salt Lake, 71-73, 186
Green River (Río de San Buenaventura), 14, 57, 59, 169, 170-172, 184
Gualpi, 2, 123, 234, 235, 246
Gualpis (Indians), 235
Guide's Fountain (La Fuente de la Guía), 37, 148
Gunnison River (Río de San Javier, Río del Tomichi), 7, 11, 31, 40, 41, 44, 59, 107, 153
Gypsum Canyon (Cajón del Yeso), 34
Gypsum Creek (Cajón del Yeso), 33, 146

H

Hackberry, 4
Hauscari (Indians), 204
Havasupai Canyon, 2, 4
Havasupais (Cosninas, Ancamuchis) (Indians), 2, 4, 10, 31, 38, 85, 88, 92, 99, 103, 104, 108, 121, 196, 199-202, 207, 208, 212, 216, 246
Hesperus, 26, 140
Hernández, 16
Hidden Water (Agua Escondida), 31, 143

High Sierra, 14
Highmore, 165
The Hill of the Scare (La Cuesta del Susto), 54
Hobble Creek (Río de San Nicolás, San Nicolás), 70, 74, 184, 187
Hopi Land, 2, 4, 12
Hopi Mesas, 2
Hopi Towns, 120
Hopis, 2, 3
Horsefly Creek, 38
Horseshoe Bend, 172
Hotchkiss, 44, 155
House Rock, 110, 218
House Rock Valley, 110
Hualapai Indians, 4
Hualapai Valley, 4
Huascaris (Indians), 94, 103, 119, 212
Hunting Knife Creek (Arroyo del Belduque), 20, 136
Hurricane Cliff, 210
Hurricane Fault, 99
Hurricane, Utah, 96, 206

I

Ignacio, 25, 139
Indians, 106, 109, 123, 188, 200, 202, 210
Indians, *see* names of
Isleta (San Agustín de la Isleta), 1, 9, 239

J

Jacob's Pools, 111
Jadito Springs, 124, 237
Jamajab (Indians), 207, 208, 246
Jensen, Utah, 57, 170
Jicarilla Indian Reservation, 19
Jila Apaches, 247
Jila River, 247, 248
Joaquin, 59, 64-66, 74, 90, 105, 161, 170, 187, 199, 200, 211, 214
Johnson Creek, 104, 213
José María, 68, 74, 82, 182, 187, 194
Juan Bautista de Anza, 17
Juan de Oñate, 73

K

Kaibito Creek, 122, 229
Kaibito Plateau, 122
Kanab Creek, 104, 213
Kanab Plateau, 104
Kanarra Creek, 91
Kanarraville 91, 201

INDEX

Kayentá district, 23
Keams Canyon, 124, 237
Kianatuna (Ojo de San José), 124, 238
Kimball Creek, 162
Kimball Valley, 104, 213
Kingman, Arizona, 4
Kino, 9

L

La Asunción, 29
La Asunción de Nuestra Señora, 142
Laberinto de Miera, see Miera's Labyrinth
La Boca, 25
La Cañada de los Chizos, 123, 232
La Cañada Honda, 38, 150
La Ciénega de San Francisco, 38, 150
La Contraguía, 53, 54, 165
La Cuesta del Susto, see The Hill of the Scare
La Fuente de la Guía, see Guide's Fountain
Laguna Colorado, see Uncompahgre River
Laguna de Miera, 243
Laguna de Olivares, see Horse Lake
Laguna de Timpanois, 196
Laguna (Indians), see Timpanogos
Laín, Don Joaquín, 11, 53, 58, 87, 133, 165, 170, 201
Lake Timpanogas, see Utah Lake
La Natividad de Nuestra Señora, 54, 166
La Piedra Alumbre, 17, 133
La Plata Mountains, 7
La Puente, 19
La Purísima Concepción de la Virgen Santísima, 119, 226
Las Ánimas, 245
La Santísima Trinidad, 20
Las Fuentes de Santa Clara, see The Fountains of Saint Clara
Las Golondrinas, see Canyon of the Swallows
Las Llagas de Nuestro Padre San Francisco, see The Wounds of Our Father St. Francis
Las Mimbres, 250
Las Vegas del Puerto, see The Meadows of the Pass
La Vega de San Cayetano, 25
La Vega de Santa Cruz, 57, 170
La Verkin, 95, 96
La Verkin Creek, 96
Lazear, 44
Lees Ferry, 112

Levan, Utah, 75, 188
Lipanes (Indians), 249
Little Colorado River, 5
Little Gypsum Creek, 146
Little River of San Lino, 178
Llano Salado, 80, 192
Logsill Mesa, 38
Long Bearded Yutas, see Bearded Indians
Long Beards, see Bearded Indians
Los Angeles, 127
Los Pinos River, 139
Lost Canyon Creek, 141
Lucero, Simón, 11, 82, 133, 194
Lucrecio, 113, 116, 117, 159
Lumberton, 20
Lund, Utah, 89

M

Mancos, 27, 141
Mancos River (Río de San Lázaro), 26, 27
Mapimí (Bolsón), 249
Marble Canyon, 111
María, José, see José María
Mártir, San Antonio, 173
McElmo River, 313
McIntyre Canyon, 145
McPhee, 29
Meadow of the Most Sweet Name of Jesus (Vega del Dulcísimo Nombre de Jesús), 65, 179
Meadows of the Pass (Las Vegas del Puerto), 82, 193
Meadows of the Valley of Señor San José, 89
Mendinueta, Don Pedro Fermín de, Governor, 2, 10, 243
Mesa de Los Viejos, 17
Mesa of Gualpi, 2
Mesa Verde, 14, 23
Mescalero Apache, 103, 212
Miera, Captain Don Bernardo y Pacheco, 1, 13, 16, 27, 34, 41, 52, 72, 73, 77, 80, 87, 89, 99, 100, 104, 106, 122, 126, 127, 133, 138, 143, 146, 167, 198, 199, 209, 213, 215
Miera, Don Luis de, 11
Miera's Labyrinth (Laberinto de Miera), 144
Miera's Maps, 128
Miera's Report to the King of Spain, 243-250
Miguel River (Río de San Pedro), 36
Milford, 86, 87, 197
Mills, Utah, 76, 77, 87, 189
Minersville, 197

INDEX

Mission of Nuestro Padre Santo Domingo, 125
Moenkopi, 231
Moenkopi pueblo, 123
Mojave Indians, 3
Mona Reservoir, 74, 188
Monero, 20
Monterey, 2, 9, 10, 68, 84, 88, 196, 199, 244
Monterey River, 14
Montrose, 38, 39
Moqui (Indians), 12, 85, 121, 196, 201, 232-237
Moquinos (Indians), 2, 10, 108, 207, 216, 235
Mora, Pedro, 7, 152
Mossonganibi, 233, 235
Mountain of the Roan Deer (Sierra del Venado Alazán), 44, 151, 155, 162
Moving Mountain, 25
Muddy Creek, 156
Muhuaches (Muhuachis) (Indians), 29, 32, 35, 37, 119, 144
Muñiz, Andrés, 7, 11, 32, 46, 65, 87, 105, 113, 116, 133, 144, 152, 154, 156, 159, 179, 198, 214
Muñiz, Lucrecio, 11, 115, 133, 222
Myton, Utah, 60, 173, 174, 189

N

Nabuncari, see San Silvestre
Napeste River, see Arkansas River
Narraguinnep Creek, 29
Natajees (Indians), 249
Naturita, 35, 147
Navajó Apaches, 235
Navajo Canyon, 120
Navajo Creek, 120, 122, 228
Navajo Mountain (Tucané), 119
Navajo River, see San Juan River
New Harmony, 93
New Mexico, 128, 244
North Fork of Gunnison River, 155
North Jadito Wash, 124, 237
North Mam Peak, 161
Nucla, 147
Nuestra Señora de Guadalupe de Zuñi, see Zuñi
Nuestra Señora de la Luz, 197, 200
Nuestra Señora de la Merced, see Our Lady of Mercy
Nuestra Señora de la Merced de los Timpanogotzis (Timpanocutzis, Come Pescados), see Utah Valley
Nuestra Señora de las Nieves, see Our Lady of the Snows

Nuestra Señora de los Dolores de Sandía, 125, 239
Nuestra Señora de los Timpanogotzis, 65
Nuestra Señora del Pilar de Zaragoza, 91, 93
Nuestro Padre Santo Domingo, 239
Nueva Galicia, 244
Nueva Vizcaya, 247, 249
Nutrias Creek (Río de las Nutrias), 18, 135

O

Ojito del Peñasco (Estiladero), 124, 238
Ojito de Moqui (El Ojito del Cañutillo), 124, 237
Ojo de Cisneros, 190
Ojo de Laín, 38, 150
Ojo de San José, see Kianatuna
Ojo de San Pablo, 74, 188
Ojo de Santa Lucía, see Soldier Springs
Okiappá, 124, 238
Olathe, 39, 152
Old Albuquerque, 239
Old Fort Pierce, 96, 206
Old Temple Road, 100
Olivares, Laguna de, 136
Olivares, Lorenzo de, 11, 105, 133, 213
Ollyquotequiebe (Salvador Palma), 126
Oñate, Don Juan de, 1, 16, 128, 245,
Ophir, 3
Oraibe (Oraybi), 2, 5, 37, 233, 234, 246
Orth, 44
Oso Colorado, see Red Bear
Otermín, Governor, 9
Our Lady of Mercy (Nuestra Señora de la Merced), 70
Our Lady of the Snows (Nuestra Señora de las Nieves), 21, 64, 137
Ouray, 59
Overland Reservoir, 44, 155

P

Pacific Coast, 9
Pagampachis (Indians), 113, 119, 220
Pagosa Springs, 22
Pahvant Butte, 193
Painted Canyon (Cañon Pintado), 55, 167, 169
Pajarito Plateau, 24
Palma, Chief Salvador, 127

Palóu, 9
Paonia, 44
Paradise Valley, see Utah Valley
Paradox Valley, 36
Paria Plateau, 110, 111, 218
Paria River (Santa Teresa), 106, 112-114, 219
Park View, 19
Parras, 249
Parusis (Indians), 103, 119, 205, 207, 209, 212
Payatammumis (Indians), 103, 119, 212
Payson, Utah, 74, 187
Payuchis (Indians), 119, 201, 226
Peach Springs, 4
Pecos, 12
Pedro (Indian), 235, 237
Pichardo, 127
Piedro Parada, see Standing Rock
Pimería Alta, 244
Pintura (Town), 94, 95, 203, 204
Pipe Spring, 105
Plateau City, 51
Posada, Fray Alonso de, 169
Presidio of El Carrizal, 249
Presido of Elceareo, 249
Preston Mesa, 122
Province of Jila, 249
Provo River (Río San Antonio de Padua), 65, 70, 179
Provo, Utah, 65, 179
Provo Valley, 41
Puaguampe, see Witch Doctors
Pueblo Colorado Wash, 124, 238
Pueblo (Indians), 1, 2
Pueblo Land, 4, 9
Pueblo of Oraibi (Pueblo of Oraybi), 121, 123, 229
Pueblo Revolt, 24, 25, 246
Pueblo of Zuñi, 11
Pueblos of Moqui, 246
Puerco River, 239
Puerto de San Pedro, 74, 187

Q

Quetzal Point, 5

R

Randlett, 60
Rangely, see San Clements
Raven Ridge, 56
Red Bear (Oso Colorado), 47, 157
Red Creek, 62, 174
Ribera de San Cosme, 173
Ridge's Basin, 26

Río Colorado, see Colorado River
Río Cosnina, 91, 201
Río de Aguas Calientes, see Spanish Fork
Río de Chama, 135, 136
Río de la Cebolla, 134
Río de la Piedra Parada, 23, 138
Río de La Plata (Río de San Joaquín), 26, 139
Río de las Ánimas, 25, 139, 140
Río de Las Nutrias, see Nutrias Creek
Río de las Paralíticas, see Disappointment Creek
Río del Norte, 248
Río de los Dolores, 142, 143, 163
Río de los Mancos, see San Lázaro
Río de los Pinos, 25, 138
Río de los Zaguaganas, see Río Colorado
Río del Pilar, 203, 205
Río del Tizón, see Colorado River
Río del Tomichi, see Río de San Javier
Río de Navajó, 20, 137
Río de Nuestra Señora de los Dolores, see Dolores River
Río de Nuestra Señora del Pilar de Zaragoza, 201
Río de San Antonio de Padua, 185
Río de San Buenaventura, see Green River
Río de San Cosme, 173, 174
Río de San Damián, 172
Río de San Francisco, see Uncompahgre River
Río de San Francisco Javier, see Río de San Javier
Río de San Javier (Río del Tomichi, Río de San Francisco Javier), 152-155, 162
Río de San Joaquín, 140
Río de San Lázaro, see Mancos River
Río de San Nicolás, see Hobble Creek
Río de San Pedro, 147
Río de Santa Ana, see American Fork River
Río de Santa Catarina de Sena, 173
Río de Santa Rosa de Lima, 155
Río de Santa Teresa, 219
Río de Santa Ysabel, see Sevier River
Río Grande River, 12, 16, 239
Río Grande de los Cosninas, see Colorado River
Río Grande de Navajó, 22, 138
Río Florida, 25, 139
Río San Antonio de Padua, see Provo River

Index

Río San Clemente, see White River
Río Sulfúreo, see Virgin River
River of Nabajóo, see San Juan River
Rivera, Don Juan María de, 6, 7, 36, 152
Roan Creek, 53, 54
Roan Creek Valley, 165
Roan Mountain, 55
Roan Plateau, 166
Roberts, Frank H. H., 23-25
Rocky Mountains (Cordillera de las Grullas), 8
Roosevelt, Theodore, 110
Rubí, Marqués de, 12

S

Sabuaganas (Indians), 31, 37, 53, 107, 119, 146, 148, 153-165, 171, 215
Salahkai Mesa, 124, 238
Salt Lake, 190
Salvador Palma, see Ollyquotequiebe
San Agustín de la Isleta, see Isleta
San Agustín el Grande, 39, 152, 153
San Angel, 100, 210
San Antenógenes, 82, 83, 194, 195
San Antonio, 23, 138, 187
San Antonio Mártir, 45, 156, 160
San Atanasio, 51, 161
San Bartolomé, 110, 217
San Benito de Salsipuedes, 112, 219, 221
San Bernardino, 75, 188
San Bernardo, 144, 145
San Buenaventura, 189
San Carlos, see Glen Canyon
San Clemente, 56, 189
San Clemente River, see Douglas Creek
San Clements (Rangely), 55, 167
San Daniel, 94, 203
San Damián, 189
San Diego, see Wahweap Creek
San Dónulo (Arroyo del Taray), 97, 206
Sandoval, Gregorio, 7, 152
San Elueterio, 86, 87, 197
San Estéban de Acoma, see Sky City of Acoma
San Eustaquio, 61, 174
San Felipe, 147
San Francisco, 9, 126
San Francisco Javier de Alburquerque, 125, 239
San Fructo, 111, 218.
San Gabriel, 3
Sangre de Cristo Mountains, 16
San Hugolino, 95, 204

San Jacinto, 122, 230
San Joaquin Valley, 3, 14
San José, 239
San José de la Laguna, 125
San Juan Bautista, 249
San Juan Capistrano, 105, 214
San Juan de los Caballeros, 16
San Juan River (River of Nabajóo, Navajo), 7, 21, 26, 31, 119, 137, 190, 245, 246
San Lázaro (Río de los Mancos), 140, 141
San Lino, 63, 177
San Luis, 147
San Mateo, 63, 176
San Miguel, 120, 121, 227
San Miguel River (Río de San Pedro), 35, 36, 147, 148
San Nicolás, see Hobble Creek
San Pasqual, 248
San Pedro de Alcántara, 248
San Proto, 122, 229
San Rafael, see Colorado River
San Ramón Nonnato, 44, 155
San Rústico, 86, 197
San Samuel, 102, 211
San Silvestre (Nabuncari), 51, 161
Santa Bárbara, 104, 213
Santa Brígida, 84, 86, 195, 197
Santa Catarina de Sena Stream, 60
Santa Clara, 133
Santa Clara Mission, 16
Santa Delfina, 54, 166
Santa Fé, 3, 9, 14, 47, 133, 173, 196
Santa Francisca Romana, 116, 223
Santa Gertrudis, 104, 213
Santa Monica, see Austin
Santa Rosalía, 51, 163
Santa Rose de Abiquiú, 133
Santa Rosa de Abiquiú Mission, 16
Santa Rosa de Lima, 44
Santa Teresa, see Paria River
Santa Ysabel, 77, 190, 193
Santísima Trinidad, 136
Santo Domingo, 135
San Vincente Ferrer, 117, 224
San Xavier del Bac, 1
Scipio (town), 78, 190
Second Mesa, 233
Senatoa Spring, 124, 238
Señor San José, see Ash Creek
Señor San José de la Laguna, 239
Serra, 9
Sevier Bridge Reservoir, 78
Sevier Lake, 81
Sevier River (Río de Santa Ysabel), 76, 78, 189-191
Sierra Blanca, 151

264 INDEX

Sierra Blanca de los Lagunas, see Uinta Mountains
Sierra Blanca de los Timpanosis, 187
Sierra de Abajo, 151
Sierra de Cobre Virgen, 248
Sierra del Almagre, 151
Sierra de la Grulla (Sierra de la Plata), 20, 26, 52, 140, 148, 151, 163
Sierra de la Sal, 36, 151
Sierra del Dátil, 151
Sierra del Sacramento, 4
Sierra de los Tabehuaches, see Uncompahgre Plateau
Sierra del Venado Alazán, see Mountain of the Roan Deer
Silvestre, Father Fray, 112, 234
Silvestre (Indian Guide), 43, 46, 49, 53, 59, 62-66, 74, 157, 171, 179, 181
Sky City of Acoma (San Estéban de Ácoma), 125, 239
Soldier Springs (Ojo de Santa Lucía), 62, 175
Soldier's Fork, 64
Solís, Rubén de, Captain, 12
Sonora, 244, 247
Spanish Fork (Río de Aguas Calientes), 65, 178, 187
Spanish Fork, Utah, 179
Spring Creek, 166
Springville, 74
Standing Rock (Piedra Parada), 20, 136
Starr, 74, 188
Strawberry Creek, 62
Strawberry Reservoir, 62, 175
Strawberry Valley (Valle de la Purísima), 62, 175
Sumas (Indians), 12
Summit Canyon, 143

T

Tabehuache Sierra, 34
Tabehuaches (Indians), 35, 37, 119, 148
Tamarón, Bishop, 12
Tanos (Indians), 12, 235
Taos, 9, 10
Tatas, see Friars
Tehachapi Pass, 3
Telluride, 36
Tierra Amarilla, 18
Tiffany, 25
Timpanogos Basin, 74
Timpanogos (Laguna, Timpanogotzis, Timpanois, Come Pescados, Fish Eaters, Timpanogó) (Indians), 41, 70, 153, 154, 179, 184-187, 210, 239, 243
Timpanogos Lake (Lake Timpanogotzis), 71, 184-187
Timpanogos Valley, 184-187
Timpanogotzis, see Timpanogos
Timpanois, see Timpanogos
Tirangapui, see Bearded Indians
Toquerville, 95, 96, 204
Truxton Wash, 4
Tuba City, 122
Tucané, see Black Creek
Tucané, see Navajo Mountain

U

Uinta Mountains (Sierra Blanca de los Lagunas), 61, 174
Una, 52, 163
Uncompahgre Plateau (Sierra de los Tabehuaches), 7, 36, 147, 148, 151
Uncompahgre River (Río de San Francisco, Ancapagari, Laguna Colorado), 7, 34, 38, 39, 41, 150, 153
Utah Lake (Lake Timpanogos), 41, 63, 65, 70-72, 177, 179, 244, 246
Utah Valley (Nuestra Señora de la Merced de los Timpanogotzis, Paradise Valley, Valle de Timpanogos), 70, 73, 178, 184, 245
Utah's Dixie, 95
Ute Indians, 9
Valle de la Purísima, see Strawberry Valley
Valle de las Salinas, 74, 75, 187, 189
Valle de Nuestra Señora de la Luz, see Bear River Valley
Valle de Timpanogos, see Utah Valley
Valle Grande Range, 16
Valle, Marín del, Governor, 12
Valle Salado, 243
Valley of Las Salinas, 190
Valley of Señor San José, 91, 200, 212
Vega del Dulcisimo Nombre de Jesús, see Meadow of the Most Sweet Name of Jesus
Vega de San Cayetano, 139
Vernal, 59
Villa de San Gabriel de Yunqui, see Chama
Villa de Santa Fé, 125, 235, 238, 239
Virgin River (Río Sulfúreo), 90, 96, 205

W

Wahweap Creek (San Diego), 114, 221

Wanrhodes Canyon, 63, 177
Warm Creek Canyon, 116
Wasatch Mountains, 63
White River (Río San Clemente), 55, 56, 167
Whitmore Pools, 122
Witch Doctors (Puaguampe), 186
The Wounds of Our Father St. Francis (Las Llagas de Nuestro Padre San Francisco), 59, 172

X

Xipaolabi (Indians), 233
Xongopabi, 123, 233

Y

Yampa Plateau, 57, 168
Yamputzi, Chief (Indian), 47, 160
Young, Brigham, 74

Ytimpabichis (Indians), 119
Yubuincariris (Indians), 103, 105, 113, 119, 212, 220
Yuma, 5
Yumas (Indians), 127, 246
Yutas (Indians), 119, 144, 149
Yutas Barbones, see Bearded Indians
Yutas Nation, 138
Yutas Payuchis (Indians), 120, 149
Yutas Sabuaganas (Indians), 153, 155
Yutas Tabehuaches (Indians), 32, 144, 148

Z

Zion National Monument and Park, 94
Zuñi (Nuestra Señora de Guadalupe de Zuñi), 2, 3, 85, 124, 196, 237, 238